Social Work Methods and Skills

Social Work Methods and Skills

The Essential Foundations of Practice

Karen Healy

palgrave
macmillan

First published 2012 by
PALGRAVE MACMILLAN

Palgrave Macmillan in the UK is an imprint of Macmillan Publishers Limited, registered in England, company number 785998, of Houndmills, Basingstoke, Hampshire RG21 6XS.

Palgrave Macmillan in the US is a division of St Martin's Press LLC, 175 Fifth Avenue, New York, NY 10010.

Palgrave Macmillan is the global academic imprint of the above companies and has companies and representatives throughout the world.

Palgrave® and Macmillan® are registered trademarks in the United States, the United Kingdom, Europe and other countries

ISBN: 978–0–230–57517–2

This book is printed on paper suitable for recycling and made from fully managed and sustained forest sources. Logging, pulping and manufacturing processes are expected to conform to the environmental regulations of the country of origin.

A catalogue record for this book is available from the British Library.

A catalog record for this book is available from the Library of Congress.

10 9 8 7 6 5 4 3 2 1
21 20 19 18 17 16 15 14 13 12

Printed and bound in Great Britain by
the MPG Books Group, Bodmin and King's Lynn

Contents

List of Figures and Tables

Figures

Tables

Acknowledgements

The Chinese philosopher Lao Tzu stated that: 'The journey of a thousand miles begins with a single step', which reflects the journey this book has been for me. I began this book with the ambition of presenting a comprehensive and accessible introduction to the methodological foundations of professional social work practice. As an academic with a special interest in practice methods, I was well aware of the diverse traditions and methods of social work practice and I was often frustrated by their separation into specialist publications. To me this was a denial of the reality and importance of the diverse foundations of professional social work practice. However, I had not quite realized what a challenge it would be to present a comprehensive introduction to the range of social work methods within the one book. By the time I realized the challenge I had set myself, this work had taken on the quality of a marathon and I had to pace myself over a much longer distance than I had originally imagined.

There are many people who have sustained me in the writing of this book. I want to thank my colleagues at the University of Queensland and the University of Sydney whose collegiality has been important to me as I have completed this journey. Particular thanks to Professor Gabrielle Meagher for her friendship and insightful thoughts about social work and social policy. Thank you also to my dear friend Julie Conway for encouraging me to keep body and soul together in the course of this work. I also want to thank the students in the direct practice courses I have taught for the past seven years, who have helped me to clarify my thinking on best practice in social work. I am also grateful for my partnerships with people in several social and welfare service agencies in government and nongovernment sectors who have provided me with opportunities to maintain a connection with direct practice. These agencies include Micah Projects Inc., the Benevolent Society, Lifeline Community Care Queensland and the Queensland Department of Communities. Within these agencies, I especially want to thank Bri Stevenson, Shelley Neilsen, Anne Hampshire, Annette Michaux and Jo Clarke-Jones. I also acknowledge and thank my colleagues internationally who have sustained our conversation about best practice in social work over several years. Thank you to Liz Beddoe, Eileen Munro, Aron Shlonsky, Siv Oltedal, Rolv Lyngstad, Gunn Strand Hutchinson, Synnöve Karvinen-Niinikoski, Michael Longstaff, Marie Sallnäs and Tommy Lundström.

There are four people without whom this book would not have been possible. First, to Catherine Gray, commissioning editor at Palgrave Macmillan, thank you for your patience and perceptive feedback at every stage of the development of this work. Second, to Karyn Walsh, director of Micah Projects Inc., thank you for your inspirational practice. I hope this book conveys something of what I have learned from you about enabling people to move from isolation and vulnerability to being participants in a community in which they are valued and can flourish. Third, thanks to my neice Khloe Larnach-Healy for being a fun young person in my life. Finally, to my husband Dennis Longstaff for your support particularly in the final months of this effort. It takes someone special to insist that I keep writing as the severe floods of January 2011 inundated our home and our city, Brisbane, Queensland. So again, it is to you, Dennis, that I dedicate this book.

Preface

This book is inspired by my interest in the diverse methods of social work practice. Professional practice embraces a diverse range of social work methods including direct work with individuals, families, groups and communities and policy work to achieve the purpose of professional social work. The International Federation of Social Workers (IFSW, 2000, p. 1) defines the purpose of professional social work as the promotion of 'social change, problem-solving in human relationships, and the empowerment and liberation of people to enhance well-being'. Social workers seek to improve the interaction between people and their social environments by facilitating change at a variety of levels, including personal change and change in families, groups, communities, formal institutions and societal systems that impact on people's lives. As social workers, we must be equipped with a broad knowledge, method and skill base if we are to intervene effectively in the variety of systems influencing the lives of the people with whom we work.

As a social work teacher and researcher, I see many benefits in social workers having a solid foundation in a broad range of practice methods. These benefits include that a broad practice foundation enables us to respond more flexibly and creatively with service users and communities than is possible if our practice base is narrow. A broad practice foundation also enables better cooperation among social workers as it enhances our appreciation of the value of different practice approaches offered by agencies and practitioners. For example, from this broad foundation, a statutory social worker can appreciate how the interventions offered by a community worker may be beneficial to users of statutory services. Similarly, a community worker with a foundational knowledge of the range of social work methods is well positioned to identify when a community member may benefit from casework or groupwork interventions. Our capacity to articulate the value and practice of a diverse methodological base can also help us to defend the social work profession against some of the assaults it faces from new public management, which I shall refer to as managerialism throughout this book. The assaults include the efforts by managerialists to reconceptualize social work practice as a fragmented set of activities focused primarily on the management of risk (Healy, 2009; Saario and Stepney, 2009). Under these conditions, social workers face great challenges in creating spaces for practice that are holistic, critical and creative (McDonald, 2006). Being able to articulate the diverse methods and skills we can bring to achieve positive change in service users' lives is important to extending the spaces in which social work may be practised thoughtfully and creatively.

Despite the benefits of a broad practice foundation in social work, in recent years I have observed a trend towards specialization in the social work practice literature. As I search for practice methods texts, I find a proliferation of specialist material focused on specific methods and edited collections where specialists present material on their chosen methods or fields of practice. This specialist material offers readers opportunities to learn from experts in, and advocates of, specific methods. Yet I am concerned about what this trend towards methodological specialization communicates to students and newly qualified practitioners in the field. It may communicate a view that one must be a specialist in order to competently use any of the diverse practice methods of social workers. In addition, it may imply that advanced practice is specialist practice, thus contributing to a lack of recognition of, and support for, the development of advanced practice that embraces a range of methods. Finally, the trend towards specialization within the practice literature suggest that the student or newly qualified social worker should choose an area of methodological specialization in the course of their study even though such a choice may be detached from the specific contexts and the needs, interests and strengths of the service users and communities with whom they will practise. For example, social work students may be expected to identify whether they will commit to clinical work or community work or policy practice before they have graduated. This approach may limit social workers confidence to engage, even at a foundational level, in the practice methods that best suit the needs and interests of the service users and communities with whom they work. This trend towards specialization is curious, given that the International Federation of Social Workers (2000) asserts that professional social work is characterized by a diverse methodological base.

Of course, to say that the profession should recognize a broad range of methods does not mean that every social worker should exercise a broad range of practice methods. Undoubtedly, some level of specialization in field and method is necessary for some within the profession as a response to the increasing complexity of practice. For example, social workers in mental health, child protection or homeless services need a detailed knowledge of matters such as indicators of risk, signs of strengths and evidence of best practice within their specific field. Similarly, I recognize that we need methodological specialists in the wide variety of fields in which we practise. I use the term 'methodological specialists' to refer to social workers who commit significant proportions of their working lives to developing a deep understanding of, and capacity to use, a particular practice method. Just as the profession needs advanced specialists, this should be balanced with recognition of and support for the development of the advanced generalist practitioner. The advanced generalist is a practitioner who can work at a sophisticated level across a range of methods in ways that respond to the service user and community needs.

Where practitioners choose to specialize, I consider that such choices should be made on the basis of a comprehensive understanding of the diverse methods of social work practice. Also, given the practice principle that the social worker should prioritize service user interests over their own, I suggest that our choice about methods should be made in the context of our practice as a response to the needs, challenges and capacities facing the service users and communities with whom we practise. We need to ask: How do I best serve the service user from the range of methods available to me? Further, if we find that we lack skill in a particular method that might well serve those with whom we work, it behoves us to address this gap in our capacity either by referral of the service user to other services or development of our own skill base.

In this book, I introduce the diverse range of social work practice methods including interpersonal work in voluntary and statutory services, practice with families and groups, and community work and policy practice. My intention is to equip the reader with a foundation in the history and application of diverse practice methods within a coherent approach informed by theory, values and an analysis of our institutional context. I hope this knowledge about our diverse methodological base will assist the reader to make informed choices about the methods of practice that best match the needs and capacities of the service users with whom they work. Whether the reader chooses in the longer run to engage in specialist or generalist practice, I hope the material presented in this book deepens respect across the profession for the diverse methods we, as social workers, use to create positive change in the lives of the service users and communities with whom we practise.

Part 1

The Core of Professional Social Work Practice

This book is divided into four parts, as shown in the figure below.

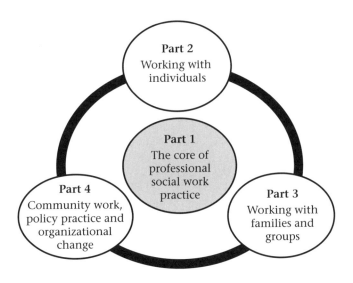

In Part 1, I introduce the professional core of social work practice that underpins our use of the diverse range of social work methods. Part 1 comprises two chapters. In Chapter 1, I describe how our sense of purpose and use of methods is shaped by the interaction between service user and community needs and capacities, our institutional context and our professional practice base. I define critical reflection and its relevance to the construction of our professional purpose and our application of practice methods. I outline the common base of professional communication skills and the phases of practice that underpin the range of practice methods outlined in the book.

Chapter 2 provides an introduction to professional communication skills. I will discuss how professional communication skills are similar to and different from the communication skills we use in nonprofessional contexts. In this chapter, I will consider how we can use professional communication skills to support the achievement of our professional purpose with service users, communities and the teams with whom we work.

1

Social Work Methods in Context: Purposeful Practice

In this book I aim to provide a comprehensive introduction to social work methods and skills. The book is intended for students of social work practice and for social workers seeking to develop, or consolidate, their knowledge of a range of methods and skills for professional social work practice. In this book, I seek to explain the rich diversity of social work practice methods and skills and to demonstrate the importance of grounding our use of these methods in a theoretically and practically informed sense of purpose.

The integrated approach to social work methods outlined in this book recognizes that micro, mezzo and macro methods are all part of the professional practice foundation of social work. 'Micro methods' refers to practice with individuals who voluntarily seek the help of social workers and those who are compelled by law to do so (covered in Part 2), 'mezzo methods' refers to direct work with families and groups (covered in Part 3), while 'macro methods' refers to community work, policy practice and organizational change (covered in Part 4).

An integrated understanding of micro, mezzo and macro methods and skills is important for a variety of reasons. A comprehensive and integrated approach can help us to recognize a common body of social work skills underpinning the range of practice methods. As we shall see in Chapter 2, professional communication skills, such as effective listening and demonstration of empathy, are relevant to the range of practice methods. In addition, a diverse practice base is important for social workers in nonspecialist roles. For example, a social worker delivering family support services or aged care services may provide individual casework services, facilitate groups and engage in community development activities. Even where we, as social workers, are in specialist roles, a comprehensive understanding of social work skills and methods can enhance our options for intraprofessional collaboration to meet client needs. For example, a social worker offering counselling services may collaborate with a community social worker to assist a client to achieve a goal such as increased social support.

In this book, I introduce social work methods and skills as integrated with, and shaped by, our practice purpose. As I shall outline, our sense of purpose is dynamic and influenced by client needs, our institutional context and our professional practice base. Our purpose is constructed in every practice interaction and so the application of practice methods and skills involves both conceptual and practical capacities. In other words, social work involves practical activities, but it is more than this, it also demands the capacity to construct our sense of purpose in ways that best serve the service users and communities with whom we practise. In this chapter, I outline the elements of a dynamic approach to methods and skill use and provide an overview of the contents of the book.

Social Work Methods and Skills: A Dynamic Approach

Social work involves the practical application of methods and skills. Our choice of method and skill use and our approach to applying them is, necessarily, informed by our sense of professional purpose. As outlined in Figure 1.1, our professional purpose is shaped by our field of practice and is informed by three key sources: service user needs and expectations; institutional requirements; and our professional practice base.

In Figure 1.1, I suggest that one's professional purpose is shaped by, and also shapes, service users' needs and expectations, our institutional context, and our professional practice base. Our professional practice refers to the combination of theories, knowledge and values that informs our approach to social work practice. The dynamic model of methods and skills recognizes that, in every interaction, the social worker actively constructs their sense of purpose in ways that recognize the complementaries and tensions between service users' or communities' needs and expectations, our institutional context and our professional practice base. Often this is a challenging task. For example, in many Anglophone countries, child protection social workers may experience tension between parents' expressed needs, such as the need for assistance to manage a drug addiction, and the expectations of our institutional context, which may prioritize children's needs and give scant recognition to our role in responding to parents' needs (Healy and Oltedal, 2010). In most social work practice contexts, there are tensions between the various factors influencing our sense of purpose, which make the task of developing a coherent sense of purpose important and challenging.

In this dynamic model of methods and skills, I recognize that social work is both a conceptual and practical activity. In every interaction, the social worker needs to construct their sense of purpose from a variety of sources, each of which may present different, and sometimes contradictory,

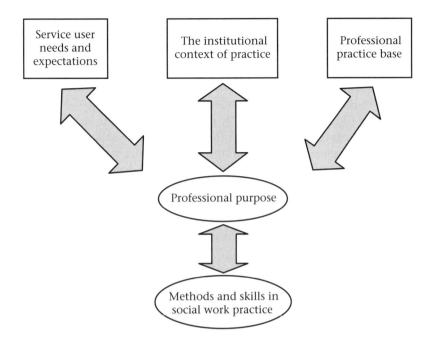

Figure 1.1   A dynamic model of methods and skills in social work practice

expectations of our purpose. I turn now to consider how critical reflection can assist us in constructing our professional purpose that is integral to our choice and deployment of methods and skills.

Constructing our Sense of Purpose through Critical Reflection

Our sense of purpose as social workers is constantly constructed by us and by other people, including politicians, policy-makers, employers and service users. Our sense of purpose may change in each interaction with an individual, group and community, and is certainly likely to alter over time in most practice situations. For example, at the formation stage of a group, the social worker may have an explicit leadership role, yet over time, group members may assume an increasing proportion of the leadership role, thus leading to changes in the social worker's purpose.

How do we construct our sense of purpose from the different sources influencing the nature and purpose of social work? One option is to passively let our professional purpose emerge, that is, to allow others to determine our professional purpose. However, we are vulnerable then to allowing the most powerful voices, such as those from employing or funding bodies, to entirely determine our practice. We can see this is a problem, given that funding bodies or employing agencies may be somewhat removed from the daily realities of practice and service users' lives, and so it is necessary for us to negotiate how we practise. Such negotiation with funders, employers and with service users is founded on a clear sense of purpose.

Critical reflection has been identified as a process through which professionals, particularly those in caring professions, can build their sense of professional purpose (see Schön, 1983). Fook and Gardner (2007, p. 51) describe critical reflection as a structured process designed to 'unsettle the fundamental (and dominant) thinking implicit in professional practice in order to see other ways of practising'. Critical reflection views all dimensions of social work practice as socially constructed and we can improve our practice by critically analysing how our practice is constructed by us and by others. Through this process of critical reflection, we can better understand how our purpose is constructed and how we may take an active role in negotiating our purpose in practice. This view is consistent with the contextual approach to social work outlined earlier, where I emphasized that our sense of purpose is constructed through an interchange between service users, communities, the institutions in which we work and our professional practice base.

A critical reflection approach also recognizes our practice experience as a base for knowledge development. Proponents of critical reflection criticize the notion that scientific knowledge can be applied to practice without an appreciation of the context in which that knowledge is applied and the nature of the relationship between the social worker and the service user or community with whom they work. For example, we can see that ideas about the use of self and role clarification must change according the context of practice and can present different challenges according to whether a service user voluntarily engages with the practitioner or is compelled to do so by law.

Proponents of critical reflection recognize that social workers (and other caring professionals) can learn much through 'doing' social work and then reflecting on the experience of practice. The use of simulated and 'real' practice experiences is important to a critical reflective approach to learning about, and becoming, a social worker. In this book, I have provided practice exercises that are intended to assist you in critically reflecting on the application of the methods and skills as I introduce them.

Service User Perspectives

So far I have suggested that our sense of purpose in social work is important because it shapes our use of methods and skills in social work. I have also outlined that our sense of purpose is negotiated from a number of sources. I turn now to consider one of these sources: service user perspectives on their needs and expectations of social work services. Later sections of this chapter consider how the requirements of our institutional context and our professional practice base shape our sense of purpose. We will discuss service users' perspectives first because we want to demonstrate the important position these perspectives should hold in determining our practice purpose.

Even though social workers, and the agencies we work for, often assert that our primary purpose is to respond to service users' needs, service user perspectives in defining those needs are often undervalued or invisible. There are at least five reasons for this apparent contradiction in the mission of social work services to serve service users' needs and the relative absence of service users' voices in shaping service delivery:

- users of social work services often have limited capacity to pay for the social work services they receive. Many social work and health and welfare services are paid for by government funders or philanthropists rather than by those receiving the service; known as a *third party funding arrangement* (Gibelman, 1999). In these arrangements, the perspectives of those paying for services may be prioritized over those receiving services, unless there is commitment from those funding the service or those providing it to ensure that service users' voices are heard (Carr, 2004)

- the service user may have limited capacity to speak directly for themselves because of a condition, such as a psychosis or dementia, that limits their capacity to rationally form or express their preferences

- there may be ambivalence by funders or service providers towards recognizing the needs of particular groups of service users. For example, in Anglophone countries, there is debate about the extent to which parents are, or should be, recognized as primary clients in child protection services (Dumbrill, 2010)

- the diversity of service user views can be difficult to weigh up; for example, in a criminal justice setting, it can be difficult to balance society's and sometimes the victim's wish to see an offender punished, with the service user's own wish for assistance. Even within one practice context, service users may express a variety of views. For example, in child protection services, some children and young people observe that child protection services waited too long before removing them from harmful situations, while others wish to stay with their families despite the harm they experience because of the importance of their family bond to them

- the compulsory nature of some service provision also creates tensions in seeking service user views. In the context of statutory service provision, such as child protection services or the prison service, services have developed despite client ambivalence, or opposition, to service delivery. This does not mean that service users' views should not be sought but it does mean that these service agencies may not have developed a culture of seeking service user perspectives on service delivery and may consider service user dissatisfaction to be inherent to the compulsory nature of service delivery.

Despite the various factors in practice that can lead to the silencing of service users' voices, it is important that social workers understand what service users desire from social work services. Understanding service user perspectives is the first step in realizing the value of supporting self-determination. According to Banks (2006, p. 48), supporting self-determination involves 'helping someone to reach a state where they have the capacity to see what choices might be available', and supporting them to undertake their preferred course of action with due regard for one's ethical framework, legal responsibilities and practical limitations. In addition, effective social work practice relies on the establishment of purposeful and constructive relationships with service users (Trotter, 2004). This means that collaboration between workers and service users is at the heart of effective social work practice (Saleebey, 2006).

Research on service users' experiences of social work services has focused primarily on social casework services in both voluntary and involuntary environments. This research indicates that service users often have many fears about, and negative perceptions of, social work services. These fears include that they will be humiliated, judged, their wishes ignored and that they will be disrespected (Maiter et al., 2006; Trotter, 2002). These fears appear to be especially acute in statutory practice settings where social workers are involved in implementing laws that can carry enormous threats for service users, such as the threat of losing their children or losing access to a benefit or service. Fears about social work services are exacerbated by the lack of control service users often experience in determining the nature of services, for the reasons outlined above, such as the overarching power that funding agencies have in determining the nature of these services.

Many studies of service users' views of social work services reach the common conclusion that many service users want the worker to engage with them in an open, authentic and warm manner. For example, in a review of evidence on effective social work engagement, Sheldon and Macdonald (2009) report that service users want social workers to demonstrate:

- **Nonpossessive warmth:** the service user perceives that the worker likes them and supports them to make their own choices; in other words, the warmth of the worker does not depend on the service user's compliance with them but instead arises from an unconditional positive regard for the service user

- **Genuineness:** the service user perceives that the worker cares about them and their situation

- **Accurate empathy:** the service user perceives that the worker listens to them and is able to demonstrate that they understand the service user's thoughts and emotions in relation to their experience.

Other researchers have also pointed to the importance of the perception that social workers are nonjudgemental, willing and able to help the service user (Healy et al., 2011). Several studies have found that service users appreciate social workers being willing to 'go the extra mile', that is, being sufficiently flexible to offer help in a way that is appreciated by service users (Frederick and Goddard, 2008; Maiter et al., 2006).

There are several practical ways that we can demonstrate a respectful and helpful approach in our engagement with service users, without negating the control aspects inherent in many social work roles (Miller, 2009; Trotter, 2004):

- being punctual – this demonstrates to service users that you value their time

- being reliable – if you commit to undertake a task, it is important that you honour that undertaking in order to create a sense of mutual responsibility within your relationship

- courteousness, for example asking service users how they would like to be addressed

- communicating clearly by using jargon-free language

- clarifying the nature of your role, particularly if there are tensions in your role such as care and control aspects of your role, and being willing to discuss and where possible negotiate that role

- being yourself rather than sticking rigidly to a professional role. Being yourself can include engaging in limited self-disclosure and practising in ways that demonstrate human care and compassion for those you serve. It is important, of course, that you maintain appropriate professional boundaries so that the service user is not confused about the nature of your role.

The Institutional Context of Practice

The term 'institutional context of practice' refers to 'the laws, public and organizational policies, and accepted practices shaping the institutions where social workers are located' (Healy, 2005, p. 4). Our institutional context shapes, but does not entirely determine, our purpose, tasks and methods as social workers. The institutional context prescribes our formal responsibilities, including our legal responsibilities, and the terms of reference for our role. These formal terms are often outlined in our job description. However, as professionals, we must also interpret these responsibilities in terms of our professional practice base, particularly in relation to our ethical responsibilities to service users. In some instances, social workers may experience compatibility between their institutional context and their practice framework. Regrettably, however, tensions between our institutional context and other sources of influence, such as our professional knowledge, values and clients' needs, are common.

Tensions between institutional context and professional frameworks are not unique to social workers; indeed, such tensions are frequently encountered in a range of professions, particularly caring occupations, due, in part, to resource constraints in most service environments. For example, medical professionals may experience tensions between their ethical responsibility to do what is possible to save a patient's life and the budgetary constraints that limit the availability of some pharmaceuticals and surgical procedures. The tensions for caring occupations, such as teaching and social work, can also be intense because of the relational and, to some extent, indeterminate character of some of the work undertaken by these occupations. Despite the significant inroads made by the evidence-based practice movement, social workers remain some way from being able to demonstrate the evidence base for many forms of professional intervention. The intensely political environments in which many social work services operate, being highly reliant on government funding, also create tensions, particularly where some forms of intervention, such as services to prisoners or vulnerable families, may not be politically popular. From a critical social work perspective, tensions between our institutional context and social work practice frameworks are inevitable because our institutional context usually frames service users' problems individualistically, while neglecting to acknowledge or address the societal factors contributing to service users' disadvantages, such as social inequality and institutional forms of discrimination (Dominelli, 2002; Healy, 2000; Mullaly, 2007).

Developing a clear sense of purpose when there are conflicts between the institutional construction of the social work role and our professional knowledge and value base is challenging. In the context of the rise of managerialism (also known as new public management), which has contributed to pressure to narrow the role of social workers to focus on the management of risk, social workers may encounter resistance to a view of social work as a thoughtful, holistic or creative activity (Healy, 2009). For example, over the past decade, many child protection authorities have moved towards an increasingly forensic orientation (Lonne et al., 2009); similar changes have been observed in probation services. At the very least, social workers need to consider how the inroads being made by managerialism are reshaping public expectations of social work services and how they can strategically resist those aspects of managerialism that threaten our capacity to actively participate in the construction of our purpose based on a thoughtful integration of employer and service user expectations and our professional practice base.

Our Professional Base

Our professional base refers to the theory, knowledge, values and skills that inform professional social work practice. Theory refers to conceptual frameworks through which we make sense of our world and different theories can provide very different sets of assumptions about the nature of social work practice. Knowledge refers to information and perspectives used by social workers to understand aspects of practice such as assessment of service users' needs. Some examples of knowledge used by social workers within specific fields of practice includes reference to diagnostic information, such as the *Diagnostic and Statistical Manual of Mental Disorders*, knowledge about human development and local knowledge of service systems.

In social work, as in other fields, there is an overlap between the theoretical and knowledge bases of our practice. There are two distinguishing features of the theory and knowledge on which social workers rely. The first is that social workers draw extensively on 'received ideas' for the theoretical and knowledge bases of their practice (Rojek et al., 1988). This means that much of the theory and knowledge on which social workers rely has not been developed in the context of social work practice and so must be adapted by practitioners to their practice contexts. The second distinguishing feature of social work theory and knowledge is its diversity. The diverse nature of social work practice itself, which can involve a range of methods from casework to policy work, limits our capacity to develop a common theoretical and knowledge base.

Studies on theory and knowledge use in social work practice have repeatedly found that social workers rarely use theory consciously in practice (see Fook et al., 2000). This is not to say that social workers do not use theory; however, it is perhaps the case that social workers do not often articulate, or reflect upon, the theoretical frames that guide their work. This failure to reflect on our theoretical frames of reference is a problem because it means that we are unaccountable to these assumptions and these assumptions may remain underdeveloped. Throughout this book, I seek to make clear links between theories for social work practice and the choice and application of a range of micro, mezzo and macro methods. I turn now to an explanation of the three theoretical approaches informing the use of methods discussed in this book.

Theoretical Perspectives Informing this Book

The theoretical frames informing this book are critical social work theory, systems theory and the strengths perspective. These theoretical perspectives have been selected for a variety of reasons that we will outline in this section. These perspectives are all social work theories for practice, which means that although they draw on received ideas from other disciplines, they have been developed by social work researchers and practitioners for social work practice.

The primary theoretical frame shaping this book, and much of my previous work, is critical social work (Healy, 2000, 2005; see also Fook, 2002). At its core, critical social work recognizes that most service users experience profound disadvantage and oppression and that this shapes service users' capacities to address their needs without the support of social work agencies. Many social workers, not only those writing from a critical social work perspective, recognize that social workers' primary purpose is to work with disadvantaged citizens. As Sheldon and Macdonald (2009, p. 3) aptly define it:

> Social work's disciplinary territory is the poor, troubled, abused or discriminated against, neglected, frail and elderly, mentally ill, learning-disabled, addicted, delinquent, or otherwise socially marginalized up-against-it citizen in his or her social circumstances.

From a critical social work perspective, it is important that social workers not only engage in a humane and compassionate way with disadvantaged and oppressed citizens but that we also work towards creating a more just society. This involves challenging the unjust social conditions that contribute to the troubles experienced by service users.

At its core, critical social work demands that social workers reflect upon the ways in which social disadvantage and oppression shape our sense of purpose as practitioners. This perspective demands that a social worker should, at the very least, have a critical understanding of social disadvantage and how to respond to individuals living in oppressed or difficult circumstances. Indeed, in order to give practical expression to social work values of acceptance and equality, it is often necessary for social workers to critically reflect on the broader societal attitudes that contribute to the discrimination and oppression experienced by service users. Theory can help social workers to make the cognitive shift necessary to working with service users in a way that moves beyond a focus on individual pathology to an approach that offers hope, recognizes service users' strengths, and is oriented towards creating conditions for change.

Over to you ...

Understanding and responding to social disadvantage

Social workers provide services to people who experience social disadvantage, marginalization and oppression. It is important that you are able to engage with service users in a nonjudgmental and supportive way and particularly in ways that avoid blaming them for the difficult conditions they face. Consider:

1. What individual and social factors might contribute to a person living in poverty or becoming homeless?

2. What theoretical frameworks do you already know about that seek to explain disadvantage, marginalization and oppression?

3. How might these theoretical frameworks be helpful for you in engaging in a nonjudgmental and supportive way with clients who are experiencing disadvantage?

A second perspective that informs this book is systems theory. Systems perspectives have had a powerful influence on the theory and knowledge base of the profession. During the 1960s and 70s, systems theories became widely accepted within the profession, although many systems concepts were well established in the profession prior to this (Healy, 2005). Most notably, Mary Richmond (1917), a social work pioneer, outlined the importance of understanding and responding to the person in their social environment. Frank Hankins, a sociologist and educator at Smith College in Northampton, USA, is credited with introducing 'systems theory' to the professional in the 1930s (see Woods and Hollis, 1990). A wide variety of schools of systems theory have influenced the profession (for an extended discussion of these perspectives, see Healy, 2005, Ch. 7).

This book is informed by a systems perspective, sometimes referred to as an 'ecosystem perspective', which came to prominence in the 1970s and which continues to be influential within the social work profession today. This branch of systems perspective focuses on social workers' role in understanding and enhancing the interaction between the individual and the systems that influence them, such as family and health and welfare service systems. Using a systemic approach, Pincus and Minahan (1973, p. 9) defined the purpose:

> Social work is concerned with the interactions between people and their social environment which affect the ability of people to accomplish their life tasks, alleviate distress, and realize their aspirations and values. The purpose of social work therefore is to (1) enhance the problem-solving and coping capacities of people, (2) link people with systems that provide them with resources, services, and opportunities, (3) promote the effective and humane operation of these systems, and (4) contribute to the development and improvement of social policy.

Pincus and Minahan, like many other theorists associated with the ecosystem perspective, emphasized the multisystemic nature of the challenges facing service users and the responsibilities of social workers to address these challenges. According to this perspective, the social workers' role could not be limited to any one system, even though some might chose to specialize in practice with a specific system type, such as families or communities. The ecosystems perspective is appealing to many social workers because it is consistent with the core value of social justice, in that it turns our attention to the systemic context of apparently private troubles.

The strengths perspective is the third perspective informing this book. This perspective seeks to emphasize and build on service users' capacities. It is a future-oriented approach that 'concentrates on enabling individuals and communities to articulate, and work towards, their hopes for the future' (Healy, 2005, p. 152). The strengths perspective encourages us, as social workers, to:

- Recognize that all people (service users and peers) have strengths and capacities and that these assets can assist in creating change

- Ensure that, in our engagement with, and assessment of, service user need, we recognize and build on service users' resilience and capacity, rather than focus on deficit

- Challenge our colleagues, and broader society, to recognize the strengths and assets of service users. In other words, we must challenge a problem-saturated view of the client

- Engage in a collaborative relationship with service users and respect and build service users' capacity for self-determination.

While proponents of the strengths perspective have made significant contributions to casework practice, this approach is also making inroads into group and community work practice, as we shall see in Chapters 6 and 7 (see also Green and Haines, 2002; Saleebey, 2006).

Values in Practice

Values are important to how we, as social workers, understand our professional purpose. Despite considerable debate about values in social work practice, some values are common to the profession across many countries. For example, in her review of social work ethical codes across several countries, including the UK, Australia and the USA, Banks (2006, p. 47) identified that these codes shared variations of the values of: 'human dignity and worth; service to humanity; and social justice' (see also IFSW, 2004). However, the application of these values is not clear-cut. Social workers often have to weigh up competing values in practice as, for example, when we seek to recognize the 'dignity of the individual, but also to make and implement difficult decisions (including restriction of liberty) in human situations that involve the potential for benefit or harm' (QAA, 2008, p. 7). Our values inform our use of practice methods through, for example, requiring that service users and community members have access to practice methods that best promote their dignity and achieve social justice with and for them.

Values shape the nature of our relationship with service users and community members. Social workers' professional codes of ethics, like those of other caring occupations, assert the professional nature of the relationship between social workers and service users. Indeed, our ethical codes in social work, and in many other caring occupations, demand that we prioritize service users' needs over our own needs or interests. In the IFSW/IAASW code of principles (2004), it is asserted that: 'Social workers should not subordinate the needs or interests of people who use their services to their own needs or interests.' In the professional practice literature, the relationship between social workers and the individuals, groups and communities they serve is widely considered to be the vehicle of change. Furthermore, given the emphasis in the social work literature on equality and collaboration, and therefore on rejecting traditional notions of professional hierarchy, there is some room for confusion for both service providers and service users about the nature of the relationship. It is important, therefore, that we critically reflect on the nature of our professional relationships and ensure that these relationships are consistent with social work values and also with our professional purpose. We also need to be clear with ourselves and those with whom we work about the professional nature of our relationship with service users and community members.

Integrating Diverse Methods

A professional approach to social work practice requires that social workers have a foundation in the broad range of methods for achieving change with individuals, families, groups and communities, and in the institutional contexts of our practice. Undeniably, it is challenging to develop a broad practice foundation. Yet to fail to do so can limit our capacity to initiate or support change in the lives of the people with whom we work and the institutions that shape their lives and our practice. In this book, I anchor this diverse methodological base of social work in a common set of communication skills and also within a structured approach to the use of each method.

As I shall outline in Chapter 2, all methods of practice are underpinned by a common set of communication skills. The communication skills we use in professional practice include many of the skills we use to communicate in everyday life. These skills include spoken, observational and nonverbal skills. While social workers have paid much attention to the use of these skills in micro and mezzo forms of practice, I will argue that the purposeful deployment of these communication skills is central to all practice methods, although how we use these skills may differ according to the methods.

I also link the diverse practice methods to an integrated approach to practice. In this integrated approach, I consider that all practice methods, from micro to macro, are underpinned by four phases. These phases, which are outlined in Figure 1.2, are engagement, assessment, intervention and evaluation/termination.

I suggest that all methods of practice involve the phases outlined in Figure 1.2:

- **Engagement** refers to the point at which the social worker joins with the individual, group, family, community organization or policy process.

- **Assessment** refers to developing an understanding, usually in collaboration with others, about the nature of the problem to be addressed and the capacities present within the situation to creating positive change.

- **Intervention** is where the social worker is involved in achieving identified change goals.

- **Evaluation and termination** refer to the assessment of the extent to which the intervention process has achieved change goals and the development of strategies for the achievement of unmet goals. In the termination phase, the period of professional engagement concludes.

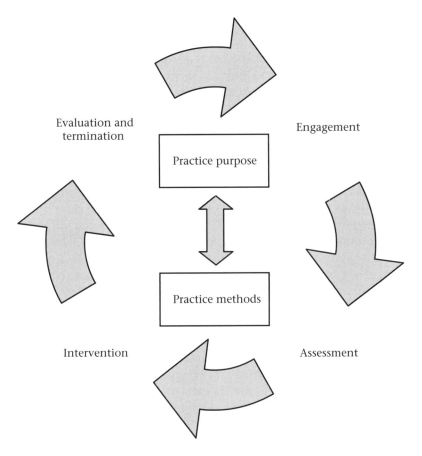

Figure 1.2 Phases of social work practice

I have conceptualized these phases of social work practice as being in a circular, rather than linear, relationship with each other. This is because each phase can and, in fact, often does blur into other phases in the application of all the practice methods I outline in this book. For example, the engagement process involves elements of evaluation and termination, insofar as the social worker establishes a baseline of information about the nature of the problem facing an individual or community against which progress will be assessed and clarifies the period of their involvement in the life of the service user or community. Our sense of purpose and the methods of practice we use to achieve that purpose are represented in the centre of Figure 1.2. This is because, as we shall see throughout this book, our purpose and our practice method shape our work in each of these phases.

Overview of the Book

We turn now to an outline of the contents of this book. The remainder of this book is focused on providing a sequenced and comprehensive introduction to a range of social work methods and skills. A unique feature of this book is that I include 'micro' methods, which involve working with individuals in both voluntary and involuntary practice contexts, alongside 'mezzo' methods such as groupwork, and 'macro' methods such as community work and policy work. Hopefully, in this chapter, I have demonstrated why these methods all belong to the foundation of social work practice. Essentially, I consider that, drawing on the theoretical and ethical frames identified in this chapter, all social workers should have the capacity to critically understand a range of forms of intervention and, better still, have the capacity to engage in this range at least at a foundational level. I do not claim that any of these methods are unique to social work. Indeed, a range of practitioners engage in the methods discussed in this book. Nonetheless, I will discuss how we, as social workers, use these methods to achieve our purpose in a variety of practice contexts.

The book is divided into four parts. In Part 1, I introduce the professional core of social work practice. In this first chapter, I have outlined the theories, ideas and values that inform the approach to social work practice discussed in this book. In Chapter 2, I will outline the professional communication strategies and skills used by social workers as we engage with the range of practice methods and communicate with our work teams and with the general public.

In Part 2, I introduce social work methods for practice with individuals. This section comprises two chapters. In Chapter 3, I discuss the methods social workers can use to work with individuals to resolve life's problems. My focus is on interpersonal practice with service users who are voluntarily involved with social work services, in the sense that they are not required by law to receive these services. In Chapter 4, I introduce practice with mandated individuals, that is, service users who are required by law to receive social work services. I concentrate on how social workers work towards achieving safety with service users and their families and the community in the face of risk and resistance. The reader may be aware that the terms used to describe interpersonal practice are controversial and contested. In Chapter 3, I will argue that 'social casework', a term once commonly used to describe interpersonal practice, remains the best way of describing how social workers practise with individuals to resolve problems. In Chapter 4, I will argue that the term 'statutory social work' is a better description than other commonly used terms, such as practice with involuntary clients, to convey individual work with mandated individuals. I ask the reader to bear with me as I make the case for the use of these terms for describing our work with individuals even though these terms may be controversial.

In Part 3, I introduce social work methods for practice with families and groups, referred to as 'mezzo' practice. In Chapter 5, I introduce the variety of methods social workers use when working with families and I describe methods for meeting families and involving members in decision-making. In Chapter 6, I discuss the rationales for groupwork in social work practice, diverse methods of groupwork used by social workers, and I will introduce how social workers can foster change through groupwork.

In Part 4, I introduce social work methods for practice with communities, policy work and in organizational change. In Chapter 7, I discuss the rationales for, and tensions around, including community work as a method of social work practice. I discuss the skills required in working with communities for creating change. In Chapter 8, I discuss policy work as a method of social work practice and discuss how social workers, working in direct practice, can participate in and foster the participation of service users and community members in policy practice. In Chapter 9, the concluding chapter, I review the themes underpinning the diverse methods of social work practice and I discuss how social workers can engage in organizational change.

Each chapter ends with review questions and practice exercises to consolidate your learning, as well as annotated further reading. The review questions are intended to assist you to recall key messages from the chapters. Through practice exercises, I aim to facilitate your reflection upon how the concepts and methods discussed in the chapter may apply, or be adapted, to your own practice within specific fields of service delivery.

Conclusion

In this chapter, I have introduced the approach to social work practice methods that underpins this book. I have argued that our sense of professional purpose, which varies across the contexts and circumstances of our work, influences our use of methods in social work practice. I have identified a range of influences on how we develop our sense of professional purpose in practice, which include the needs and preferences of service users and community members, our institutional environment, and our professional practice base. My intention in outlining these factors is to assist you in critically reflecting on how your professional purpose is shaped in practice and how it varies between practice contexts and circumstances. As we become aware of how varied and variable our professional purpose is, so too we may recognize the need for a diverse methodological base to achieve our purposes. The rest of this book is dedicated to introducing this diverse methodological base in the hope that it will provide you with the foundations for achieving your professional purpose in the diverse, and often challenging, environments of social work practice.

Review Questions

1. What are the key messages in this chapter about service users' views on what they are seeking in their relationships with social workers?

2. The social work profession is committed to supporting service user self-determination and promoting social justice. What do these terms mean? How would you practically achieve these values in practice? Thinking of a specific field of practice, consider what challenges you might face in implementing these values.

3. Social workers' sense of professional purpose is shaped by service user needs and expectations, the demands of our institutional context, and our professional practice base. In a field of practice that interests you, what do you see as the professional purpose of social workers?

4. What are your views about the nature of professional boundaries in social work practice? What might be the challenges for you in communicating your professional boundaries to individuals, groups and communities with whom you work?

Further Reading

● Banks, S. (2006) *Ethics and Values in Social Work*, 3rd edn. Basingstoke: Palgrave Macmillan.

   Comprehensive introduction to values and ethics in social work and health and welfare services practice.

● Berg, I.S. and Kelly, S. (2000) *Building Solutions in Child Protective Services*. New York: Norton.

   Offers an insightful and practical analysis of the use of strengths-based and solution-focused practice with vulnerable children and their families.

● Fook, J. and Gardner, F. (2007) *Practising Critical Reflection: A Resource Handbook*. Maidenhead: Open University Press.

   Accessible, practical introduction to the practice of critical reflection as a base for building knowledge and skills in practice.

● Germain, C. and Gitterman, A. (1996) *The Life Model of Social Work Practice: Advances in Theory and Practice*, 2nd edn. New York: Columbia University Press.

One of the foundational texts on the ecosystems approach to social work practice.

● Healy, K. (2000) *Social Work Practices: Contemporary Perspectives on Change*. London: Sage.

Outlines the theory of critical social work practice.

● Pincus, A. and Minahan, A. (1973) *Social Work Practice: Model and Method*. Itasca, IL: FE Peacock.

One of the enduring classics of the systems approach to social work practice. Clearly outlines different types of systems impacting on service users and provides insights into how social workers can strategically intervene to create systemic change.

● Saleebey, D. (ed.) (2006) *The Strengths Perspective in Social Work*, 4th edn. Boston, MA: Allyn & Bacon.

Includes a range of papers on the theoretical foundations and practical application of strengths-based approaches to a broad range of practice fields. Excellent introduction to the strengths perspective.

2

Professional
Communication Skills

Social worker professionals spend a great deal of time communicating with service users, community members, members of their team and the public. To be an effective social worker, one must be an effective communicator. Professional communication in social work draws on the skills we use in everyday interactions. The key difference between everyday and professional communication is that in the latter we need to be aware of our purpose and ensure that our use of communication skills supports the achievement of that purpose.

I begin this chapter by outlining a contextual approach to communication. I will consider the ways in which our purpose as a social work professional shapes our use of communication skills. I will discuss the communication skills that underpin direct practice with individuals, families, groups and communities, which are also central to communication in teams and with the public. This includes skills in listening, nonverbal communication, observation and verbal or spoken skills. Throughout, I consider the challenges in communicating with people from cultures other than one's own.

A great deal of attention is paid to communication skills in the social work literature. Allen and Langford (2008, p. 53) assert that:

> Communication skills are the range of learnt techniques that help social work professionals to communicate clearly, warmly with a wide range of people, even those who may have impaired communication, or whose first language might not be English.

Much of the literature on communication has emerged from interpersonal practice with voluntary clients. Yet social workers often engage with service users in involuntary relationships. Our practice may involve meeting more than one individual in groupwork, family work and community development work or working with teams. I now outline a core set of communication skills that are needed in a diverse range of practice settings and which are central to the use of the practice methods discussed in this book.

Listening Skills

Perhaps the most important skill a social worker has is the capacity to listen well. Listening is an active process of engaging with, and facilitating articulation of, the perspectives of the individual, family, group, community and team members with whom you are working. Listening is an essential skill for building purposeful relationships and for gaining the level of understanding needed to form assessments and implement effective interventions.

How we listen as a social work professional has many similarities with how we listen in everyday life; for example, in both professional and nonprofessional contexts, we demonstrate listening by being attentive to the speaker. But there are also important differences. One of the most important being that listening in social work is a purposeful activity. Even while listening, the social worker will often subtly direct the speaker to particular topics that are important for developing an assessment or intervention plan regarding the issue at hand. While you may consider yourself to be a good listener in most situations, as a social work professional, you are likely to further develop your listening skills to respond to the many challenges of listening well in your professional role.

In most social work practice environments, it is important that the social worker listens in an empathetic way. *Empathetic listening* refers to the message receiver accurately understanding what the 'sender is feeling and thinking' and conveying this understanding in their nonverbal behaviour and verbal tone and expression (Boyle et al., 2006, p. 107). To demonstrate that we are listening, we need to create a physical environment in which we can give our undivided attention to the service user. Many practice environments present practical obstacles to achieving this; for example the lack of physical space for private conversation can be an obstacle. Similarly, interruptions by colleagues, telephones or pagers as we interact with service users can disrupt our capacity to give them our undivided attention. There is a danger that we fail to notice these obstacles because we have become used to them. Nonetheless, they can convey to those with whom we are communicating that we do not have the time to listen to them.

Another component of empathetic listening is that of understanding the speaker's perspective. Our own expectations of the conversation and our prejudices can form barriers to understanding the perspective of another. For example, the expectation that we should focus on risk assessment can prevent us from hearing the service user's perspective on the matter at hand. In contexts where we are listening to a group of people, such as in groupwork or community development practice, we need to ensure that we are able to hear the range of perspectives present, not only the loudest or most influential voices. A lack of focus on service users or the diverse views of community members' perspectives can contribute to a lack of rapport and is likely to deny us important information we need to make sense of the situation in which we are engaged.

Facilitation is also an important element of listening in all methods of direct practice. *Facilitation* refers to the listener directing the speaker, often in subtle ways, to express their thoughts and feelings in a way that will help them and the worker to understand and act on their situation. An important way we can facilitate discussion is by the use of 'continuers' or 'minimal encouragers', short verbal utterances or nonverbal cues for the other to continue the conversation (Harms, 2007, p. 129). Examples of verbal minimal encouragers are 'hmm', 'yes', 'I see'. Encouragers can also extend to brief statements of empathy, such as 'that must be difficult', or specific invitations for more information, 'tell me more about that'. Nonverbal encouragers include nodding to show you understand, or agree with, the speaker's view, or leaning forward to show interest in the speaker's words. Verbal and nonverbal signs of encouragement can also enable you to steer the conversation towards the disclosure of information needed to form an assessment and intervention plan with the individual, family, group or community or team with whom you are working.

In a nutshell, we can demonstrate that we are listening by:

● Minimizing distractions and interruptions to the conversation

● Approaching the conversation with an open mind, which may involve being aware of, and putting aside, our pre-existing assumptions

● Encouraging the speaker to express themselves. We can assist this by purposeful use of encouragers and focused questions aimed at bringing attention to parts of the narrative that appear important either for the service user or the professional purpose on which we are focused.

Listening Exercise

Over the next week, take note of how you listen in conversation. For this reflective exercise, chose three conversations in which you have been engaged over the week. Try to ensure there is some variation in the examples you choose. Ideally, you should choose an example where you believe you listened well, another where you were dissatisfied with your listening and a third example somewhere in the middle of these two levels of satisfaction. This variation is likely to help you to reflect on your strengths and areas for development as a listener. Complete the following table as you reflect on your examples. In each row, briefly describe the example, such as 'conversation over lunch with my friend'. Then provide a rating from 1–5 (with 1 being completely untrue to 5 being completely true) for each of the following statements:

1. I focused entirely on the speaker – consider what helped you focus and what prevented you from focusing, such as distractions.

2. I maintained an open mind – consider what helped you maintain an open mind and any challenges you faced to keeping an open mind.

3. I encouraged the speaker to express themselves – consider how you created or limited opportunities for the speaker to express themselves.

In the final column, note your reflections on any other aspect of how you listened, or what prevented you from listening well in the conversation.

	I focused entirely on the speaker	I maintained an open mind	I encouraged the speaker to express themselves	Other reflections
Example 1	(rating 1–5)	(rating 1–5)	(rating 1–5)	
Example 2	(rating 1–5	(rating 1–5)	(rating 1–5)	
Example 3	(rating 1–5)	(rating 1–5)	(rating 1–5)	

After you have completed the listening exercise, consider the following questions:

1. What have learned about your strengths as a listener?

2. What have you learned about your areas for further development?

3. Identify two strategies for improving your listening skills.

Listening with Two or More People

Many social work practice situations involve listening to more than one person. For example, in family work practice, it is important that we hear the perspectives of all family members and in group and community work, it is vital to listen to all group and community members. Listening well to each person is important for:

● Building their confidence in you as someone who is open to all participants' viewpoints

● Ensuring that you have a comprehensive picture of the situation that recognizes similarities and differences in the viewpoints of members of the family, group and community.

There are a number of strategies that social workers can use to ensure that they are able to listen equitably to different viewpoints. These strategies include:

● Establishing ground rules or principles at the outset of a meeting that encourage recognition of all perspectives.

● Ensuring that equivalent time is allocated to hearing different perspectives.

● Subtly facilitating equivalent speaking space to each person. For example, in a family meeting, the social worker may direct open questions to specific individuals, rather than asking open questions to the whole family group.

● Being explicit about ensuring equal speaking space, for example stating that a particular group member has already spoken and asking for another person to speak.

● Increasing awareness within the family, group or community of patterns of inequality in speaking and inviting the group to take responsibility for ensuring greater equality in speaking. For instance, we can provide members of the group with visual cues that show who is speaking most often in a group.

● Ensuring the safety of each person to speak. In some situations, such as abuse or violence within the family, it may be necessary to hold separate meetings for different family members.

Nonverbal Communication

We turn next to nonverbal communication. This refers to communication through our physical presence and behaviour. Nonverbal behaviour includes facial expressions, posture, nonvocal cues, such as pitch and tone of voice, and nonverbal cues such as nodding, distance to the other person. It is important that you, as a social worker, give at least as much attention to your nonverbal communication as your spoken communication for two reasons. The first is that nonverbal communication is a highly influential form of communication. Studies on communication have indicated that up to 85% of the communication is conveyed through nonverbal interaction (Harms, 2007). The second reason is that attention to nonverbal communication is vital to beginning to address the fear, distrust and resistance that many service users feel towards social workers, and other helping professionals.

Achieving congruence in nonverbal communication with those with whom we are communicating will assist us to build appropriate professional relationships. Social workers need to be able to reflect on their nonverbal behaviour and adjust this behaviour to the communication needs of service users and their specific practice environment. One of the challenges in communicating nonverbally is that much of this behaviour is unconscious to us, and we may be unaware of a habit that can, in a practice environment, become distracting to the service user. Also, nonverbal communication 'habits' that we may have developed in one context may be inappropriate in another context. For example, in some practice environments, it may be appropriate to have open, smiling and engaging facial expressions and in others, such as some legal contexts or dealing with clients who are facing sudden trauma, such facial expressions may be inappropriate.

A number of models of nonverbal communication have been developed to assist social workers and other helping professionals to reflect on and demonstrate nonverbal behaviour that is appropriate for facilitating a constructive and purposeful interaction. Most of these guides have been developed for counselling and casework interactions but, nonetheless, have utility for other situations where social workers seek to demonstrate engagement, interest and empathy with others. One of the most well-known models of nonverbal communication for health and social care professionals is SOLER. This model was developed by Gerard Egan (2010) for counsellors and caseworkers, but can also be used as a framework for reviewing our nonverbal behaviour in other contexts. The meaning of the acronym SOLER is as follows:

S: **Sitting squarely** – that is, facing the person we are communicating with

O: **Open body posture** – this involves avoiding crossing one's arms across one's body or placing an object across one's body, such as a folder. However, crossed legs are acceptable as long as it is does not compromise the perception of an open body posture

L: **Leaning towards the other** – sufficiently to demonstrate interest and engagement but not so far as to imply a level of intensity that could be uncomfortable for the person with whom we are communicating

E: **Eye contact** – maintaining an appropriate level of eye contact with the service user to demonstrate that we are listening and interested in their story but no so much as to intimidate

R: **Relaxed** – appearing relaxed in one's facial expression and body posture is important for putting those with whom we are communicating at ease.

Egan's model is helpful on a number of levels. SOLER covers many dimensions of nonverbal behaviour and it is easy to recall, enabling us to quickly assess and adjust our nonverbal behaviour even in the midst of a practice situation. While some may regard the model as prescriptive, it is sufficiently broad to be relevant to a range of contexts of professional communication.

Nonetheless, the model does not address some cultural, gender and contextual differences that can impact on effective nonverbal communication. The model places great emphasis on the postural aspects of nonverbal communication but less on other equally important aspects of nonverbal communication, such as facial expression, interpersonal distance and appearance. We now turn to consideration of how we can demonstrate cultural sensitivity in our nonverbal communication.

Cultural Diversity and Nonverbal Communication

Inevitably as social workers we will find ourselves working with service users from cultures other than our own. By culture, I refer to a set of beliefs and values that are shared by a group and which may have their foundation in a particular geographical or historical location (Yan, 2008). While some social workers may work with a specific cultural groups, in many practice contexts social workers come into contact with service users from a wide variety of cultures. As we seek to engage service users in culturally sensitive ways, it is important to ensure that we recognize differences yet avoid stereotyping service users and denying their individual experience or expression of cultural identity. There are two ways we can achieve this balance. The first is becoming informed of evidence on cultural differences in communication so that we can be sensitive to differences in communication that *may* be present in our interactions with people from cultures other than our own. This is especially important if we are engaging regularly with people from a specific cultural community other than our own. The ways you can become informed include participating in learning opportunities relevant to communication with that community, seeking advice from members of that community, and seeking out research on communication with the community. The second way is to attune yourself to the communication strategies of people within the communities you work with, such as taking time to observe communication styles and reactions to different forms of communication. This involves being able to adjust your communication to better match the communication of others.

There is a large body of work on cultural competence in professional communication (Reynolds and Valentine, 2004). In the field of social work, there is a great deal of critique of the concept of cultural competence. To attempt to gain cultural competency can ignore the dynamic and diverse character of culture. Further, Johnson and Munch (2009) argue that tensions exist between the concept of cultural competence and social workers' responsibility to recognize the unique experience of the individual, to learn from the client and to value the individual's right to self-determination.

In essence, in understanding cultural difference, it is important that we walk a fine line between understanding differences among cultural groups while also seeking and valuing the unique experience of the individual. In our consideration of cultural difference in nonverbal communication, we will confine ourselves to some key differences in nonverbal communication observed in cross-cultural research and practice. It is especially important to be aware of cultural differences in nonverbal communication because as Chen and Han (2001, p. 118) observe: 'nonverbal communication is more culturally bound than verbal communication, it can quickly elicit confusion and irritation, leading to ethnic stereotyping'. The key differences we will focus on in patterns of communication include variations in:

● The use of eye contact

● Level and nature of facial expression

● Comfort with silence

● Interpersonal distance

● Norms about interactions between genders.

Cultural norms about the use of eye contact vary considerably. Some level of eye contact is important for building rapport with service users and for engaging in an assessment of service users' situations. However, people from Western cultures, such the dominant cultures of Europe, North America, Canada, Australia and New Zealand, tend to have a preference for high levels of eye contact in interpersonal interaction. Because many of the casework and counselling texts are written by authors from the dominant cultural groups within these nations, it has been widely accepted that high levels of eye contact are important for effective engagement in casework contexts. Yet in many Asian and indigenous cultures, high levels of eye contact can be viewed as impolite, invasive or intimidating (Chen and Han, 2001). It is important then to be alert to the possibility that service users from these cultural backgrounds may not be comfortable with high levels of eye contact. However, do not assume that 'all' service users from indigenous or Asian cultures would prefer limited eye contact. If the service user appears uncomfortable with eye contact, it is important that you take steps to reduce the level of eye contact in the interaction. Some ways of doing this include: changing the seating arrangements into a V shape, so that you are more side on, rather than squarely facing service users; be conscious of increasing your visual focus in other directions, such as looking down at your notes, or outwards in the same direction as the service user's visual gaze, rather than directly at the service user; and mirroring the nonverbal behaviour of the service user.

Cultural norms in relation to facial expressions, like the norms governing eye contact, vary markedly by culture. Drawing on a large body of research, Butler et al. (2007, p. 31) assert that: 'Western European values such as independence and self-assertion encourage open emotion expression in most situations' and, by contrast, 'Asian values such as interdependence and relationship harmony might encourage suppression equally.' In many Western cultures, an open, highly expressive face is regarded as engaging and, hence, many counselling and casework texts emphasize the importance of open facial expressions, such as smiling, in building rapport. However, in some cultures, such as some Asian cultures, there is much emphasis on the containment of facial expression. Like all other forms of nonverbal expression, it is important that you are aware of the nature and impact of your facial expression. Being able to adapt your facial expression to more closely mirror that of the client is an important dimension of all communication but appears to be especially important in culturally sensitive practice.

Expectations regarding the presence of silence in conversations appear to vary considerably by culture. In many dominant cultures of many Western nations, silence may be regarded as uncomfortable or as an invitation for the other person to speak. By contrast, cross-cultural researchers observe that silence appears to play an important role in many non-Western cultural contexts. Reflecting on groupwork practice, Chen and Han (2001) assert that Asian participants may remain silent to avoid disagreement or keep a low profile in the group. Further, Chen and Han (2001, p. 118) assert: 'In these cases, silence is not necessarily a signal inviting others to take over the conversation.' Similarly, indigenous social workers urge practitioners to allow space for silence in their interactions with service users. For example, in reflecting on child welfare work with indigenous clients, Skuse (2007, p. 26) remarks:

> it's important to understand different ways of communicating, both verbally and non-verbally (for example eye contact). They [the client] may be sitting there thinking about what you are saying and you may think they're ignoring you. They may not even give you an answer then; they may give you an answer tomorrow.

Silence can be important for participants in any interaction, including social work interactions, to process information and emotions and to gather ideas.

Assumptions about the appropriateness of interpersonal distance also vary between cultural groups. Sue and Sue (1977) suggest that people from Anglo-Celtic cultures, by which they mean the dominant cultures of Western nations, tend to expect greater interpersonal distance than those from some African and Asian cultures. Again, the issue here is for the worker to moderate their behaviour to more closely mirror that with which the service user feels comfortable. At the same time, it is important that the worker does not compromise themselves to the point that they become uncomfortable in the interaction.

All cultures have rules that govern the norms of interaction within and across genders. Interactions among people of the same gender are also governed by rules that are often unacknowledged. For example, in many Anglophone cultures, physical touch among women is relatively common but among men it may be regarded as inappropriate. In some indigenous cultures, there are strict rules about issues that might be regarded as 'women's business' and 'men's business' and it would be considered inappropriate, for instance, for a male social worker to discuss some aspects of women's business (Corporal, 2007, p. 14). If you are working regularly with a particular cultural group other than your own, it is vital that you become knowledgeable about, and demonstrate respect for, the norms governing interactions within and across genders. If, on the other hand, your work brings you into contact with people from a wide variety of cultural backgrounds, it may be difficult to be aware of all the cultural variations concerning appropriate forms of interaction within and between genders. In these cases, it is important that you are alert to cultural differences in interactions between and within genders and ensure that, as far as possible, you avoid contravening cultural protocols. Until you are certain of these protocols, it is advisable to err on the side of caution by maintaining a polite and respectful distance in your contact with service users of the opposite gender. It is helpful to be especially alert and responsive to signs of discomfort in others. For example, if you offer to shake the hand of a person of the opposite gender and that person appears reluctant to do so, be ready to withdraw that offer in a low-key way so as to avoid embarrassment to them.

Appearance, Identity and Communication

Our physical appearance, particularly our clothing, personal grooming and general demeanour, communicates a great deal about ourselves, particularly our identity, to others. This information can be important to service users' assessment of whether they regard us as a credible source of assistance to them. Like all aspects of ourselves, our appearance is also a dimension of the use of self in social work and, no less than our verbal and nonverbal communication, should be subject to critical reflection. Some aspects of our appearance reflect aspects of our identity and, as such, we may not want to change these aspects of our appearance or these aspects may be unalterable. How we manage these aspects of our appearance and identity in our inter-actions with service users is likely to be quite different to those aspects of our appearance, such as our clothing and general demeanour.

Let's turn first to those aspects of our appearance that are amenable to change and which may have significant influence on service users' percep-tions of us and our capacity to be of assistance to them. These aspects include our clothing, our personal grooming and our general physical appearance and demeanour. Very little attention is paid in the social work literature to these aspects of our appearance. This is surprising, given the large body of literature in other fields, such as business, on the importance of appearance to effective impression management and engagement with service users. In some practice contexts, such as health services, there are formal dress codes that apply to a broad range of staff including social workers. Beyond these specific practice contexts, the issue of appearance is rarely discussed. It is as though many of us assume, incorrectly, that our presentation has little impact on our relationships with service users or in service users' assessment of our capacity.

Like all aspects of self in social work, our appearance should be subject to critical reflection. In addition to sending a message of respect for others, social workers should convey in their words and actions a clear statement of their professional purpose, which should always include the ability and willingness to be of assistance to service users and community members (Sheldon and Macdonald, 2009). In reflecting a capacity for personal self care, our appearance can also promote service users' confidence in our capacity to be of assistance to them.

A clean neutral appearance helps to reduce the chance that your appear-ance will be a distraction for the service user. Our attire and demeanour should reflect the accepted standards of the variety of services and individ-uals with whom we are likely to engage in our daily work, not only the standards of the service we are employed within. For example, working in a service for young people, we will be likely to interact not only with the young people, but perhaps also their families, the police service, schools and the legal profession. We need to ensure that we respect the dress codes of courts of law and other environments, such as public talks, where you seek to advocate for or publicly represent service users. Failure to reflect these codes will limit your credibility and may negatively affect your capacity to convey your message.

Let's turn now to those aspects of our appearance that may be difficult or impossible to alter. Unalterable or difficult to alter aspects of ourselves that are likely to influence our appearance can include age, gender, height and weight, skin tone and facial shape, and signifiers of ability or disability. These elements of our appearance reflect aspects of our personal and cultural identity (or identities) to service users and can be the subject of positive or negative assessment by them. For example, the service user may comment that they would prefer to have a social worker of a different age, gender or ethnicity to your own. In some cases, you may be required by law to accommodate these requests, such as in some services, clients will have a right to be served by a person of the same gender or same ethnic group. In some, but not all cases, you may work in a service where the workforce is sufficiently large and diverse to accommodate the service user's request for another worker based on perceived greater compatibility between themselves and a worker with a similar set of identities to them.

Anti-oppressive practice theory emphasizes that practitioners should be able to critically reflect on their identities and how this shapes their interactions with service users (Dominelli, 2002; Healy, 2005). Accordingly, it is important that you are able to critically reflect on your appearance and your identity and, as appropriate, to explore service users' concerns with them. For example, a child protection service user may complain about the involvement of an 'older worker whose kids are grown up' or a 'young, childless worker'. The social worker could respond to this by acknowledging and exploring the service user's concerns; these concerns may include the perception that the worker will not understand or may judge them. If the social worker can explore these concerns and commit, both in their words and actions, to the values that the service user would like to see in the relationship, such as understanding and a nonjudgmental attitude, the worker is likely to overcome the service user's concerns. While it is easy to become defensive when aspects of our identity are questioned, it is more productive for your relationship with the service user if you can explore the basis of their concerns and put strategies in place to address these concerns. In so doing, you demonstrate a genuine willingness to be of assistance and this attitude is positively correlated with client satisfaction with social work services (Maiter et al., 2006; Sheldon and MacDonald, 2009).

Observation Skills

Observation refers to taking note of and analysing what we see and experience either in our direct interaction with service users and community members or when we observe them in interactions with others, such as family or community members. The profession's recognition of the importance of observation has varied at different points in our history and among different groups in the profession (Le Riche, 1998). Observation of infants and children, particularly in interaction with their parents, has been a cornerstone of psychodynamic approaches to social work (Tanner, 1998). Within the psychodynamic approach, observation is distinct from active engagement with service users and may involve the social worker in observing the service user(s) from a distance, such as behind a two-way mirror (Trowell and Miles, 1991, cited in Tanner, 1998). Recently, Harry Ferguson (2011, p. 206) has argued for a renewed acknowledgment of the role of observation as part of what he defines as 'intimate social work practice', that is, practice which recognizes 'the centrality of the emotions and the body and the mind of the worker and service user in doing and experiencing' social work. In this section, I refer to observation as part of the active engagement between us as social workers and those with whom we work.

Observation provides us with information about the emotional state and reactions of those with whom we work. This information can enhance our capacity to communicate with a diverse range of individuals and communities. For example, in working with a family where there is conflict between a young person and their parent, we may use our observations about the relative disengagement of the young person to allow them as much space as possible in determining whether and how they will join our meeting with their family.

By sharing some of our observations with service users, we can also build a common understanding of their circumstances. Sharing observations can be seen as a form of clarification, in that we invite the service user to comment on our observations. For example, as part of developing a case plan with a young person leaving out-of-home care, we might share with them that while they appear to be relieved to have left the care system, they also seem sad about the loss of connection with a foster parent. This reflection could help us to explore the service user's experiences in care and what points of connection, if any, they would like to maintain with their foster family or the care system.

In a cross-cultural context, much information is to be gained by observing norms about interaction. For example, you may observe that there appears to be age hierarchy determining who speaks first in any interaction or you may notice that facial expression and vocal tone are subdued. By observing and reflecting these patterns, you enhance your ability to communicate effectively with people from cultures other than your own.

Observations about service users and community members' response to us, as workers, can also provide a basis for critical reflection on our practice

(Le Riche, 1998). By reflecting on circumstances in which we experience an unexpected or unpleasant response from a service user, or community member, we might reflect on what contribution we have made to that reaction. It may be that the service user's response has valuable information for us about our role and how we might improve our communication in this role. For example, reflecting on a situation in which we appeared to trigger an angry response from a service user, we may find that we failed to communicate difficult information in a sufficiently sensitive way or that our timing of the communication contributed to the service user's response. Of course, it also needs to be acknowledged that the very nature of some social work roles is more likely to give rise to negative responses from service users, for example any role that involves curtailing service user's individual rights, such as roles in statutory social work services. Even so, reflecting on how we might most clearly and sensitively communicate with service users is likely to enhance our capacity to build an effective working relationship in these roles (Trotter, 2004, 2006; see also Miller, 2009).

Observations about our own responses to circumstances we encounter in our practice are important to critical reflection. Our own reactions to situations, particularly strong reactions, should not be ignored. By subjecting our reactions to critical scrutiny, we may uncover personal biases but, equally, we may also recognize that there is an issue that needs further exploration. For example, a strong negative 'gut' reaction to a parent we meet in the context of a child protection assessment may, on reflection, be because the parent has similar physical features to an abusive parent with whom you have previously worked. This insight can enable us to avoid allowing previous practice encounters to negatively impact on the current practice situation. Alternatively, on reflection, we might conclude that our reaction was a response to the parent's negative description of the child and the sad demeanour of the child, and we may decide that further assessment of the situation is required.

Effective Speaking in an Interpersonal Context

The relationship between workers and the people with whom we work is an important vehicle of change in all forms of social work practice. A great deal of attention has been paid to the nature of the 'helping' relationship in the interpersonal practice literature, but it is the case that the relationship between worker and client is central to all methods of social work practice. Drawing on our ethical framework and evidence on best practice, the relationship that social welfare professionals seek to develop is characterized by:

- a focus on understanding the views of service users and/or community members

- acceptance and a nonjudgmental attitude

- respect for service users' and community members' right to participate in decisions that affect them.

Staying on Track and Focused

In many contexts of social work practice, we need to develop an accurate and detailed picture of service users' or community members' perspectives. Developing this understanding is an active process requiring good listening skills, facilitation skills and the capacity to check the accuracy of our emerging understanding with those with whom we are interacting. Whereas in everyday conversation, we might engage in a two-way expression process, in social work practice our communication process should be focused on enabling the other person to express themselves. For example, if a client tells us they are grieving for the breakdown of their relationship with a partner, it is more important for us to explore with them their experience of grief than to share our experience of grieving over a similar loss. Of course, it may be appropriate to share that we have had a similar experience, but only insofar as it enables the service user or community member to express themselves. In a professional practice context, the focus of the interaction should remain on the service user or community member and not be an expression or exploration of the social worker's experience.

We now turn to communication skills that enable you to stay on track, demonstrate to the service user your emerging understanding of their perspective, and enabling them to correct any misunderstandings. *Paraphrasing* involves a brief statement reflecting back to the service user or community member our understanding of the thoughts or feelings underpinning or evident in what they said, which may also be evident in the demeanour of the service user. For example, in response to a young person happily discussing the apartment they have just moved into, we might say: 'it sounds like you are very happy in your new home.'

Paraphrasing demonstrates that the caseworker is listening. Paraphrasing helps to ensure the accuracy our understanding, as through paraphrasing we can provide the service user with an opportunity to correct our view. Paraphrasing is used more frequently in casework and counselling than in everyday conversation. This is because one function of paraphrasing is to keep the discussion focused on the issue at hand and on enabling the service user to express their views; this contrasts with the mutual exchange of viewpoints that characterizes everyday conversation.

Parroting involves repeating back the exact words of the service user and is used to emphasize key points in the statements to you. For example, in the following statement, 'after hearing the news, I went into shock', we might parrot back 'went into shock'. Parroting can be part of demonstrating understanding and empathy of the service user's situation.

The third of these tracking and focusing skills is the skill of *clarification*, which involves seeking a more complete understanding of the person's situation. Clarification is important for ensuring that you understand who and what is important to the service user or community member. In seeking clarification, it is important to avoid sounding inquisitorial. For example, it is important to avoid terms like 'please explain' when asking for further information. Instead, it can be helpful to put forward your understanding as a clarifying question, such as: 'so Joanne is your daughter, is that right?' This question allows the service user to clarify their relationship to 'Joanne'. We can also avoid sounding inquisitorial by asking in a sensitive way for more information, such as: 'Can you tell me a little more about your relationship with Joanne?' Clarifying statements and questions can also relate to service users' experience of an event. For example, at a community meeting, you might ask: 'Can I please clarify then, the community was not informed about the government consultation of the plan to build a block of apartments on the land?' It is important that clarifying statements include the option for respondents to correct your interpretation. An explicit question, such as 'have I interpreted that correctly?' can help to let respondents know you are seeking their viewpoints.

While clarifying questions, paraphrasing and parroting are important for keeping us on track and for ensuring the alignment of our interpretation with the view of the service user, clarification needs to be used sparingly. An overuse of clarifying questions can create an impression that we are not listening attentively or that we do not have the capacity to understand the service user's or community member's story. A person can become frustrated if they are asked, too frequently, to explain or clarify points that they believe should be obvious to the service provider. For example, a community worker would be expected to have some understanding of recent events, particularly high-profile events in the community, and of key members of the community, such as formal and informal leaders.

The skill of summarizing refers to the use of statements that bring together the key issues raised and points covered and will often involve a statement of future action. Because of the range of topics covered, summaries will tend to be significantly longer than paraphrases. Summaries can also facilitate some power sharing in the casework interaction by providing service users with both clarity about the caseworker's understanding of the major themes and proposed directions for future action and the opportunity to clarify misinterpretation. Summaries need to be used sparingly as their overuse can lead to too greater focus on the sense the worker is making of the interaction rather than facilitating the service user's expression of views.

The Use of Questions

The effective use of questions is important in all forms of social work to gain a clear understanding of service users' situations. Yet the inappropriate use of questions can have a negative effect on your relationship with the service user. Perhaps most obviously, the overuse of closed questions can lead the service user to feel they are being interrogated. As we develop our communication skills for practice, it is important that we consider the different forms of questions and their effects on our professional relationships.

Open questions are intended to encourage the client to answer in an extended or narrative form. According to Boyle et al. (2006, p. 123): 'Open-ended questions allow the client to answer as he or she chooses, giving whatever detail the client deems appropriate based on the client's interpretation of the situation.' Open-ended questions can be helpful in indicating to the service user that you are actively seeking their view of the situation and, as such, are important for building rapport and gaining a shared understanding of the situation.

Open-ended questions may begin with words such as 'what', 'how', 'when' and 'who' or with questioning statements hinting at information you might be looking for. For example, we may say: 'John, can you tell me a little more about what has happened at home to make you so unhappy there.' This hinting style of questioning, which is intended to invite the service user to tell of their perspective, can be especially important when working with services users from non-Western cultures. For instance, Aboriginal service users can find direct questions including open questions quite intimidating (Department of Justice and Attorney General, 2000).

It is important to avoid questions beginning with 'why' because such questions can appear inquisitorial and imply that the worker does not believe, understand or empathize with the service user's view. For example, the question 'why didn't you leave the situation?' can imply that the service user should have left the situation. Similarly, 'why did you take the pills?' can imply that the person should not have taken the pills or that the worker is finding it hard to understand their actions. The intention to explore the motivations for taking 'the pills' could be put more openly as: 'What were you feeling when you took the pills?'

Open-ended questions can be limited or create problems in some situations. Open-ended questions may not be helpful in situations where specific information is needed, such as in possible medical emergencies or in referring clients to services. For example, in a situation where you suspect a client has overdosed on medication, you may need to know the amount of medication taken. Similarly, open-ended questions may not be helpful in gaining information needed to determine client eligibility for a service. Open-ended questions can also be unhelpful when the client is an emotional state that can impede their capacity to express themselves fully. For example, a person in a state of emotional shock may be too overwhelmed to answer open questions. Also, it is important to limit open-ended questions in situations where you have limited time to hear the answers. When you are under significant time pressure, it is better to communicate this to the service user than to cut off the service user as they respond to questions from you.

Closed questions are questions that call for a short answer of a single word, such as yes or no, to a short sentence. Closed questions can be helpful for gathering specific information. This information may be needed to gain an overview of the service user's situation, to determine their eligibility for a service, or to investigate a particular concern. In some instances, these questions might form part of the initial engagement with the service user, such as: 'I just need to ask some questions before we can discuss your matter in more detail.'

Closed questions should be used sparingly in social work practice. A key problem is that closed questions reinforce the power of the worker to direct the interaction. For this reason, the extensive use of closed questions can be a direct contradiction of our value of promoting the service user's capacity for self-determination. The extended use of closed questions creates an inquisitorial tone to the interview that is likely to alienate the service user. Boyle et al. (2006, p. 124) also suggest that the overuse of closed questions can reinforce the view of the service provider as expert and so erroneously lead the service user to believe that 'once they have supplied all the answers, the social worker will provide a solution'.

In recent years, with the growth of strengths-based, narrative and solution-focused approaches to practice, there is increased development of questions as part of the assessment and intervention process. Despite their different philosophical origins, narrative, strengths-based and solution-focused approaches all recognize the power of language in shaping service outcomes. Across these different approaches, language is recognized as much more than a vehicle for expression and instead can shape our awareness of the possibilities open to us. One of the shared characteristics of these different approaches is the optimistic view of human capacity and hence there is some emphasis on questions that reveal and explore those capacities. We turn here to some examples of these types of questions:

- **Coping questions** explore how the client has coped with their situation. For example, instead of only exploring a range of problems a service user is experiencing, the worker may also ask: 'Given everything that's going on for you right now, how have you managed to get the children to school every day?' Coping questions can help to focus our and the service user's attention on the service user's capacities and in so doing counter the focus on failure or pathology that can easily dominate social work interactions, such as risk assessments. Coping questions can also demonstrate that you are seeking to understand and empathize with the service user's circumstances.

- **Exception questions** ask service users to report on situations where they experienced a breakthrough, or at least a break from, the issue of concern. For example, when working with a young person who has missed two of the past five days at school, the worker might ask: 'What was different about the three days that you were able to get to school?' Like coping questions, exception questions challenge a focus on the problems facing the individual and instead draw attention to exceptions to the problem. We can use these exceptions as a way of assisting people to develop solutions that may work for them.

- **Scaling questions** ask the service user to rate their experience on a continuum. For example, the worker might ask: 'On a scale of 1 to 10, with 1 feeling completely anxious and 10 feeling completely calm, can you tell me how you feel about your anxiety today?' The scaling questions enable a person to 'externalize' a problem. This means that the worker and the person with whom they are working view the issue as something external to the client and this can assist us to reconceptualize a problem as more amenable to change than if it were an integral part of the person. For example, a person might reconceptualize themselves a person who battles, and sometimes beats, anxiety, rather than as an 'anxious person'.

- **Miracle questions** invite the service user to consider their situation without the problem or issue of concern. The term 'miracle' is used to refer to the fact that the worker is inviting the client not to engage in a step-by-step analysis of their concern but rather to imagine a completely different situation. For example, the worker may ask: 'If this nightmare was over tomorrow, how would your life be different?' or 'If a miracle happened tonight, what would your life be like tomorrow?' Like coping and exception questions, the miracle question is intended to counter a focus on pathology or failure. It is also intended to invite us, as workers, and those with whom we work to spend at least as much of our energies on creating a different and more positive future as we do on understanding the problems of the present.

Demonstrating Sympathy and Empathy

In many social work contexts, the demonstration of sympathy and empathy is important for expressing concern for the service user and understanding of their situation. These concepts are helpful to building rapport with the service user.

Sympathy refers to acknowledging and being moved by the experience of the other. For example, on hearing about a young mother's struggle to complete school, a social worker may sympathetically comment on the difficulty of the young person's struggle, with words such as 'that must be really difficult'. Similarly, on hearing that a service user has recently been widowed, the social worker might say 'I'm sorry for your loss'. An expression of sympathy shows that you hear the difficulty being experienced, and expressed, by the other person. Sympathy has been described as 'passive understanding' (Trevithick, 2005, p. 154) because it requires only that the sympathizer observe and reflect back the other's expression of their experience. Even so, sympathetic responses can be helpful for demonstrating our willingness to acknowledge the experience of the other. On the other hand, too much sympathy can be experienced as unhelpful because it can lead the service user to conclude that the social worker did not 'really understand' or could not 'identify' with their situation.

Empathy refers to a willingness to imagine and, in that imagining, experience some of the pain or difficulty of the service user. By empathizing, we put ourselves in the position of the other person and reflect back to them what we imagine their experience to be like. Empathy is often regarded as more active than sympathy because it requires us to more fully enter into the experience of the service user. The demonstration of empathy involves a number of elements, including:

- identifying the experience of the service user

- imagining what that experience is like for the service user, in other words, trying to enter into the lived experience of the service user

- putting that understanding, born of imaginatively entering into the service user's world, into words

- providing them with the opportunity to further explore that understanding.

The following example demonstrates the difference between a sympathetic and empathic response.

Practice example

Service user: 'Since the diagnosis, I feel I can't go on, I have no motivation, everything seems bleak.'

Practitioner's sympathetic response: 'I'm sorry this is such a difficult time for you.'

Practitioner's empathetic response: 'The diagnosis has left you feeling sad and frightened. It seems that it is difficult to find a reason to go on with your future seeming so uncertain, is that right?'

I have concluded the empathic response with a question because it is important for the service user to have the opportunity to correct your understanding of their situation. This can be achieved by including a vocal inflection at the end of the sentence, to indicate that a correction is welcome, or by the inclusion of a direct question, such as 'have I understood you correctly?'

Over to you ...

Developing sympathetic and empathetic responses

Consider the following service user statements and develop a sympathetic or empathetic response to the statements.

- Statement from a young woman whose partner has become increasingly verbally hostile towards her: 'Rob has been really angry lately and, after last night's violent outburst, I'm frightened to go home.'

Sympathetic response:

Empathetic response:

- Statement from a community member living on a housing estate: 'The estate used to be a great place to live but now I can't get any peace. I wish all these new families with teenage kids would leave. They are ruining the neighbourhood.'

Sympathetic response:

Empathetic response:

Strengths and Limits of Empathy

The demonstration of empathy is widely regarded as a cornerstone of effective social work practice because of its potential to demonstrate care for the service user, build rapport, and promote service user insight into how their experience may be viewed by others. Trevithick (2005, p. 155) states:

> the importance of being understood by another human being is enormously important, not least because it can lead to self-understanding. Self-understanding can last a lifetime: longer than our professional involvement, which may be fleeting. Nevertheless our role in this process of self-discovery may be deeply significant.

Many social workers view the demonstration of empathy as integral to achieving change, especially in interpersonal and groupwork practice. When we demonstrate empathy, we can create a safe space in which the service user and community member can explore the challenges facing them.

Demonstrating empathy is also important in community practice and policy contexts; however, much less has been written on empathy in macro practice contexts. Empathy is important in macro practice contexts for demonstrating to community members or other participants in the policy process that you understand their point of view. Indeed, if the community worker or policy worker is unable to demonstrate empathy for a range of positions on an issue, they risk being perceived as 'captured' by a particular interest group or community. Empathy is important for negotiating across differences, such as differences within a community or different perspectives on a policy outcome, and thus for achieving a workable solution to community or policy problems.

The capacity of the worker to demonstrate empathy has been shown to be an important factor in service user satisfaction with service provision (Maiter et al., 2006; Trotter, 2002). Workers' use of empathy has been linked to positive outcomes in child protection, for example children being in care for shorter periods, families making more progress (see Trotter, 2004). Lack of empathy, as indicated by workers making judgemental comments about families or individuals, has been linked to negative outcomes, such as greater levels of continued offending among juvenile offenders than would be anticipated by their case history (Trotter, 2006).

While the importance of the capacity to demonstrate empathy is well established, research points to some problems with the use of empathy. The first is that workers' inappropriate use of empathy has been linked in some circumstances to negative service outcomes. For example, referring to research on juvenile offenders, Trotter (2006) concluded that workers who demonstrate high levels of empathy may inadvertently imply that they not only understand but endorse the service user's behaviour, including antisocial behaviour. In his study of child protection services, Trotter (2002) stated that it was necessary for workers to combine an empathetic and positive approach to service users with clear expectations and a willingness to gently confront families with abuse and neglect concerns.

Trotter (2004, p. 137) states that empathy should be linked to a clarity of purpose and a 'prosocial' perspective on the part of the service provider. Prosocial perspective means reinforcing behaviours and attitudes that are consistent with the goals you are trying to achieve with the service user, for example reduced violence, increased school attendance, and challenging antisocial or criminal comments or actions (Trotter, 2004). Trotter (2004) identifies four steps in promoting prosocial attitudes in our communication with service users:

1. The worker identifies prosocial attitudes or behaviour by the service user or community member, for example attending a parenting group

2. The worker rewards and encourages prosocial attitudes and behaviours by, for example, noticing and praising these attitudes and behaviours

3. The worker models prosocial actions and comments on the way they relate to the service user, for example being respectful, punctual

4. The worker challenges antisocial or pro-criminal comments, for example 'everybody does it', 'it doesn't harm anyone'.

A further limit to empathy is its potential to lead us to overidentify with the service user and in so doing leave us unable to confront aspects of the service user's outlook or behaviour that may harm others. Writing on the problems of overidentification in child protection work, Killen (1996, p. 793) defines overidentification as

> a form of projective identification where we project onto the parents our own feelings and qualities or feelings and qualities we believe that we have towards children, instead of empathizing with and facing the parents' and children's realities.

Avoiding overidentification can be a particular challenge because the demonstration of empathy inherently relies on our capacity to imagine what it would be like to walk in the service user's shoes. Assuming how we would feel and react if we were in the service user's situation can prevent us from understanding service user motivations or attitudes that may be far different from our own, or at least those motivations we are willing to attribute to ourselves. In other words, we are likely to attribute to ourselves and to service users more positive motivations than might necessarily be the case. At its most problematic, overidentification can prevent us from seeing how the service user may hold attitudes or engage in behaviours that inadvertently or deliberately harm others. For example, the belief that all parents care for their children, if given the right circumstances, may prevent us from identifying the small proportion of parents who present a true danger to their children. Similarly, assuming that the juvenile offender's violent behaviour was an expression of their desperate circumstances can lead us to underestimate the experience of the victim and perhaps underestimate the violent intent of the offender. Engaging in critical reflection with peers and with a professional supervisor can be helpful in recognizing when we have begun to overidentify with service users and it can help us in facing the service user in their 'reality' rather than in the reality we might imagine. Of course, it is important that your supervisor has the capacity themselves to stand outside the practice situation. This can be a particular problem where the supervisor also has developed a position or perspective in relation to particular cases, as can happen when the supervisor is also involved in the same practice situation. In some instances, therefore, it may be necessary to seek external supervision.

Communication in Teams

So far, I have considered communication skills in direct practice with service users and community members. I want now to turn to communication in a team environment. Being able to communicate well in teams is vital, given that social workers often work in teams (Martin and Rogers, 2004). Some teams share a common disciplinary base, although in many health and welfare service contexts teams are multidisciplinary. The terms 'multidisciplinary' and 'interdisciplinary' refer to 'a team of individuals with different training backgrounds, who share common objectives but make a different but complementary contribution' to achieving these objectives (Marshall et al., 1979, cited in Leathard, 2003, p. 5).

Teams provide many advantages for enhancing direct practice outcomes. Teams can enhance decision-making by providing opportunities for members of the team to critically reflect on practice situations and, in multidisciplinary teams, by providing opportunities for the application of complementary professional knowledge and skills to practice (Anning et al., 2006; Leathard, 2003; Martin and Rogers, 2004). However, teams also present many challenges. These challenges include managing differences in relation to the definition of purpose, equitably recognizing the contribution of each team member to the achievement of that purpose, conflicts over power and authority and over the distribution of workload among team members (Anning et al., 2006; Leathard, 2003). Notwithstanding these challenges, as social workers, it is likely we will work in teams and our capacity to communicate in these teams will not only affect us, individually, but also our capacity to achieve outcomes with and for the clients with whom we work.

To effectively communicate in teams, we require a clear sense of the objectives of the team. The specific nature of these objectives is likely to vary between and within organizations (Anning et al., 2006). For instance, the objectives of a team in a child protection service will differ from those in a mental health service. It is important therefore that when you join a team, whether as a student on placement or as a worker, you familiarize yourself with the organizational mission and where your team fits in with that mission. This can be achieved, in part, by reviewing the formal statements of the organization about its mission and the policies and procedures for the achievement of that mission. However, these formal statements will only provide part of the picture. To understand the objectives of your organization and your team, you need also to observe and speak to organizational and team members about how they see the mission of the organization and the team.

Developing a clear sense of our role in a team is also important for effective communication with the team (Quinney, 2006). If you are a student on placement or a new worker to a team, it is likely that roles will have been established and that there is some agreement within the team about the role you are expected to play as a social worker on that team. There is likely to be formal statement of your role, sometimes referred to as the job description. While elements of one's role may be explicit, other elements will be implicit, that is, expected but unstated. For example, in some teams, the social worker may be expected to address the emotional support needs of team members in work that is emotionally demanding. We can establish the implicit elements of the social work role by observing other social workers in our practice context and also by initiating discussions with team members about their expectations of our role.

In addition to clarifying our role in a team, we may also need to negotiate elements of our role. Negotiations over roles are often sources of tension, particularly within multidisciplinary teams (Leathard, 2003), yet negotiation is necessary if team members are to maximize their contributions to the achievement of their shared objectives. For example, as social workers, we may need to negotiate our role because the existing role definition does not reflect, or allow us to exercise, the full range of skills we possess relevant to our role. Negotiation of our role requires that we clarify with team members the expectations of our role and that we understand the roles of other team members (Quinney, 2006). Role negotiation may also involve educating team members on the scope of your knowledge and skill as a social worker. For example, we might inform team members that we, as social workers, have the capacity to use a range of practice methods.

Beyond role clarification, there are several ways we can enhance communication in the teams within which we work. These include being aware of and responsive to the communication norms within the teams in which we practise. Most teams tend to develop a shared knowledge base and set language practices, such as acronyms, that are recognized by the team. Social workers often work in host organizations where other professional discourses dominate and in these contexts, we need to learn new terminology in order to communicate with the team. For example, social workers working in health settings often need to familiarize themselves with biomedical terminology so that they can translate this terminology to patients and families, and communicate credibly with their team (Opie, 1995).

We need to attend to the diverse sites of communication in teams, which can include team meetings, case conferences and, of course, written case notes (Opie, 1995). In each of these contexts, we can enhance our communication with the team by demonstrating our understanding of the team's shared purpose and ensuring that, through our communication, we support the achievement of this purpose by, for example, providing information or supporting decision-making processes. In communication with professional teams, we should avoid terms that undermine the professional nature of our work; for example, we may use the words 'interview' or 'conversation' rather than 'chat' to describe to team members our interaction with the family of a service user.

At their best, teams can contribute to reflective practice by providing members with the opportunity to review their perspectives in a blame-free environment and to build knowledge drawing on the collective insights of the team. Yet teams can be difficult contexts to maintain open communication because of clashes in different professional outlooks and also because the institutional arrangements around teams can promote competition among team members and the dominance of some disciplinary perspectives over others (Leathard, 2003; Quinney, 2006). While these challenges appear to be an inevitable feature of health and welfare service provision, there is still much we can do to support effective communication in teams. Some strategies and skills we can use to support open and respectful communication in teams, while also highlighting our contribution as social workers, include:

● Sharing relevant information openly with the team and in the appropriate forums. For example, case notes should be completed in a timely and accurate manner and the information and insights we have gained through our direct practice must be brought to decision-making venues, such as case conferences.

- Demonstrating that we can be relied on to play our role in the team by being prepared and punctual for team meetings and by ensuring that we assist our team to achieve its outcomes. For example, if our role involves liaising with service users' families, we should ensure that our team has the information they need about service users' family environments to help in team decision-making.

- Listening to the viewpoints of other team members and encouraging others to listen to these views as well by, for example, avoiding interrupting others and by probing further the information they have presented and their decision-making processes.

- Being willing to argue for our views and doing so respectfully by building on the evidence in the practice situation at hand and drawing on the best evidence available to us.

- Being willing to revise our own positions in the face of competing viewpoints of team members. It has been shown repeatedly that decision-making is enhanced in environments where individuals can subject their practice to rational scrutiny in a nonjudgemental environment (Munro, 2008).

- Being willing to reach a compromise with team members if we believe that the compromise will enable the team to achieve their objectives.

- Promoting inclusive communication by limiting the use of jargon, particularly jargon that is not familiar to team members, and by ensuring that team members are kept informed about details in the practice matter.

- Initiating reflection on the effectiveness of existing communication channels for the achievement of team objectives. For example, we might discuss with the team how the quality of case notes could be improved so that this site of communication can better inform decision-making among team members.

Effective Speaking in a Public Context

Many social workers are called on to speak in public contexts, such as appearing in court, presenting information at public meetings or pitching a case for funding to a funding body. Later in your career, you may also be asked to appear in the media. However, as this book is focused on foundational skills in social work practice, we will stay with the examples of public speaking skills that many newly qualified social workers are required to use – speaking in court and presenting information at public meetings. Despite the differences in the public contexts in which you, as a social worker, may be required to speak, there are some common rules to speaking effectively across all of them.

Effective public speaking in a public context involves having a clear message that is credible to the audience. Preparation is essential to effective communication and it involves three elements. The first element is *understanding our audience*. The key question here is: Who is the primary audience to whom we will be speaking? For example, in a court of law, the primary audience may be a magistrate or judge. Once we have established our audience, we need to consider what they are likely to know and what they will expect from us. For example, in a court, the magistrate will know the relevant legislation and is likely to expect that we can answer questions about the service user and their situation to help the magistrate develop a legal ruling on the situation. In a public meeting context, we should consider who is likely to attend the meeting and the issues that are likely to be foremost for them. Demonstrating that we understand our audience and their concerns lays the foundation for effective engagement with them.

A second principle is helping our audience to *visualize our message*. The use of pictures, numerical information (such as numbers of people affected by a community problem) and metaphors can be helpful. In a legal context, it is important that we are able to convey the image of our work context and the service user's context succinctly and clearly to the court. Key information about the service user that is likely to be relevant in a court may include current living circumstances and family circumstances, the nature of the problems facing them, the steps we have taken with service users to address these problems, areas of success and continuing problems, and the current intervention plan.

In public meetings, we are likely to have more scope, than in a court setting, to present visual images to our audience. The presentation of visual images, such as pictures of locations that are of concern to the community, or information, such as demographic data or study findings, can help to build a common base for discussion among participants. While the use of images and research data can stimulate discussion, it is important not to overwhelm participants with too much information.

A third principle of effective communication in public speaking is *attention to the process of delivery*. Our process of communication needs to be appropriate to the context. In a courtroom, it is important to directly answer the questions asked, with limited use of examples. If needed, the magistrate/judge or legal counsel will ask for further illustration of the points made. By contrast, in public meetings, it is helpful to involve the audience. There are several ways of doing this, including:

● Asking participants for their expectations about the meeting. In large meetings, we will need to consider strategies for enabling people to state their expectations, such as a survey prior to the meeting or asking people to write their expectations on notes, which are then posted for public viewing at the meeting.

● Creating specific question points in the meeting. Often it can be helpful to have such question points at regular intervals throughout the meeting, especially if the meeting is an hour or more in length. It can also be helpful to ask participants to talk to each other about their questions before inviting questions from the group as a whole. This approach, of small group discussion, can help people to formulate their questions in a way that may be most constructive for participants.

● Arranging a panel discussion as part of the meeting, where members of the panel represent different viewpoints. This can assist in stimulating discussion from a range of perspectives.

Conclusion

Social workers communicate with a broad range of people including individual service users, families, groups, community members, team members and the general public. All forms of social work draw on a common base of communication skills; however, how we deploy these skills varies according to our context, purpose and practice methods. The communication skills discussed here underpin the diverse practice methods that I introduce in the remainder of this book.

Review Questions

1. Why is it important for social workers to listen well in practice?

2. How does nonverbal communication affect a social worker's capacity to effectively engage with people from diverse cultural groups?

3. Why is observation an important part of communication in social work?

4. What are the benefits and challenges of working in teams? Give three strategies for promoting open and respectful communication in teams.

Critical Reflection Questions

1. Consider the circumstances in which you listen well and those in which your capacity to listen is compromised. What are the differences between

these situations? What can you do to ensure that you listen well in social work practice?

2. Consider an area of practice you would like to work in as a social worker. What challenges might you face in empathizing with service users in this practice context? In which situations might you overidentify with service users? How might you ensure that you are able to empathize in ways that are constructive for achieving positive outcomes in practice?

Practice Exercises

1. Role-play the following situation to experiment with the use of different types of questions.

    Imagine you work in the rehabilitation ward of a hospital where your role involves helping people who have experienced a range of health challenges to move back into the community. Part of your role involves assessing the level of support the patients have in their home and community. In this role-play, imagine you are meeting Betty Miller, a 75-year-old widow who lives at home. She is about to return home after two weeks in hospital following a hip fracture sustained after a fall in her home. Following the fall, she spent a night on the floor of her home unable to move or reach a phone to call for help. Although the rehabilitation team has organized a help alarm for Betty to wear at all times and planned a range of home improvements, Betty is anxious about returning home. Other members of the team have noted that Betty seems anxious not only about another fall but also about returning to living alone as she appears to be socially isolated.

    In this role-play, your purpose is to explore with Mrs Miller her concerns about returning home. Try first to explore these concerns using closed questions. Note what impact the use of closed questions has on the interaction. Try conducting the role-play again, this time using more open questions and at least two of the following question types: coping questions, exception seeking questions, scaling questions and miracle questions. What impact do these questions have on the interaction with Mrs Miller?

2. Imagine you were asked to conduct a community meeting to discuss the possible purchase of a small plot of land for a community garden for the community groups who attend the neighbourhood house where you work as a community social worker. You have been asked by the president of the community gardens committee to prepare a 10-minute opening address to outline the origins of the garden project and the plans for further consultation with the community about the garden. What steps would you take to ensure that your opening speech is informative and engaging?

Further Reading

● Anning, A., Cottrell, D., Frost, N. et al. (2006) *Developing Multi-professional Team-work for Integrated Children's Services: Research, Policy and Practice.* Maidenhead: Open University Press.

Provides an evidence-based approach to working effectively with multiprofessional teams. While the evidence is drawn from a study of integrated children's services, the lessons learned about the challenges of, and approaches to, teamwork are relevant to communication teams in other health and welfare environments.

● Lamerton, J. (2004) *Public Speaking: Speak in Public with Confidence.* Glasgow: HarperCollins.

Although intended as a general guide to public speaking, this practical and accessible handbook provides useful tips on how to speak with credibility and confidence in a range of social care and community service contexts.

● Lishman, J. (2009) *Communication in Social Work,* 2nd edn. Basingstoke: Palgrave Macmillan.

Practical guide for communication skills in direct practice with individuals and families.

● Reynolds, A. and Valentine, D. (2004) *Guide to Cross-cultural Communication.* Upper Saddle River, NJ: Pearson Prentice Hall.

While intended for a general audience, this theoretically informed and accessible handbook provides an excellent overview of key issues in cross-cultural communication.

● Seymour, C. and Seymour, R. (2007) *Courtroom Skills for Social Workers.* Exeter: Learning Matters.

This practical guide outlines the written and spoken communication skills for social workers whose work requires them to appear in court.

● Twelvetrees, A. (2008) *Community Work,* 4th edn. Basingstoke: Palgrave Macmillan.

Provides practical strategies for communicating effectively with individuals and groups in a community work context.

Part 2

Working with Individuals

Many social workers work with individuals. Indeed, the general public image of social workers is of practitioners meeting individuals in their home or in the social worker's office. In Part 2, I focus on the methods of practice with individuals. As indicated in the figure, these methods of practice draw on the professional core of social work and, while linked to mezzo and macro practice methods, are also distinct from them.

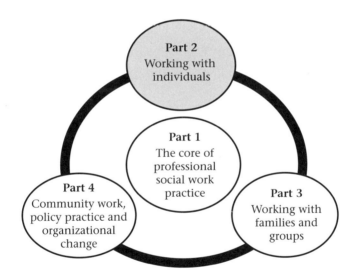

Part 2 comprises two chapters. In Chapter 3, I outline how social workers work with individuals to assist individuals in resolving life's problems. My focus is on practice with individuals who are voluntary service users, in the sense that they are not mandated by law to receive social work services. The practice methods I discuss are social casework and counselling. I define these methods and describe how they are similar to, and different from, other forms of interpersonal work such as case management and clinical social work practice.

In Chapter 4, I outline practice with mandated service users, that is, practice with individuals who are compelled by law to receive social work services. I discuss the dual nature of social workers' role in working with mandated individuals and the strategies social workers can use to balance the helping and social control aspects of the statutory social work practice method. I consider how social workers work towards achieving safety with service users, while managing risk and service user resistance to the involvement of social workers in their lives. In both chapters, I discuss how the phases of engagement, assessment, intervention and termination and evaluation, outlined in Chapter 1, are applied to the interpersonal practice methods outlined in this part of the book.

3

Working with Individuals to Resolve Life's Problems

Many social workers work with individuals to assist them in addressing life's challenges. These challenges are diverse and may include coping with life transitions, personal crises or managing life in the face of a chronic condition, such as an illness. In this chapter, I consider interpersonal work with individuals who are not mandated to receive casework assistance. The specific methods of interpersonal work I focus on in this chapter are social casework and counselling. Social workers deploy these methods in a range of contexts including with individuals who voluntarily seek professional help to manage a life problem, such as dealing with grief and loss. Service users may also receive social casework or counselling services as part of a suite of services offered by a multidisciplinary team in a health and welfare service context. In this chapter, I define social casework and contrast it with other forms of interpersonal practice in which social workers and other helping professionals engage. I consider the history of social casework and key debates about casework as a method of social work practice. I then outline and discuss the implementation of social casework and counselling methods.

What is Social Casework and Counselling?

In this chapter, I will focus on social casework and counselling as practice methods that involve understanding and responding to individuals in their social environment. Both social casework and counselling involve a purposeful and planned approach to working with individuals. Social casework was the first fully articulated method of social work practice. Mary Richmond (1861–1928), in her classic work *Social Diagnosis* (1917), outlined a 'scientific' framework for casework practice. Mary Richmond used the term 'social casework' to refer to direct practice with individuals and families. Today, practice with families is more commonly referred to as 'family social work' or 'family work practice' and we will consider this practice approach in Chapter 5. Similarly, today the term 'social casework practice' as referring to practice with individuals is also contested. Sheldon and Macdonald (2009, p. 112) assert that the term 'social casework' is rarely heard today, although 'it long described the essence of what social workers did – they worked with people and their problems (cases), and they still do'. In this chapter, I argue that social casework remains the best term for what social workers do when working with individuals in many health and social care settings, and cannot simply be interchanged with terms like 'counselling' or 'clinical social work'.

Social casework is a method of interpersonal practice developed by social workers to assist individuals resolve life's problems. Its focus is primarily engaging with the individual to enhance the interface between the individual and their social environment by achieving change in how the individual engages with their social environment and to create change in their social environment (Christensen et al., 1999; see also Fook, 1993; Perlman, 1968). Understanding and enhancing the interaction between the individual and their social environment is commonly referred to by caseworkers as a 'psychosocial' approach to practice (see Fook, 1993; Germain, 1970; Reid, 1978; Woods and Hollis, 1990). It is this focus on understanding *and* intervening, where necessary, in the social environment that distinguishes social casework from other closely aligned fields of interpersonal practice such as counselling. Certainly, many counsellors and psychotherapists seek to understand the social environment of the service user but their interventions remain focused primarily on changing service users' approach to that environment rather than intervening in the environment itself. In differentiating social casework from counselling, Seden (1999, p. 14) states that: 'counselors do not have to engage with service delivery or directly with clients' social environments', whereas caseworkers do.

Both social casework and counselling are informed by a range of theories. Contemporary social casework practice is informed by a wide variety of theoretical approaches, including psychodynamic theory (Woods and Hollis, 1990), cognitive behavioural theory (Reid, 1978), problem-solving theory (Perlman, 19957), radical theory (Fook, 1993), and solution-focused and narrative theories (Christensen et al., 1999). Despite the wide variety of influences, all these theories endorse some common principles found across a range of social casework approaches:

● an emphasis on a staged approach to social casework that begins with a comprehensive analysis of the problems or concerns to be addressed

● collaboration with the service user in establishing a clear shared understanding of the purpose of the relationship and the nature of the intervention

- recognition and enhancement of service users' capacities to address the challenges they face.

Yet there are important differences in the theoretical assumptions under-pinning various schools of social casework practice. A key way in which these different approaches to casework differ is in their interpretation of 'psychosocial' orientation of social casework. For example, while psychody-namic casework emphasizes psychological change, that is, change in the way the individual service user interprets and experiences the world, critical approaches to casework place much greater emphasis on encouraging change between the service user and their environment (Fook, 1993).

Social casework can include a number of methods and techniques of interpersonal work that are also widely deployed by other health and welfare service professionals and which may be regarded as specialist areas of social work practice:

- **Counselling:** a form of interpersonal practice that provides the 'client with an opportunity to explore, discover and clarify ways of living more resourcefully and toward greater well-being' (British Counselling Asso-ciation, cited in Seden, 1999, p. 14).

- **Psychotherapy:** interventions, often referred to as 'treatments', using verbal techniques, such as therapeutic counselling, or creative tech-niques, such as art therapy, to achieve improvements in the mental, emotional or behavioural wellbeing of the service user (Mojtabai and Olfson, 2008).

- **Case management:** practice aimed at 'connecting clients to appropriate services and coordinating utilization of those services' (Sheafor and Horejsi, 2006, p. 60). The purpose of case management is to ensure the comprehen-sive provision of appropriate services to the service user. As case managers, social workers are responsible for assessing service user needs and goals, developing a plan for achievement of these goals, coordinating, moni-toring and evaluating service access (Roberts-DeGennaro, 2008).

Social Casework and Other Forms of Interpersonal Practice

The term 'social casework' is sometimes used interchangeably with other terms, including 'counselling', 'direct practice' and 'clinical social work'. Although, as I have commented, social casework can involve counselling, psychotherapy or case management, none of these terms adequately encapsulates social casework. Counselling can be a 'stand-alone' form of practice but it can also be a technique incorporated into social casework practice. For example, a social worker working in care services for older people with increased physical dependency may conduct grief and loss counselling to help these people identify and transition to hostel or nursing home care. Moreover, a wide variety of health and welfare service professionals, such as psychologists and nurses, also use counselling methods and techniques, whereas the term 'social casework' tends to be used only by social workers. Some authors use the term 'direct practice' (see Boyle et al., 2006) to refer to practice with individuals, couples and families; however, this application of the term seems too narrow, given that any form of direct work with service users, including community work, is also direct practice.

There is some debate about the similarities between clinical social work and casework. In my view, clinical social work is an important social work specialty that shares many similarities with, but also key differences from, social casework. As the National Association of Social Workers (NASW, 2005, p. 7) defines it:

> Clinical social work has a primary focus on the mental, emotional, and behavioral well-being of individuals, couples, families, and groups. It centers on a holistic approach to psychotherapy and the client's relationship to his or her environment. Clinical social work views the client's relationship with his or her environment as essential to treatment planning.

The key similarity between clinical social work and social casework is the level of social work engagement: both describe social work practice primarily with individuals, couples and families. A major difference is the orientation of this practice: psychotherapy is integral to clinical social work practice, but is not always part of social casework. Indeed, the term 'clinical social worker' is often used interchangeably with psychotherapist. For example, according to Specht and Courtney (1994, p. 125), almost all clinical social workers in private practice 'refer to what they do as "psychotherapy"' rather than social work. Furthermore, the clinical social worker's orientation to individual or interpersonal change is further highlighted by the reference to their interventions as 'treatment' (NASW, 2005, p. 7), a term rarely used now by social caseworkers or social workers involved in other modes of practice.

In contrast to clinical social workers, social workers using social casework interventions may focus on change in the service user's social or structural environment rather than focusing their change efforts towards influencing the intrapsychic or interpersonal world of the service user. For instance, a hospital social worker may use a casework approach to improve a service user's access to home and community care services within their own community in order to maximize the service user's capacity to achieve a better quality of life within their own community. Radical caseworkers appear to reject a psychotherapeutic approach to casework, focusing instead on assisting the individual to develop a critical analysis of their circumstances and to achieve change in their interpersonal environment and in the broad social structural conditions (see Fook, 1993).

Another important difference is that social casework is a method of practice that may be used by social work practitioners in a wide variety of practice settings, while clinical social work is strongly linked to a specific occupational identity, that of the 'clinical social worker'. For example, a community social worker or a professional social worker may engage in casework in order to assist a community member to access a service or explore an issue of concern, but the worker would not describe this work as clinical social work practice or psychotherapy. Furthermore, unlike casework and counselling, clinical social work may be regarded as a practice specialty involving specific education and training requirements. In the USA, for example, the term 'clinical social worker' refers to those who have a licence in clinical social work. To achieve a clinical licence, social workers must complete postgraduate qualifications in clinical social work and undertake a postqualifying period of supervised practice in this method (Gibelman, 1995). By contrast, in most countries, accredited social work programmes are required to include basic education in direct practice with individuals, meaning that all qualified social workers should have basic casework skills.

Key Debates: The Evidence-based Practice Movement and Social Casework

More than any other method of social work practice, the social casework method has been the subject of considerable challenge about its evidence base. The focus on the evidence base, or lack of it, of social casework practice is justified, according to Fischer (1973), on the grounds that this is the most common method used by the profession. It may be also that casework, more than any other method, has carried the hopes of the social work profession to establish a truly scientific base for practice. Reflecting on the emergence of professional social work, Germain (1970, p. 8) remarks:

> The Charity Organization movement was introduced in the late 1870s as a means for making almsgiving scientific, efficient, and preventive. Charity Organization Societies (COS) developed over the next twenty-five years, and modern social casework, as their later offspring, became the twentieth-century heir of the movement's scientific aspirations.

Mary Richmond (1917) outlined a 'scientific' basis for social casework practice, and Germain (1970, p. 10) asserts that her now famous text *Social Diagnosis* was based on the assumption that 'uncovering the cause will reveal the
cure, a premise that reflected nineteenth-century science and scientism'.

From the 1920s to the 1950s, psychodynamic perspectives dominated
social work and other cognate fields, most notably psychiatry. For example,
social work practice with children and families was heavily influenced by
the work of the Tavistock Clinic in London, the leading institute in
psychodynamic psychiatry during this period. However, during the 1950s,
these perspectives came to be questioned as an evidence-based movement
began to emerge in social work and in cognate fields in mental health services, particularly psychology and psychiatry. By the late 1960s, psychodynamic casework, the dominant mode of social casework in the previous
decades, was facing serious challenges to its legitimacy by researchers
committed to a scientific approach to social work practice. Reflecting on an
emerging body of research on casework practice in the 1950s and 60s, Joel
Fischer (1973, p. 14) came to an alarming conclusion:

> Of all the controlled studies of the effectiveness of casework that could be located,
> nine of eleven clearly showed that professional caseworkers were unable to bring
> about any positive, significant, measurable changes in their clients beyond those
> that would have occurred without the specific intervention program or that
> could have been induced by nonprofessionals dealing with similar clients, often
> in less intensive service programs ... Thus not only has professional social work
> failed to demonstrate that it is effective, but lack of effectiveness appears to be
> the rule rather than the exception across several categories of clients, problems,
> situations and types of casework.

For at least a decade prior to the publication of Fischer's critique, those
committed to the scientific method in social work had become increasingly
vocal about their scepticism about the evidence base of social casework.
Serendipitously, these concerns intersected with questions from an entirely
different quarter, that of radical social workers, about the legitimacy of the
social casework as a method of social work practice. Helen Harris Perlman's
(1968, p. 235) declaration that 'In the past five years or so casework has
become the whipping boy of social work' gives some insight into the intensity of debates about social casework that emerged in the 1960s.

Whereas many radical social workers questioned the legitimacy of casework, Fischer and other academics within what is now known as the
evidence-based practice movement, or the empirical practice movement,
were (and are) committed to the creation of a scientific base for casework
practice. Indeed, William J. Reid (1978, p. 5), one of the founders of the
task-centred approach to casework, asserted 'the supremacy of research-

based knowledge over knowledge acquired from other sources, such as practice wisdom or untested theory'. Today, the evidence-based practice movement continues to be influential in social work practice and many of the studies have focused on effectiveness in casework or clinical forms of social work practice (see Fischer and Corcoran, 2007; Sheldon, 1995). This movement emphasizes scientific approaches to knowledge building, with a strong preference for research designs involving 'experimental methods, randomized control trials, single system designs and systematic reviews of research' (Plath, 2006, p. 63). Nonetheless, there is also some recognition within the movement of the relevance of other ways of knowing, such as the relevance of qualitative studies and professional wisdom in effective social work practice.

The enduring legacy of the evidence-based practice movement on casework and counselling practice is at least twofold. The first is in the emergence and widespread acceptance of systematic approaches to casework and counselling practice. In contrast to the open-ended or client-directed approaches that characterized earlier approaches to social casework, today casework and counselling conducted by social workers is often time limited and structured around distinctive tasks associated with assessment or intervention. While this orientation is due in part to the resource constraints shaping the services where social workers practice, it is also attributable to the research evidence demonstrating the comparative cost–benefit of time-limited interventions (Reid and Shyne, 1969; Reid and Epstein, 1972). A second significant influence of the evidence-based practice movement has been its emphasis on evaluation and research as integral to all practice. While the nature and use of research evidence for social work practice continues to be debated, today many social workers and their employers recognize the need to systematically evaluate practice outcomes.

Radical Critiques of Social Casework

Since the 1960s, a radical critique of casework, counselling and clinical social work has emerged within the social work profession. Of course, throughout the modern history of social work, individuals have criticized casework methods as dominant modes of social work practice. For example, during the 1930s and 40s, Bertha Capen Reynolds challenged the relevance of psychoanalytically oriented modes of social casework to the social and economic challenges facing service users during that period (Specht and Courtney, 1994). However, it was during the 1960s that a substantial radical critique emerged among social work commentators in several countries, which questioned both the nature and legitimacy of casework, and other individually oriented forms of social work practice. The rise of the radical critique of casework can be associated with the re-emerging influence of sociological perspectives on social work and the growing interest among some social work scholars in community and social action methods in social work (Healy, 2005). Radical critics of social casework practice have drawn on a range of critical sociological perspectives, particularly Marxism and critical social theories, as well as social movements, such as feminism and anti-racist movements, to challenge key assumptions and practices of dominant modes of social casework and clinical social work practice.

Radical social workers are concerned about the potential for social casework and other individually oriented modes of practice to pathologize the individual. The core concern is that a focus on the individual as the primary point of engagement all too easily becomes a focus on the individual, or their immediate social environment, as the source of the problem and the solutions, thus neglecting broader social and structural contexts of service users' lives (Fook, 1993). Beyond this shared concern, the radical critique can be divided into two forms: those who question the individual orientation of casework practice and seek to reform it to incorporate a more radical vision of casework practice; and those who question the legitimacy of casework (and other individual service modes) as dominant forms of social work practice.

The first form of radical critique centres on the concern that caseworkers (and others involved in individual service modes) have minimized or neglected the 'social' dimensions of the psychosocial underpinning of casework. For example, Fook (1993, p. 19) contends that social workers have 'lost sight of the original dual orientation (psychosocial) nature of casework. The result has been that we have relied unduly upon predominately psychotherapeutic and counselling techniques with only minimal social emphasis.' Radical critics of casework consider that casework practice has lost its way as a result of the dominance of psychological perspectives in the development of this practice approach throughout much of the last century (see Specht and Courtney, 1994). Indeed, even critics not aligned with the radical tradition challenge the dominance of psychoanalytic perspectives in the development of casework theory on the grounds that social workers' focus on these perspectives 'led to a disengagement from the poor and seriously troubled – our natural clientele' (Sheldon and Macdonald, 2009, p. 23). From the reformist radical perspective, the problem with social casework practice lies not with the level of engagement, that is, with the individual, but rather the way the individual is engaged. From this perspective, social casework can be reformed by the incorporation of critical social science perspectives, such as tenets of radical or feminist theory, to achieve a more fully developed approach to the social context of service users' lives.

The second form of radical critique questions the legitimacy of casework, and other forms of individual practice, as modes of social work practice. These critics argue that the person-in-environment focus that distinguishes social work from individually oriented helping professions should lead us to more fully engage with socially oriented modes of action. For example, Specht and Courtney (1994, p. 171) contend that 'the major objective of social work practice is to develop and strengthen community supported services and to enable participants to make use of social resources available to them' and, accordingly, social workers' primary function should be to 'draw people into social groups and community activities'. This challenge to social casework is associated with the emphasis on social action that emerged within radical and critical social work literature during the 1960s, and the emergence of community development as an increasingly important mode of social work practice. Notably, during this period, many within the profession came to recognize the validity of a diversity of practice methods, with Perlman (1968, p. 437), a leading casework theorist, observing that: 'Casework is one process in social work. It is only that: one process. The other major processes by which social work carries its purposes into action are group work and community work.'

Social Casework and the Rise of Neoliberalism

A third area of debate about casework practice centres on the changing context of social work practice. The rising influence of managerialist ideas on public services and public funding for community services is reshaping service delivery (MacDonald, 2006). Sheldon and Macdonald (2009, p. 32) observe that the increasing focus on managing the bureaucratic demands of practice has led to a substantial decline in opportunities for contact with service users, with, for example, 'visiting rates now accounting for less than 20 per cent of the working week'. There is also the concern that where face-to-face practice does occur, it is constrained to a focus on case management, with less opportunity for engagement in the core elements of social casework, such as developing a therapeutic alliance and seeking to achieve psychosocial change. Seden (1999, p. 2) observes that 'the current preoccupation with quasi-markets, commissioners, providers, resources and outcomes might lead the present observer to conclude that such skills [in casework and counselling] are no longer needed'.

In short, social workers today face many challenges to the implementation of the social casework method. More than any other method of social work practice, social casework has been subject to critique from within the profession. While there is no consensus within the profession about the nature or legitimacy of casework as a mode of social work practice, some common themes underpin the debates about casework. These themes include:

- Casework, defined as a psychosocial approach to working with individuals to improve the interaction between themselves and their social environment, continues to be an important method of social work practice.

- While sharing common features and techniques with counselling, case management and clinical practice, casework is not interchangeable with these terms.

- A broad range of theoretical influences now shape casework practice and psychodynamic frameworks are no longer the dominant theoretical influence in this tradition.

- Most contemporary casework approaches involve a structured approach to casework, with elements of engagement, assessment, intervention and evaluation integral to this mode of practice.

- Casework practice is subject to time and resource constraints. While there is some debate about whether casework is still possible in the context of these constraints, it is clear that social workers need to be aware of and communicate these constraints to service users in order to develop a realistic understanding of what can be achieved in casework practice.

A Framework for Social Casework and Counselling

We turn now to the practice of working with individuals. The approach discussed here is relevant to both social casework and counselling in social work practice settings. The approach is applicable to work with voluntary service users in a counselling setting, such as an individual seeking counselling to assist in making a life decision, through to a casework setting, such as social work practice in a hospital or health setting where the client may be offered social work services as part of a suite of health and social care services, and in this sense the goals of practice are also partly determined by the expectations of the healthcare team.

The approach draws on problem-solving, strengths-based and solution-focused approaches, and critical social work practice:

- From **problem-solving**, particularly the task-centred work of Reid (1978), the approach recognizes the notions of clarity of purpose, collaborative establishment of practice goals, structured intervention according to practice goals and time limits, and the importance of evaluation of practice.

● From **strengths-based and solution-focused practice**, the approach recognizes the importance of balancing the exploration of problems with a recognition of service users' strengths and capacities to solve the challenges facing them and honouring service users' hopes as well as practical goals for the future.

● From the **critical social work tradition**, this approach draws on both radical and critical postmodern theories to emphasize the 'social' dimension of social casework by encouraging critical reflection and recognition by worker and service user of the contribution of social conditions to the challenges faced by service users and the importance of addressing the social and structural context of service users' challenges (Fook, 1993; Healy, 2000). As Fook (1993, p. 83) defines it, the aim of radical casework is 'towards the personal change, autonomy and power, gained mainly through an awareness of the influence of the social structure on the problem situation'. The radical casework approach urges practitioners to draw attention to the links between apparently personal problems and the aspects of the social structure that support, or reinforce, these problems (Fook, 1993).

The approach discussed in this chapter recognizes four phases to social casework and counselling practice and these elements are outlined in Chapter 1 (see Figure 1.2). These phases are engagement, assessment, intervention, and evaluation and termination. The conceptualization of casework as incorporating several stages from initial meetings to termination is common in much of the contemporary casework and counselling literature. Reid and Epstein (1972), in their exposition of a task-centred approach to casework practice, emphasized the importance of a clearly structured process for ensuring that the casework relationship was structured, goal focused and effective in reaching agreed outputs. Reid and Epstein (1972) were among the first social work authors to emphasize that evaluation should be incorporated as a clear phase of the casework relationship. Many contemporary counselling texts, such as Egan's work (2010) on skilled helping, also recognize different phases in interpersonal practice processes.

Engaging the Service User: Establishing the Casework/Counselling Relationship

The first phase of the casework relationship involves engaging the service user. The key objective of this phase is to establish a purposeful and effective working relationship between the caseworker and the service user. Of course, given the centrality of the worker/client relationship to casework practice, the worker must attend to maintaining a purposeful and effective relationship at every stage of their involvement with the service user. Even so, this first phase of engagement is important for setting the tone of the practice relationship and as such is likely to impact greatly on the later phases of casework practice.

So how do we establish a purposeful and effective working relationship with service users? As discussed in Chapter 2, several studies have established caseworker behaviours that are associated with establishing an effective casework relationship. These studies have pointed to the importance of the social worker demonstrating personal warmth, empathy, genuineness and helpfulness (Healy and Darlington, 2009; Healy et al., 2011; Sheldon and Macdonald, 2009). By recognizing warmth, empathy, genuineness and helpfulness/flexibility as behaviours, rather than as characteristics or dispositions, we see that social workers can learn to demonstrate these important behaviours even when challenged to do so. These challenges can include the worker's own personal disposition, for example the worker may have a reserved manner, or the worker's negative personal reactions to service users in some circumstances. While the value framework of social work practice, particularly the emphasis on nonjudgementalism and acceptance, can help increase our capacity for warm and authentic engagement, it is still possible (in fact likely) that there will be certain circumstances in which we have a negative emotional reaction to a service user. Moreover, it can be difficult to know what might trigger such a reaction. In the interests of developing or maintaining a therapeutic alliance with the service user, it is usually important for social workers to contain the strong emotional responses to the service user, particularly in the phase of engagement (Crago, 2008). By exploring our reactions to service users in an emotionally safe environment, such as in supervision, we can also learn to predict the situations in which we may have these reactions and develop ways of managing them to ensure our focus remains on the best interests of the service user.

Several social work researchers, particularly those working within the problem-solving tradition (Reid and Epstein, 1972; Reid, 1978; Trotter, 2002, 2004), argue that an effective casework relationship also involves the caseworker demonstrating:

● Clarity of professional purpose

● A primary focus on the needs and goals of the service user

● Clarity about the limits to the relationship, such as it is time limited.

We can see that there is a balance to be struck here between the warm and authentic relationship that many service users' prefer and the need for caseworkers to place professional boundaries around the casework relationship. Our ethical responsibility to focus on the needs of the service user means that the relationship is not entirely a mutual one and further that there is a responsibility for workers to contain their emotional involvement with the service user. For example, it is recognized in professional ethical codes that it is inappropriate and harmful to service users for caseworkers to become sexually involved with service users.

The principle of collaboration between service providers and service users is central to most contemporary casework theory and practice (see Reid, 1978; Saleebey, 2006). Critical approaches to casework practice take this further to indicate that workers should seek to recognize and address the power inequalities inherent in the casework relationship. According to Fook (1993, p. 103), 'the radical casework relationship is best seen as one of joint learning through an exchange of impressions, rather than an imposition of one person's interpretations on another'. Some ways in which greater equality can be achieved include acknowledging the power inherent in the relationship, being prepared to share out assumptions and making them 'accessible for debate' with the service user, avoiding jargon, and the use of self-disclosure in ways that highlight commonalities with service users without compromising the primary focus on the service user's needs (Fook, 1993).

So how do we, as caseworkers, establish an appropriate and constructive relationship with service users?

● Being clear about the nature of the relationship ourselves, particularly any time limits to involvement or responsibilities to third parties, and sensitively communicating these boundaries to the service user. Time limits include not only the fact that the casework relationship will end, either because of time restrictions of the agency or because the caseworker may leave their role, but also due to daily time limits regarding your availability to the service user, for example your role may involve being available during office hours and also taking into account the needs of other service users on your caseload. It is also vital that we acknowledge any responsibilities we have to third parties, such as writing court reports, and how we will negotiate these responsibilities with the service user and the third party. For example, in some circumstances, we may be able to invite service user feedback on our report or allow a space for them to make additional comments.

● Using appropriate language to describe your practice or engagement. There is an important balance to be struck between recognizing the formality of your role while also demonstrating warmth and a commitment to engage collaboratively with the service user. For example, to state to a service user that you've 'just popped in for a chat' may underplay the formality and seriousness of your role in their life, and it is usually more appropriate to begin with a more formal description: 'I'd like to discuss your care needs once you leave hospital with you.'

● Using accessible language by, for example, using plain English and avoiding jargon.

Over to you ...

Imagine you are working in a family support service on a large public housing estate. You are just about to meet Jodie, a 22-year-old single mother who has two young children. Jodie has asked to speak to someone about the stresses she is experiencing, having told the receptionist that she is 'at breaking point'.

As you engage with this service user, how would you communicate warm, authentic empathy and helpfulness/flexibility in a casework/counselling relationship, while also being clear about your professional purpose?

1. What words might you use to introduce yourself?

2. What do you see as your professional purpose(s)?

3. How would you express your sense of purpose (what words might you use)?

4. How would you appear? Consider your facial expression, body posture and clothing.

5. What else might you want to communicate in the initial phase of engagement?

6. How would you communicate this?

How might your approach to engagement be different if:

1. The service user was a different age (much older or younger than the young mother in this case study)?

2. If the service user was a male rather than a female?

3. If the service user was from a cultural or linguistic community other than your own?

Assessment

The objective of the assessment phase is to develop a shared understanding, with the service user, of the service user's situation so as to form the basis for action in the intervention phase of practice. A holistic understanding of the person's situation, demanded by a person-in-environment perspective of social casework, takes time and systematic attention to the person's view of their situation and an analysis of their social context. Caseworkers often encounter personal and organizational pressures to quickly move to problem-solving before conducting a holistic assessment with the service user of their situation. Yet without a comprehensive assessment, the caseworker risks developing inaccurate or inappropriate understandings of the service user's situation, alienating them and failing to fully engage them in addressing the challenges they face.

The assessment phase will usually begin with a statement of 'the problem' or 'concern' to be addressed in the casework situation. A clear statement of the initial problem is part of the foundation of a collaborative relationship with the service user and it should never be assumed that both the worker and the service user have a common understanding of the problem, instead a shared understanding will usually need to be developed between the worker and service user. In the case of a voluntary service user seeking counselling for a personal problem, developing this shared understanding may begin with an open question such as 'How can I assist you?' In many settings, the casework goals are at least partly defined by institutional responsibilities or expectations. In the engagement phase, it is vital that the social worker is transparent about any institutional responsibilities inherent in their role. For example, in a hospital context, the social worker may have responsibility for ensuring the timely discharge of patients. In this context, the social worker would need to ensure that the service user was aware of the worker's responsibility to enable them (the patient) to leave hospital in a timely manner and to participate in developing a community care plan that best suits their health and social care needs. In this example, the social worker may introduce their focus in the following way: 'I understand from Dr Wran that you've recovered well from the operation and you'll soon be well enough to go home. I'm here to discuss with you where you would like to go on leaving hospital and what support you will need once you leave the hospital to make sure you continue with your recovery.'

Exploration of problems and strengths

An exploration of service users' concerns and capacities occurs after, and derives from, the initial statement of the problem. Traditionally, the assessment phase of casework has tended to focus on problem exploration (Perlman, 1957; Reid and Epstein, 1972). Over the past two decades, this focus on problems has been challenged in two ways:

1. Increasingly, social workers are expected to assess risk. This focus on risk assessment, while evident in many contexts of social work practice, has

intensified in statutory casework and so we will focus on risk assessment in Chapter 4.

2. As a result of the inroads made by strengths-based, solution-focused and narrative theorists, there is an increasing emphasis in the casework and counselling literature on assessing service users' strengths, capacities and victories over the problems they face.

The notion of 'problem exploration' found in many traditional casework texts is derived in part from the psychodynamic tradition of casework, where it was believed that the 'presenting' problem often masked a deeper psychological problem and further it was proposed that it was in the service user's interest to address the deeper problem (see Woods and Hollis, 1990). Today, the notion of problem exploration remains important in casework even where caseworkers do not adopt a psychodynamic perspective. Exploration of the problem is important for developing a collaborative and constructive relationship with the service user and providing a solid foundation for casework intervention by providing a comprehensive analysis of the range of factors contributing to the concern. Moreover, from a strengths-based perspective, this phase also provides opportunities for caseworkers to understand service users' strengths and capacities to address the problems they face.

Traditionally, exploration of problems begins with the caseworker seeking to understand the 'history' of the problem. In this phase, the case-worker seeks to facilitate the service user to provide a comprehensive account of the problem and its impact on the service user's life. Key areas for exploration include:

● How long the problem has been evident in the service user's life.

● The pattern of the problem, such as points where the problem is more or less intense, and where there appear, in the service user's observation, to be events that trigger the problem.

● The practical effects of the problem in the service user's life, both positive and negative.

● How the problem relates to the family or community context of the service user's life, such as whether the problem relates to issues in the person's family of origin or current family or whether the problem is linked to community issues, for example a lack of access to resources, such as family support services.

● What responses and solutions to the problem have been tried? To what extent were these responses successful/unsuccessful?

When the problem is defined in part by others, other exploratory questions, in addition to those already outlined, are relevant to the assessment of the concern. These other questions may include:

● How does the service user see the problem, particularly what are the issues from their viewpoint?

● How, if at all, does the service user's view of the problem or issues differ from that of the 'third party' defining the problem? For example, an older person in hospital for surgery related to a hip fracture may not agree with the medical assessment that they should be transferred to a supported living arrangement and they may seek, instead, the social worker's assistance in returning them home.

As mentioned earlier, the workers may also be required to undertake a formal risk assessment, often using standardized risk assessment tools. The risk assessment component of casework will be discussed in Chapter 4.

Insights from strengths-based, solution-focused and narrative traditions

Proponents of the strengths-based, solution-focused and narrative traditions have criticized the exploration of problems as unbalanced and leading to a wholly negative and often discouraging view of the service user's circumstance (see Berg and Kelly, 2000; Turnell and Edwards, 1999). These theorists argue that a consideration of problems or challenges and concerns must be balanced with consideration of service user strengths and capacities to respond to the challenges they face. In addition to exploring the nature of the problem, the strengths-based, solution-focused and narrative-focused practitioners would also ask:

● What victories has the service user had over the concern, such as are there times when the service user has felt depressed but managed to get on with their life despite feeling down?

● What is the service user most proud of in their life? This seeks to build a non-problem-saturated view of the service user.

● What resources are available to the service user for addressing the problem?

● In their network of family and friends, who is supportive of them and holds a positive, life affirming view of them?

A common theme in the strengths-based, solution-focused and narrative traditions is the importance of separating the person from the problem. The mantra 'the person is not the problem, the problem is the problem' is often articulated by authors within this tradition to denote this emphasis on separating the person from the problem. 'Externalization' of the problem is one technique that is used for achieving this in the exploration phase of assessment. Externalization involves a two-stage process. First, naming the problem as separate from the person. For example, rather than saying Bill is a schizophrenic, we would say that Bill is a person who experiences schizophrenia or who hears voices others are unable to hear. Importantly, this challenges the definition of Bill's identity as his mental health status, and the description of someone who hears voices others are unable to hear may challenge the stigma surrounding schizophrenia as a state of being less than others to one of being different from others.

Frequently, particularly within the narrative tradition, the worker and service user give a name to the concern, for example 'the dragon' for states of anger, or 'the voices' for auditory hallucinations. The naming of the concern also helps the worker and service user to see it as separate from the identity of the service user. The second part of the process of externalization involves analysis of the issue of the 'dragon', or the 'voices' as a point of curiosity rather than as a problem that must be defeated. For example, in relation to 'the voices', we might ask Bill to tell us about the last time 'the voices' visited him.

Another shared theme in the strengths-based, solution-focused and narrative traditions is that of enabling service users to imagine a future without the concern or at least without the concern being a major focus of their lives. In contrast to traditional problem-oriented casework approaches, which place great focus on analysis of the problem, proponents of the strengths, solution-focused and narrative traditions focus efforts with service users on building a comprehensive picture of what the service user's life would be like without the problem. The miracle question is one technique common to these traditions for achieving this outcome. The miracle question involves asking the service user to tell you what their life would be like if a 'miracle' occurred and the problem was no longer present. Examples of this question include: If a miracle happened tonight while you were sleeping and the depression disappeared, what would your life be like tomorrow? Another version of this question is asking the service user: How will you know that the voices have gone from your life? The questions enable us to focus on solutions rather than the problem and also ensure that the service user is attuned to, and can build on, the solutions that may already be present in their lives.

Insights from the radical casework approach

Radical casework approaches seek to empower the service user in the assessment process in two ways. One is to reduce the service user's distress by normalizing the problems and by recognizing the strengths and capacities of the service user. 'Normalizing' refers to highlighting the extent to which the problems and challenges faced by the service user are shared by many others, particularly those who also experience the forms of social oppression experienced by the service user. For example, referring to our earlier case study of Jodie, the young single mother, we might emphasize that many parents experience challenges and that single parents face the extra challenge of raising children on their own. Like strengths-oriented practitioners, radical caseworkers also emphasize the demonstrated strengths of the client by acknowledging what the client has achieved in the context of the challenges before them.

In the assessment phase, the radical caseworker also seeks to draw links between the 'personal' and the 'political' in assessing the service user's situation (Fook, 1993, p. 47). The term 'political' is used here to refer to how the social structures associated with capitalism, patriarchy and colonialism give rise to oppressive attitudes and a lack of opportunity for many service users. In the assessment process, the worker seeks to facilitate the service user's critical awareness of how the links between oppressive attitudes and lack of opportunity shape the service user's personal experience of the challenges they face. For example, when working with Jodie, we would seek to understand how her own attitudes, and those of others around her, may be contributing to the stress she is experiencing by leading her to feel that she should be coping despite the enormous challenges she faces.

Techniques for the assessment phase

Although philosophical differences exist among social caseworkers in their approach to assessment, a range of techniques are commonly used in the assessment phase to explore concerns and capacities. Social caseworkers use the communication skills outlined in Chapter 2 to build a shared understanding with the service user of the nature of the problem and the resources they have, and will require, to resolve these problems.

In the assessment phase, a great deal of information can be brought forth. Unless the information is organized in some way, the discussion can become confusing and directionless for the service provider and service user. Two techniques that are commonly used to organize information about family and social relationships or resources in the service user's life are the 'genogram' and the 'ecomap', sometimes referred as a sociogram. The genogram is a pictorial representation of family relationships and dynamics over at least two (and usually more) generations of a family. These relationships are represented hierarchically, with the older generations appearing towards the top of the genogram and younger generations appearing towards the bottom. The genogram is widely used in a range of health and social care contexts. The genogram is used in casework with individuals and families and we will focus on the techniques for developing a genogram in Chapter 5. The ecomap is a visual representation of the significant social relationships, including family relationships, and systems in the service user's life. Like the genogram, the ecomap assists in seeing patterns in relationships; in addition, it helps to identify gaps in social resources, such as service access, facing a service user (see Hartman, 1995).

A balanced exploration of the concerns as well as the service user's strengths and capacities provides the caseworker and service user with a comprehensive, if potentially unwieldy, view of the challenges and some initial insights into addressing them. The final part of the assessment process involves narrowing the assessment to a plan for action. The task-centred model of casework provides some helpful pointers as to how the casework and service user can collaborate on developing a workable plan. These include:

● **Placing a time limit on the intervention process**. Reid and Epstein (1972) emphasized that time limits helped to motivate change by encouraging service providers to create realistic goals and to focus their efforts on achieving those goals.

● **Narrowing the range of problems to be addressed** to those that can be managed within the time frame and context of practice. Reid and Epstein (1972, p. 151) argued for the 'rule of three', meaning that the casework intervention should be focused on addressing no more than three issues in any intervention phase. In working with the service user to decide which issues to focus on, we should take into the account any institutional obligations we have in our casework role, consider what can realistically be achieved in the context of practice, identify the problems that the service user is most motivated to work on and the issues that are likely to have the biggest positive impact on the challenges facing the service user.

● **Developing a clear set of outcome goals**. These goals should be directly related to the resolution of the problem that we have agreed to work on with the service user.

Over to you ...

Return to the case study of Jodie, introduced earlier in this chapter, and undertake a role-play of an assessment. In this role-play, try to use elements from the three casework perspectives discussed in this chapter (the problem-solving, radical and strengths-based approaches). Ideally, you should record this role-play so that you can analyse the assessment process. Once you have completed the assessment role-play, consider:

1. What insights did you and 'Jodie' gain from the different approaches to assessment?

2. Were there questions or approaches that seemed to reveal the most useful informa- tion for you, as the worker, and for the person playing 'Jodie', for assessment purposes?

3. What other impact did the role-play have on the person playing the role of 'Jodie'? Were there aspects of the assessment that enabled her to feel more or less empow- ered or respected in the process? Were there questions that gave her more sense of the direction she would like to go in to address the challenges she is facing?

Intervention

The intervention phase involves actions by the worker and/or service user aimed at achieving the agreed goals of intervention. These change goals can be at several levels and often include changes in the service user's percep- tions of the challenge, behaviour and social environment by improving access to, and use of, networks or resources.

Overall, the caseworker should assist the service user to set a framework for change, including clear goals and strategies, and assist the service user to monitor their achievement of these goals. In this section, we will consider a small range of basic casework intervention strategies. I acknowledge that there is a great deal of literature on specific approaches to casework and counselling intervention and a list of resources for further consideration of some key inter- vention approaches is provided at the end of this chapter. It is beyond the scope of this book to present a detailed guide to intervention strategies. Our aim here is to provide a beginning knowledge of casework intervention rele- vant to those in generalist rather than specialist casework roles.

The casework relationship can provide a context for directly contributing to change in thinking and behaviour through 'therapeutic' techniques, particularly cognitive behavioural techniques, challenging self-limiting and oppressive attitudes held by the service user or others in the service user's life, and providing opportunities for rehearsing new behaviours. The radical tradi- tion also encourages the caseworker to recognize the social dimensions of the psychosocial approach to casework in all these dimensions of intervention activity and to facilitate social change in the life of the service user. We will now consider how three types of change – change in thinking or outlook, change in behaviour, and change in access to resources – can be achieved in the intervention phase.

The first type of change is *change in the outlook of the client*. The type of change required may be relatively minor, such as helping the service user to work through a solution to a problem that may appear insurmountable to them. For example, a young person who has decided to continue with an unplanned pregnancy will inform their family of the situation and what they will do next with their lives. In the course of supportive counselling with this young person, the service provider may assist them to think through the meaning of their decision so as to reframe their situation in ways that empower the young person to move forward. The service provider may also work with the young person to 'rehearse' how they will inform their family of their circumstance.

Sometimes people seek social workers' assistance for problems that require fundamental shifts in the way they think about their situation. For example, a parent whose child has significant behavioural problems may seek help not only in coping with a situation but in changing their responses to their situation. In some situations, the problem may be so entrenched that specialist assistance is needed. For example, a person with agoraphobia may be best helped by a clinical social worker or a psychologist. However, in situations where the problem is less entrenched, the caseworker can help by assisting the service user to identify aspects of their thinking that prevent them from achieving their goals. These aspects can then be subject to critical scrutiny, with a focus on developing a realistic appraisal of the person's concerns and, where necessary, a plan of action if the 'worst' outcome occurs. For example, a person with a general fear of participating in social situations may be encouraged to discuss their fears about what can happen at social events, such as being ignored or being embarrassed. The caseworker can empower the service user to address these fears by, first, assisting the service user to realistically appraise the likelihood of these outcomes, second, assisting the service user to develop knowledge or skills that would help reduce the likelihood of negative outcomes, and, third, developing a plan so that the person is empowered to manage the situation even if their worst fears are realized.

Behavioural change is a second type of change that can be supported through casework interventions. According to Sheldon and Macdonald (2009, p. 149), a wide range of interpersonal problems for which service users seek assistance are 'largely a matter of social skills which may not have been acquired naturally, or which may have atrophied owing to intervening experience'. For example, Jodie, from our earlier case example, may have been isolated since the birth of her children and have lost some of her confidence in making friends.

The caseworker can assist in the development of new skills in several ways, including modelling behaviours, providing opportunities for rehearsing behaviours, and positive reinforcement of new behaviours. Modelling behaviours refers to the caseworker's demonstration of behaviours or skills that will assist the service user to develop. For example, in encouraging a service user to adopt a prosocial attitude towards others, we, as caseworkers, should model these attitudes through our own behaviour towards the service user, for example being punctual and respectful in our approach to them (Trotter, 2006). Modelling can be helpful for assisting service users to develop behaviours that may enable them to constructively engage with their social environment, such as assertiveness, rather than passivity or aggression.

A second way caseworkers can assist service users to learn new skills is by providing opportunities for the service user to rehearse these skills within the context of a casework relationship which, ideally, should be an emotionally safe relationship. For example, returning to the case example of the young person who has decided to continue with an unplanned pregnancy, the caseworker can help the young woman to rehearse different approaches to talking the matter through with their family and to consider how she will respond to a range of reactions. Rehearsal can also provide the service user with the opportunity to see the situation from the other parties' viewpoints and so both enhance their capacity to empathize with that view and anticipate how the other parties may respond to them.

The caseworker can also support new skills by noticing and reinforcing changes in behaviours that are consistent with the service user's goals. This is important because the service user themselves may not receive endorsement from others about new ways of behaving, for example the young woman may not receive support from her family about her decision to continue with her pregnancy. The caseworker's recognition and support of behavioural changes is also important because others may not appreciate the significance of behavioural changes, particularly those that might seem minor, for the overall achievement of service user goals.

A third way caseworkers assist change is by *enhancing service user's access to, and use of, social networks and resources*. By networks, I refer to relationships between people. For example, Jodie may benefit from access to a network of other young parents or to a community with whom she identifies. By resources, we refer to sources of knowledge or services that may produce a material benefit for the service user. For example, if Jodie is stressed by a lack of knowledge about how to manage her children's behaviour, she may benefit from access to parenting skills materials or programmes. Very often, users of casework services experience socioeconomic stress, and enhancing access to services that address material challenges in service users' lives, such as housing, employment and educational and economic benefit services, are an important part of casework intervention. Indeed, one way casework is differentiated from counselling is in its focus on enhancing access to services aimed at alleviating some of the social disadvantages experienced by service users.

In order to enhance service user's access to networks and services, the caseworker at a minimum requires a comprehensive understanding of existing networks and services relevant to service users and a capacity to work with the service user to identify a broader range of networks and services that may be relevant to them. However, from a radical casework perspective, it is also important that the caseworker is active in maximizing the range of networks and services available to the service user. This involves the caseworker in critically reviewing the policies of their own service and other service agencies in which they are engaged to ensure that service user access to their services is maximized. This may involve advocating for a change in eligibility requirements. For example, if particular entry requirements to services deny access to a group of service users, the caseworker may be involved in advocating for a change to those requirements (Mullaly, 2007).

Termination and Evaluation

I turn now to the termination and evaluation phase of social casework. This phase is important for the caseworker and service user to consolidate the work undertaken together, to develop plans for action in relation to goals or continuing challenges, and to evaluate the effectiveness of the casework process of helping the service user. The termination phase is important for ensuring that the service user is able to recognize and build on the gains they have made and also for providing an opportunity to address any areas of dissatisfaction with what has (or has not) been achieved. For both service providers and service users, the termination phase can spark emotions, such as loss and grief, as it marks the end of the professional relationship between caseworker and service user. A well-managed termination phase can assist the service user to leave the casework relationship with a realistic and hopefully positive evaluation of what they have achieved, and a sense of completion with the casework process.

The features of a well-managed termination include:

● it is anticipated, and expected, by the service user. From the outset of our engagement with the service user, we should ensure that they are aware of the time limits, or any other limits, to our involvement with them. For example, social work students on placement should ensure that service users know when the student placement will conclude.

● the service user is provided with the opportunity to reflect on their achievements as well as areas for further action and that, where necessary, the service user is provided with a plan for accessing the resources needed for them to move forward with that plan.

● the service user is provided with the opportunity to address with the worker any issues evoked by the termination process. For example, termination of the casework relationship may evoke a range of feelings in the service user, such as relief that the intervention process is complete through to a sense of loss or abandonment. Acknowledging these emotions may be important for the service user to draw upon the gains made in the casework process and to move forward without the continuing assistance of casework services.

At a minimum, the termination phase involves setting aside time to acknowledge the end of the social casework relationship. Sometimes service providers and service users choose to mark this conclusion formally by, for example, celebrating the final session together or marking it with a symbolic gesture, such as lighting candles for the service user's future. Bearing in mind that the termination may have enduring effects on how the service user regards the casework experience, it is important that termination activities reflect the tone of the casework relationship and are jointly agreed by the service provider and service user.

The final phase also provides an opportunity for the service provider and the service user to evaluate the effectiveness of the casework intervention overall. Evaluations are important for assisting continuous improvement of our practice, as they enable us to reflect on what has worked and what needs improvement. Evaluations can also assist the service user to realistically appraise their achievements as well as areas for further action. There are many books on evaluation of practice in health and social care (see Aveyard and Sharp, 2009) and some contemporary casework texts also give insights into how to evaluate casework intervention (see Sheldon and Macdonald, 2009; Trotter, 2006). Some key tips for evaluating casework intervention are:

● the evaluation of our effectiveness should occur systematically over the course of our work with service users. Once we have established with the service user the nature of the problem, we will address the goals of our casework with them, and collect baseline data about the problem and its impact on the service user's life. Typically, this baseline information includes data about the frequency and severity of the problem, which enables us to systematically assess the service user's progress towards achieving agreed goals over the course of the intervention. This can enable us to regularly review or revise our intervention plan in light of information about the service user's progress. This systematic approach can be especially important for understanding whether problems that arise in the intervention process, such as apparent setbacks in the service user's achievement of goals, are short-term issues or reflect fundamental problems in the intervention approach we have adopted with them.

- service users should be involved in the evaluation process so they can appraise their own progress towards service goals. Service users can be encouraged to keep diaries or to chart the frequency and/or severity of the problem they are confronting over the course of their work with you. For example, a young mother might be encouraged to rate and record the severity of the impact of stress in her life as she engages in strategies aimed at minimizing the impact of stress upon her.

- a range of evaluation information should be collected and, at a minimum, should include information about progress towards goals and service user satisfaction with the process. Service providers may consider using standardized evaluation instruments to develop baseline information about the challenge facing the service user and the progress (or otherwise) towards addressing that challenge (Fischer and Corcoran, 2007).

- evaluation information should include signs of improvement as well as signs of problem reduction.

- wherever possible, the evaluation should include both quantitative and qualitative information. Qualitative data that may be helpful includes summaries of workers' and service users' impressions of the impact of the intervention on their problem, while quantitative data includes numerical data such as data from standardized assessment instruments and scaling of service user's perceptions of the nature and impact of their problem on them.

- evaluation data should be presented in a range of ways including verbal summaries, graphs and/or symbols (such as facial symbols to indicate different emotional states). Sheldon and Macdonald (2009, p. 110) note that 'social workers seem to suffer from a kind of graph phobia … [yet] in our experience clients like to use these devices'. Visual devices such as charts and graphs can help us, and those we work with, visualize achievements as well as areas for further action.

Our primary aim in evaluating our casework is to ensure that we systematically review the service user's progress towards achieving agreed goals and the contribution our intervention has made towards the achievement of those goals. The systematic review of our work is important for enabling us to maximize the effectiveness of our intervention and, where necessary, to revise the agreed goals or intervention plans. Evaluation processes can provide service users with evidence of their progress towards achieving agreed goals and information about which ongoing issues might require further action. For example, a young mother may find that the social casework intervention has assisted her to develop effective strategies for reducing stress in her life but that isolation remains a major concern for her. She may decide that this continuing issue cannot be addressed by casework intervention but through other actions, such as participation in a local community group.

Conclusion

Social casework and counselling are core methods of social work practice. I contend that the term 'social casework' continues to be the best term for describing social work practice with individuals that is focused on understanding and responding to the person in their social environment. In this chapter, I have discussed key debates about social casework. I have also considered the four phases of social work practice as they apply to social casework methods. I have introduced strategies for assessment and intervention in social casework; however, I have also emphasized that there is much to be learned from the vast body of literature associated with each of the casework traditions discussed in this chapter. The Further Reading at the end of this chapter provides key texts on these methods of social work practice.

Review Questions

1. What does the term 'social casework' mean?

2. What types of change can social casework help individuals to achieve? Discuss two or three strategies social workers can use to assist individuals achieve change.

3. Why is the termination and evaluation phase of social casework important?

4. What sorts of information (or data) would you collect to help you and the service user evaluate the effectiveness of casework intervention for achieving the service user's goals?

Critical Reflection Question

1. In this chapter we have considered three key theoretical approaches to casework practice – the problem-solving and strengths-based approaches and radical casework. What do you see as the pros and cons of each of these approaches?

Practice Exercise

Imagine you are working in a housing service for low-income families where your role is to offer supportive casework to people housed by your service. Shane (22) and Louise (19) have lived in supported accommodation for three weeks now. Louise has come to see you because she is thinking of separating from Shane. They have been together for about a year, but Louise is unhappy in the relationship. Shane lost his job as a builder's labourer several months ago and Louise says that since then Shane has become increasingly irritable and difficult to live with. According to Louise, Shane has little interest in searching for another job and she thinks he seems depressed. Louise has a part-time job at a local supermarket and has a dream of completing school so that she can become a nurse. Louise's income is low and she cannot afford to rent a place of her own. One complication is that Louise has just discovered that she is pregnant and she does not know what to do as she is uncertain about her feelings for Shane.

1. What do you see as the key purpose(s) of your practice with Louise?

2. How would you engage with Louise to build a constructive and purposeful relationship with her?

3. How would conduct an assessment of the situation with Louise and what issues would you want to address in the assessment process?

4. Drawing on the approaches discussed in this chapter, outline what intervention strategies you think might be appropriate for working with Louise.

5. What baseline information might you collect, or encourage Louise to collect, from the outset of your work with her, in order to evaluate the effectiveness of the social casework process?

Now imagine that Shane rather than Louise has come to see you for assistance. Louise has told him that she plans to leave him. Discuss what you would see as your purpose in working with Shane and how you would develop a constructive working relationship with him.

Further Reading

- Connie, E. and Metcalf, L. (eds) (2009) *The Art of Solution Focused Therapy*. New York: Springer.

  Provides a contemporary introduction to solution-focused therapy and insights into its application with individuals, couples and families.

- De Shazer, S. (1985) *Keys to Solutions in Brief Therapy.* New York: Norton.

  An enduring classic in the field of brief therapy. Written by a pioneer of solution-focused brief therapy, it outlines the theory and practice of this approach to counselling practice.

- Fook, J. (1993) *Radical Casework: A Theory of Practice.* St Leonards, Sydney: Allen & Unwin.

  Accessible and detailed introduction to the theory and practice of radical casework. Comprehensive analysis of the consistencies and contrasts between traditional and radical casework approaches.

- Reid, W.J. (1978) *The Task-centered System.* New York: Columbia.

  Detailed description of the philosophy and practice of task-centred casework. Valuable step-by-step guide to implementing this approach in practice. Extensive use of case study material provides excellent guidance to the implementation of this approach.

- Saleebey, D. (ed.) (2006) *The Strengths Perspective in Social Work Practice*, 4th edn. Boston: Pearson/Allyn & Bacon.

  Introduction to the theory of the strengths perspective and its application to a broad range of practice fields and methods.

- Sheldon, B. (1995) *Cognitive Behavioural Therapy: Research, Practice and Philosophy.* London: Routledge.

  Comprehensive introduction to the empirical foundation of cognitive behavioural therapy and to the theory and practice of this approach for social work practice.

4

Working with Mandated Individuals

In this chapter, I introduce social work practice with individuals mandated by statutory law to receive those services. I will use the term 'statutory casework' to refer to this form of interpersonal practice because the role of the social worker in this form of practice is, in part, defined by statutory laws. In all wealthy, or 'advanced', nations, statutory laws exist in a range of health and welfare fields and, accordingly, social workers' roles are often shaped by these laws. While the purpose of statutory law in health and welfare services fields is heavily contested, justifications for the development of statutory laws include the need for governments to promote the safety of vulnerable individuals or the general community. I will refer to the service users who are subject to statutory inventions as involuntary or mandated service users to reflect the fact that these individuals are compelled to receive social work (and other related) services. However, as I shall argue, social workers should aim to develop a collaborative relationship with service users in this context wherever possible. Statutory social work is a challenging field of practice for a range of reasons, but primarily because service users are likely to resist the involvement of social workers in their lives.

I begin this chapter with a definition and discussion of the nature of statutory social work practice. I then outline debates about, and rationale for, social workers' involvement in this method of practice. In the remainder of the chapter, I will focus on how the four phases of social work practice, outlined in Chapter 1, can be applied to statutory casework.

Defining Statutory Casework

I refer in this chapter to statutory casework as a method of practice because, as we shall argue, this type of casework practice involves specific capacities. The worker's capacity to recognize and balance their legal and helping responsibilities is an essential and unique feature of statutory casework. Service users can be required by law to engage in other forms of service delivery, such as groupwork, but such requirements are usually part of a case plan developed between the social worker and service user in the course of statutory casework practice. The term 'statutory' is used to refer to the fact that the legal requirement is embedded in a statute, rather than case law. Governments develop statutes in health and welfare fields to allow for state intervention into the lives of vulnerable individuals, such as children, or those who are perceived to pose a threat of harm to themselves or others. Statutes allow for intervention in a wide variety of issues. In many countries, social workers are involved in the implementation of statutes in welfare fields such as child protection, mental health, prison, probation and parole, and public health. Social workers may not be the only practitioners responsible for the implementation of these statutes, as, for example, a range of health practitioners may have responsibilities under mental health and public health acts.

I use the term 'statutory caseworkers' to refer to social workers who are required as a central part of their role to implement statutory law to investigate, assess and/or intervene in the lives of individuals and families. Examples of this include:

- child protection caseworkers employed by the government to implement statutory child protection law to assess and intervene in the lives of children at risk of abuse or neglect

- caseworkers employed by the prison and probation services agencies to monitor and intervene in the lives of people on intervention orders related to probation or imprisonment

- mental health caseworkers who have a statutory responsibility under a mental health statute to assess and intervene in circumstances where a person with a mental health condition poses a risk of harm to themselves or others.

I do not include in this definition caseworkers practising outside statutory services but who might be required by law to report concerns, such as concerns about child abuse, to a statutory authority.

Social workers using statutory casework methods work with involuntary or mandated services users. In this chapter, I will be focusing on an important set of involuntary services users, those who receive a social work service either because of 'a court order or under the threat of some other legal sanction', such as the threat of one's children being removed (Trotter, 2006, p. 2). Even if the service user is willing to receive the services, they can be considered involuntary in that they have no real choice to refuse them.

There is another group of service users who we may refer to as semi-voluntary or even involuntary services users because while they are not subject to a mandated intervention, they seek services because they are experience some form of external pressure to do so. For example, a man seeking counselling to address his use of violence in intimate relationships may be compelled by the threat of losing his family and the threat of police intervention in his, and his family's, life. Similarly, a person with a drug addiction may seek counselling as part of a strategy to provide a court of law with evidence of their commitment to rehabilitation. Service users who are compelled by such concerns cannot be considered truly voluntary, but neither are they mandated service users. Another example of semi-voluntary service users are those who are receiving services because they have a practical need for the services offered by an organization. For example, women and children seeking refuge in domestic violence shelters or young homeless people seeking accommodation services are illustrations of service users who have a compelling practical need that leads them into contact with a range of social and healthcare services. These service users may not seek, and may actively resist, the social casework services that are often provided alongside the provision of practical resources, such as housing; however, these service users are not mandated clients because they are not compelled by law to receive services. While the main focus of this chapter is on casework practice with individuals who are mandated to receive services, the skills and strategies discussed will have relevance for services users who fit somewhere along the continuum outside the category of 'voluntary' or 'involuntary' service user.

Statutory Casework: An Inconvenient Truth?

Our involvement, as social workers, in statutory casework necessarily aligns us with the exercise of the authority power of the state. The exercise of statutory power can appear to contradict the core values of social work, such as:

- **Client self-determination:** The exercise of statutory responsibilities can require that we practise in ways that are in tension with, or contradict, the views or wishes of the service user. For example, the mental health social worker may invoke their statutory authority to require a service user to enter a psychiatric facility against their will.

- **Social justice:** In statutory casework practice, we may need to focus on assessing and reducing risk to a vulnerable individual despite being aware that unjust social arrangements have contributed to the risks faced by the individual. Similarly, the exercise of statutory power in relation to individuals often involves holding them personally accountable for acts, or failure to act, and for achieving change. Yet in many circumstances, it is clear that social circumstances such as entrenched poverty and other forms of social marginalization have contributed to the difficulties facing the individual. For example, it is well established that the prison population is disproportionally drawn from socioeconomically disadvantaged and racial minority populations (Wildeman, 2009).

Some social work commentators appear to question whether the risk management and social control aspects of statutory casework can be aligned with our helping role, especially in the increasingly bureaucratized and risk-averse contexts of practice. For example, Seden (1999, pp. 2–3) questions whether counselling skills are valued in social work education and practice, given that 'They [social workers] now find themselves overwhelmed by work of a more bureaucratic and directive kind, which meets the requirements of the legal mandates of social services.'

Beyond the longstanding philosophical tensions surrounding social workers' involvement in statutory casework, there are also practical concerns. Statutory casework is often difficult and sometimes dangerous work. The difficulty arises, in large part, from the involuntary nature of the relationship. Indeed, mandated service users are often described as '"difficult", "uncooperative", "negative" ... and "often hostile"' (De Jong and Berg, 2001, p. 361). Some researchers suggest that statutory service users have lower levels of motivation for achieving change and hence are less likely to achieve change than voluntary service users (see Lincourt et al., 2002).

Another problem is that the service user may not consider there is a problem to be addressed. For example, the young person mandated to receive social casework services to address offending behaviour may deny that they have offended or may seek to justify their actions as a reasonable response to the 'victim's' behaviour or the offender's circumstances. Different views about the existence (or not) of the problem can create a considerable obstacle for workers and service users in developing a constructive working relationship.

A further difficulty is that in statutory casework, the social worker may be perceived by the service user as part of the problem rather than part of the solution. For example, the first meeting between a child protection social worker and a service user is likely to be focused on the investigation and assessment of a concern about child abuse and neglect. Unlike casework practice with voluntary service users, wherein the caseworker/counsellor may initially focus on building a relationship, the statutory caseworker may be required by law to raise highly sensitive issues early in the first meeting with the service user.

Statutory casework can also be dangerous for a range of reasons, including the highly emotive subject matter, the fact that the statutory caseworker represents a human welfare system, such as child welfare or prison services, that the service user may have good reason to resent, or that the service user may be in an unstable state due, for example, to drug use or psychosis. Given that statutory services are often invoked when other noncompulsory forms of intervention have failed, we can anticipate that the service user may present more complex or challenging problems and behaviours than might be encountered in more voluntary service arrangements.

Ironically, in many countries, newly qualified workers are overrepresented among workers involved in statutory casework in fields such as child protection (Healy et al., 2009; Tham, 2007). The overrepresentation of newly qualified workers is due in part to the high turnover rates in some fields of statutory practice such as child protection services in some countries (see Barak et al., 2006; Healy, 2009; Tham, 2007). Another problem in many statutory services is that career pathways often promote frontline practitioners out of direct service roles into managerial roles (Healy et al., 2009; Tham, 2007). To make matters worse, the newly qualified worker may be least prepared because of the ambivalence within the profession towards statutory casework practice (De Jong and Berg, 2001), and also the wider community uncertainty about the involvement of governments in the private lives of individuals and families. This is a heavy burden for the statutory caseworker to bear, particularly newly qualified workers who are still 'finding their feet' in practice. The inherent stresses of statutory casework make it all the more important that the statutory caseworker has a clear theoretical framework for their practice and well-developed practice skills.

But is it Casework?

I acknowledge that my use of the term 'statutory casework' and my reference to it as a social work method is controversial. There is considerable debate about whether statutory practice is, or should involve, 'casework' or even social work practice (Healy, 2009; Trotter, 2006). In some countries and in some fields of practice, statutory authorities have attempted to emphasize the investigative and risk assessment parts of the statutory casework role, while marginalizing the helping components (see Annison et al., 2008; Healy, 2009). Yet I consider that the term 'casework' is relevant because frontline statutory work with service users in fields such as child protection, prison and mental health services involves both helping and social control functions. The helping dimensions of statutory casework may include case management but also go beyond it to include other helping activities such as case planning and involvement in creating change with the service user (Trotter, 2006, p. 41).

I use the term 'statutory casework' because this term recognizes the delicate balancing act involved in exercising statutory authority while also maintaining a helping focus. Further, I contend that much of the knowledge and skill associated with social casework, discussed in Chapter 3, is also relevant to statutory casework practice. Some of the key similarities are that both methods:

● Draw on a range of theoretical perspectives. The approaches discussed in this chapter, like Chapter 3, include problem-solving, strengths-based and solution-focused approaches, and radical casework perspectives

● Require that the social worker identify and work with the service user's definition of the problem and the service user's goals

● Require a nonjudgemental stance and an optimistic and positive attitude towards the service user and their potential to achieve their goals

● Demand the effective use of micro-skills, including listening, appropriate questions, tracking and reflecting service user's perspectives, and attention to nonverbal behaviour

● Require that the social worker has the skills needed to help the service user to achieve their goals.

Despite these similarities, there are also some significant differences, including:

● The statutory social work role involves at least two dimensions, the helping and social control dimensions. In the interests of transparency, it is vital that the worker is aware of these dimensions and communicates them to the service user

● Service users are compelled to receive these services. Hence, the social worker must be skilled in developing a constructive relationship in the context of service user resistance or distrust of them and their service

● The need to balance the expression of empathy with a prosocial perspective, which includes the worker being willing to take a directive stance in shaping intervention goals (Trotter, 2006)

● The likelihood that the assessment phase will involve the use of formal risk assessment tools.

Risk Assessment in Statutory Casework

The complex nature of the statutory caseworker's role is also reflected in the assessment process, which usually involves both the assessment of the individual's needs and strengths and the assessment of risk. Risk assessment involves developing a view of the likelihood of a specific kind of negative event, such as the death of a child, or negative behaviour, such as criminal behaviour, occurring in the future (Shlonsky and Wagner, 2005). While social workers assess risk in a range of contexts, in statutory social work, this form of assessment has some unique features. The first is that risk assessment is often a mandatory aspect of social casework. This means that the worker may be compelled by law or agency policy to conduct a formal risk assessment as part of their work with the service user; in other words, the completion of a risk assessment may be a non-negotiable dimension of the social worker's role.

The second is that the worker may be required to use a risk assessment tool. Structured risk assessment tools are increasingly commonplace in many contexts of social work practice, particularly in statutory casework where the worker must make decisions based on an assessment of the risk of future harm to the service user or others with whom the service user has contact. These tools are frequently used by child protection workers to assess the risk of future harm to a child, by mental health workers to assess the risk of harm a service user may pose to themselves or others, and in the prison service to assess the likelihood of future offending. There are a wide variety of structured decision-making tools and it is important that caseworkers receive training in the use of the specific risk assessment tool used in their workplace.

Risk assessment tools provide the caseworker with a list of factors to assess in their work with service users. The list comprises factors considered to be indicators of risk of future harm or the likelihood of adverse events, such as suicide or reoffending. Often these tools are integrated with case planning information technology systems. This means that the caseworker may be required to report on risk assessment information before they are able to complete other aspects of their assessment, such as the consideration of the service users' goals (Gillingham and Humphreys, 2010).

Formal risk assessment tools focus on quantifiable information, such as the number of previous investigations of the family or the number of previous hospitalizations of a person experiencing a mental illness. The quantified information may be given a weighting according to the degree of risk associated with a specific factor. For example, in a child protection risk assessment, a factor such as the presence of domestic violence may be given a higher weighting as a risk factor for future maltreatment than, say, the parent's employment status because of the stronger association between domestic violence and the likelihood of future harm to the child. Based on the information gathered and quantified, the caseworker can use the tool to predict the likelihood of future risk of specific adverse events, such as child abuse or neglect, or suicide. This information is then used to guide the caseworker's assessment of the situation and actions in relation to that assessment.

According to Shlonsky and Wagner (2005), risk assessment tools are usually developed through consensus or actuarial means. Consensus-based risk assessment tools are 'compiled by "experts" who may draw upon previous research findings, clinical experience, or a combination of both' (Shlonsky and Wagner, 2005, p. 410). Actuarial assessments are developed through statistical analysis of existing databases to 'identify a set of risk factors with a strong statistical relationship to the behavioural outcome' (Shlonsky and Wagner, 2005, p. 410). For example, in the prison service, a statistical analysis of databases of repeat offenders could reveal factors associated with an increased likelihood of continuing offending behaviour. Similarly, in child protection services, database analysis could reveal factors most associated with the likelihood of future harm to a child.

There is a great deal of debate about the use of structured risk assessment tools in casework practice (see Gillingham and Humphreys, 2010; Lonne et al., 2009). Yet one reason these tools are so widely used by statutory authorities is that they appear to substantially enhance the accuracy of practitioner assessment of risk. Numerous studies have demonstrated that 'carefully validated actuarial models outperform clinical judgment at estimating future behavior' (Shlonsky and Wagner, 2005, p. 411; see also Trotter, 2006). This enhanced accuracy in predicting risk is achieved in part because the risk assessment tool can assist the caseworker to focus on, and appropriately weight, the most significant risk factors in relation to a specific concern, such as the risk of child abuse and neglect. Without the tools, the accuracy of the assessment can be limited by the sheer volume of information available to the practitioner and because of the short timelines in which some decisions need to be made. The structured decision-making tools also require workers to focus on a range of risk factors that they may not otherwise consider, particularly if the worker is inexperienced or if their practice experience has limited their openness to a full consideration of some risk factors. For instance, if a worker has experienced a negative child protection outcome in relation to a family where mental illness was present, they may tend to overestimate the impact of risk in future child protection situations involving families where mental illness is present.

Many of the criticisms of structured decision-making tools are focused mainly on why and how these tools are being used and their potentially negative influence on the quality of casework practice. A major concern of many critics of structured decision-making is that it is used by employers to undermine professional judgement in a wide variety of statutory practice contexts. For example, some child protection authorities have argued that the presence of structured decision-making tools makes it possible to employ child protection officers without qualifications in fields such as social work or child and family social work (Healy, 2009). Yet this contradicts the view of researchers involved in the development and evaluation of these tools, who have argued that a formalized risk assessment 'is not an infallible prediction, nor is it a substitute for the exercise of sound professional judgment by the investigating worker who completes it' (Shlonsky and Wagner, 2005, p. 420). In a similar vein, several commentators have pointed to practitioner concern about the use of risk assessment tools to neglect, or dumb down, the inherent complexity of child protection decision-making (Gillingham and Humphreys, 2010; Lonne et al., 2009).

In a risk-averse environment, risk assessment tools can also contribute to more intensive and potentially harmful interventions into service users' lives (Gillingham and Humphreys, 2010). For example, a practitioner may feel compelled to adopt intrusive interventions to protect themselves from the risk of a negative outcome in a case assessed involving high risk. Yet risk assessment tools can only measure the statistical probability of an adverse outcome, and an assessment that there is a high level of risk does not mean that an adverse outcome is certain.

Another concern pertains to the potential for risk assessments to reinforce social inequalities by neglecting how these inequalities contribute to the creation of risk (Trotter, 2006). For example, many factors strongly associated with socioeconomic disadvantage, such as single parenthood, low income and having being raised in institutional care, have been identified as risk factors in various risk assessment tools in child protection settings (Shlonsky and Wagner, 2005). Through a formalized risk assessment process, these factors may be seen as a problem of the individual family, yet from a critical perspective, these factors may also be viewed as systemic problems that need systemic rather than individualized responses.

Why Do Statutory Casework?

Given the profession's and society's ambivalence towards statutory casework, we may question why the profession should bother with it at all. To engage in statutory casework is to constantly face criticisms from within the profession and within the broader community about the social control function of social workers, and also entails engaging with service users who, in many cases, will resist our involvement in their lives. Despite these challenges, there are several reasons why the profession should continue to stake a claim to this method of practice. The first is service quality. As discussed in Chapter 3, social workers adopt a person-in-environment perspective. The person-in-environment approach is important in statutory casework for challenging an exclusive focus on individual pathology, and facilitating social support interventions to prevent further harm and to improve quality of life. Furthermore, social workers have an ethical commitment to making a positive difference to service users' lives (Healy, 2009). Without this commitment, statutory casework risks becoming focused solely on social control. This is a problem from a social justice value perspective, in that the majority of service users experience socioeconomic disadvantage, which requires a change-oriented, helping response, even if there is also a socially mandated need to require change in the individual's behaviour. A focus on social control in statutory service provision is associated with service user dissatisfaction, which, in turn, is linked to reduced service effectiveness (Trotter, 2008).

The social work profession's commitment to working with vulnerable people is another reason we should engage in statutory practice. Mandated service users are among society's most vulnerable people and often have little capacity to pay for personal assistance and, for a variety of reasons, they may also avoid voluntary community service agencies. By making a positive and constructive connection with the service users, social workers can help mandated service users to access the services needed to make a positive difference to their lives (De Jong and Berg, 2001).

A third reason is that social workers can bring a critical understanding of the history of health and welfare institutions in the lives of service users and continuing inherent dynamics of power to statutory practice. To be sure, an understanding of this history and the inherent tensions in the care and control aspects of statutory work places social workers in an uncomfortable position. However, this critical understanding of the history of statutory service provision, including its oppressive aspects, can help us as practitioners to work more critically in contemporary contexts of statutory social work practice. Without this critical understanding, we risk failing to address the fear and anger that service users may feel towards this form of service provision, alternatively we may miss the responsibility of statutory service providers to use their legal powers to protect vulnerable children and adults.

Statutory Casework Practice

In the remainder of this chapter, we outline how the four phases of social work practice, first outlined in Chapter 1, apply to statutory casework. We use the same four-phase approach discussed in Chapter 3, and we now turn to consider how these phases are implemented in statutory social work practice.

Engagement

The engagement phase is often a challenging one in statutory casework, given that service users are likely to be reluctant to engage with the service provider. As discussed earlier in the chapter, this reluctance has many sources, the primary one being that the service user is compelled to receive the service. Yet the capacity to build an effective relationship with the service user is as crucial in statutory social work as it is in other methods of social work practice. In reflecting on statutory child protection work, Miller (2009, p. 116) asserts:

> While the work is complex, the essence of good practice is simple: it is about relationships – relationships that engage people in change, that build on strengths and look creatively with families for solutions that will make a difference; relationships that have warmth, and are non-judgmental, curious about the experience of each member of the family and honest.

In essence, in both statutory and nonstatutory social worker, the worker must build a constructive relationship with the service user. Statutory social workers must manage the delicate balance between the helping and authoritative aspects of their role, which involves both recognizing this balance ourselves and assisting service users to understand the nature of our role (Trotter, 2006).

From the outset of the engagement phase, the worker needs to make a clear statement of who they are and the reason for their contact with the service user. This statement of purpose should reflect both one's legal responsibilities and helping purposes. For example, a worker could state 'I am Bronwyn Carmichael and I work for the child protection service. I am here to discuss some concerns raised about your children and to hear your views on the situation.' In this statement, the worker has stated who she is (her name) and her work role (I work for child protection services), she has also briefly stated her legal responsibility to address the concerns and also an interest in the service user's viewpoint.

Making clear and frequent reference to the dual nature of the role can be difficult, partly because social workers often feel uncomfortable with the social control aspect of the role and partly because it is necessary for the worker to discuss the issues that are of concern even before they have established a relationship with the service user. For example, we may feel more comfortable asking a person about a child protection concern once we have spent time getting to know them. However, a failure to communicate your legal obligation to assess particular issues, such as child protection or mental health concerns, can confuse service users about the nature of our role. Expressing the dual nature of one's role from the outset and during the interaction is a practical way we can demonstrate our commitment to transparency and to recognize the client's right to know the true nature of our role. In addition, our communication of our dual role helps the service user understand the difference between this and other forms of health and welfare services' interactions; such understanding is vital for building trust and reducing the considerable scope for confusion in statutory work. Trotter (2006) suggests such understanding also contributes to practice effectiveness, as several studies have demonstrated that service outcomes are improved when workers help the client understand the nature of the role.

In statutory casework, the social worker needs to take an active role in determining the focus and goals of practice; this is in contrast with social casework with voluntary clients where a greater degree of self-determination of focus and goals may be possible. In the statutory casework method, we must ensure that the focus and goals are consistent with our statutory responsibilities. For example, a statutory child protection worker has an obligation to focus on the safety and wellbeing of children in the families with whom they work. So although a statutory child protection worker may assist a parent with drug dependency issues to access rehabilitation services, their primary purpose in doing so is to ensure that the harmful impact of parental drug use on the children at risk of abuse or neglect is minimized.

The dual character of the statutory social worker's role places specific constraints on the appropriate use of empathy in this method of practice. In Chapter 2, I defined empathy as a willingness to imagine the experience of the service user and, in that imagining, experience some of the pain or difficulty faced by them. By empathizing, we put ourselves in the position of the other person and reflect back to them what you imagine their experience to be like. While the demonstration of empathy continues to be important in statutory casework, we also need to be aware of its limitations in this method of practice. We need to be alert to the potential for the expression of empathy to be interpreted as 'some kind of subtle permission or sanction' for behaviours that have contributed to the problem or issue of concern (Trotter, 2006, p. 33). For example, in empathizing with the young violent offender's anger arising from their experience of childhood neglect, we must still communicate our non-tolerance of violent behaviour.

To recognize the tensions in the expression of empathy in statutory practice is not to say that the building of empathy is not necessary, indeed it is vital to building effective relationships with service users. However, it is necessary for the worker to be able to critically reflect on their use of empathy and the extent to which it helps and hinders the realization of our complex, and sometimes competing, responsibilities as statutory workers. By having regular and open discussions with service users about the dual nature of our role, including our statutory responsibilities, we can minimize the chances that our expression of empathy will be misinterpreted as an endorsement of antisocial behaviour and we also maximize our opportunities to recognize with the client our legal obligations in practice. For example, in our expression of empathy for the parent struggling with their own childhood experiences, as statutory child protection workers, we should continue to ask them, and ourselves, what their experiences mean for their parenting today.

Finally, in the engagement phase, it is important to openly and sensitively acknowledge any differences between yourself and the service user that may constrain the development of a constructive working relationship. This provides an opportunity for you to demonstrate to the service user your concern with being responsive to their needs and your concern with building a constructive relationship with them. For example, age, gender and cultural differences may act as significant barriers to effective working relationships. Indeed, in some cultural groups, it may be regarded as unacceptable for a female social worker to work with a male service user in relation to certain matters, such as discussions of sexuality or family concerns. Acknowledging these barriers can be important for providing the service user with an alternative worker where there are immovable barriers to an effective working relationship with the service user, or, at the very least, to find ways of accommodating the service user's concerns and interests. For example, while a service provider may not be able to accommodate a service user's request for a worker of a specific cultural background, they can commit to engaging in a culturally sensitive way by, for example, finding out more about the service user's cultural identity and its importance to the service user.

Over to you ...

Engaging in a statutory context

Imagine you work in a mental health support service where one of your statutory responsibilities is to conduct mental health assessments. You have the statutory authority, in consultation with another health worker, to place a person in secure care for a time-limited period if you believe they present a risk of significant harm to themselves or others. A housing worker from a community housing support service has asked for an assessment of a young man residing in their accommodation. The housing worker, David Bright, has reported that the young man, Jed, has expressed his wish to 'end it all' to his two housemates. You are about to meet Jed, an 18-year-old young man who was born in Ethiopia but left with his parents when he was five years old. He has had lots of conflict with his parents and no longer lives with them. Jed has had a long struggle with depression and has been involved in the harmful use of alcohol and amphetamines. Jed has been studying to be chef but has taken a six-month break from his apprenticeship, because he was having problems with the restaurant owners and he has decided to undertake his apprenticeship elsewhere. Jed has resided in supportive housing for six months and shares a house with two young men with whom he has a positive relationship.

Ideally, you should role-play this situation, with you and your partner each taking a turn at being Jed and the mental health social worker. As you role-play, or reflect on, this case study, consider the following questions:

1. How would you introduce yourself to Jed, and in particular, how would you sensitively communicate the dual nature of your role?

2. How would you describe the reason for your visit?

3. How would you demonstrate your dual responsibilities to help and to assess the safety issues for Jed (and possibly others) in the way you engage with Jed?

4. How would you recognize cultural differences between yourself and Jed?

After you have completed this role-play (or written responses to the questions), consider the following:

1. What was it like for you in the role of Jed? What were your fears and hopes for the interaction with the mental health social worker? What could the person in the role of social worker do to most clearly and sensitively communicate their role?

2. In the role of Jed, what would help you to feel confident in the worker's capacity to help you?

3. How do you feel about the social control aspect of the worker's role, that is, that the worker is there, at least in part, to assess the level of harm you pose to yourself and possibly others?

4. What was it like for you in the role of the mental health worker? To what extent were you able to communicate the dual nature of the role? What was easy and what was difficult?

Assessment

A goal of the assessment phase in statutory social work is to develop a shared understanding of the service user's situation based on a comprehensive review of both the risks and dangers as well as the strengths and capacities present in the situation. The practical tasks to be achieved in this stage include:

● Explanation of the focus of assessment, particularly that it will involve the consideration of risks, dangers, strengths and capacities within the individual and their social environment. In this phase, the social worker needs to continue to reinforce the dual nature of their role and the specific focus of their responsibilities. For example, in accordance with their legal obligations, a child protection worker must assess risks and strengths in relation to children's protection and wellbeing needs, and, similarly, a mental health social worker must assess the mental health status of the service user.

- A clear statement of the situation to be assessed. For example, we might say to Jed that we are concerned about his emotional state as we have received information that he is thinking of self-harming, so we need to assess whether he does, in fact, present a risk of self-harm and how we might keep him safe from harm.

- Exploration of the service user's view of their situation.

- Completion of a comprehensive assessment of risks, harms, strengths and capacities, often with the aid of structured risk assessment tools.

The core task of this phase is to develop a shared and comprehensive understanding of the service user's situation, and this understanding should form the basis of your ongoing work together. The importance of developing a shared understanding is common to both statutory and nonstatutory forms of social work. As Trotter (2006, p. 27) emphasizes: 'Research consistently points to the need to work with client definitions of problems and goals with both voluntary and involuntary clients.' Yet developing a shared definition of the problem has specific challenges in statutory social work for several reasons. Here we will consider these challenges and what you can do as a statutory worker to address them.

The first challenge is the likelihood that the service user will be reluctant to engage in a shared assessment of the concerns. This resistance can be for many reasons, including a perception that a problem does not exist, a lack of trust in the willingness of the statutory authority to fairly assess the concerns, or a fear of the consequences of acknowledging the concerns. Yet it is vital that the worker helps the service user overcome these reservations, given that, as De Jong and Berg (2001, p. 327) have emphasized: 'co-constructing a basis for cooperation is the sole productive way to engage mandated clients'. Some practical ways you as a worker can help to address service user reservations is to practically demonstrate that you want to involve the service user in defining the issues to be addressed and in developing a plan for addressing those concerns. From a strengths-based perspective, you can also demonstrate that you are keen to build on what is good or positive about their situation, not only the problems facing the service user. For example, in a child protection interview, you might ask not only about risks and concerns but also about those aspects of family life that are positive and give the parents pride in their family (Berg and Kelly, 2000).

Of course, it is possible that after exploring the issue with the service user, we arrive at a different assessment of the situation from the service user. One of the most challenging circumstances is when the worker's and service user's assessment of the level of risk or concern differs significantly. Most commonly, tension arises where the social worker perceives a much greater level of risk than the service user. A solution-focused approach is helpful for addressing this impasse by encouraging us to move beyond a shared view of the problem to a shared view of a solution (Miller, 2009). For example, we could explore with the service user what they would most like to change about their circumstances; this could include, for instance, exploring what role if any the service user wants statutory or other services to have in their lives. If, for example, the service user asserts that they want no involvement with statutory services, we might incorporate this wish as a goal for us to work on together. So in the case of Jed, we might state the goal as: to achieve enough stability in his life that the involvement of statutory mental health services is no longer required. This means that we could explore with the service user what would need to happen for the statutory services to no longer be present in their lives. This refocusing of the goal from a focus on the problem to a shared intervention focus can help to build a collaborative partnership between the service provider and service user, while still allowing us to recognize our statutory obligations.

The second challenge is that of building service user collaboration in the assessment process. While there is a great deal of debate about the uses and limits of structured risk assessment tools, social workers are now required to use these tools in many contexts, particularly in statutory social work. A challenge for both service providers and service users is to ensure that risk assessment tools are used to assist in the decision-making process rather than replacing the views of service providers and service users in the assessment process (Gillingham and Humphreys, 2010). There are several ways the service provider can reduce the chances that the risk assessment tools will create a barrier to collaboration. The first is to begin by exploring the service user's view of the situation, such as how they view the issues, risks and strengths in their situation. It is important that the service provider takes time to introduce the risk assessment tool to the service user and to explain its role as a tool for supporting, rather than determining, part of the assessment, that is, the assessment of risk. The service provider can further enable collaboration in the risk assessment process by inviting service users' comments on each of the items and noting within the case record, shared and different views between themselves and the service users on each of the standardized items. The service provider should share with the service user the outcome of the structured risk assessment process, and discuss any differences between the findings of the risk assessment and the service provider's and service user's perceptions of the level of the issues and the service user's strengths and capacities alongside the nature and level of risk within the situation.

A third challenge is that the worker must take a more proactive role in defining the problem and focus of assessment than in other contexts, such as work with voluntary service users. The service provider is obliged to ensure that their assessment incorporates their statutory obligations. For example, in a child protection context, the worker must understand not only the service user's perspectives on matters such as their experience of mental illness or drug use, but how these matters impact on their capacity to keep their children safe and address their needs. Similarly, in a mental health context, where the social worker may have a statutory obligation to assess the level of risk of harm a service user may pose to themselves or others, it is necessary that the impact of the service user's mental health status on their level of risk to self or others is considered. As a statutory social worker, you have a responsibility to help the service user to understand the nature of your role. Not only does this include explaining the care and control aspects of your work, it also means that you should help the service user to understand the boundaries of your role.

Over to you ...

Returning to Jed, consider the following:

1. How would you describe the assessment focus and process to Jed?

2. What risks and dangers would you like to explore with Jed in the assessment process?

3. What strengths and capacities do you see in Jed's situation and what areas of strength and capacity would you like to explore?

4. Imagine that you are required to perform a formal risk assessment in your work with Jed. How would you introduce this formal assessment to him?

Intervention

We turn now to the intervention plan, which includes the development of a plan, implementation and monitoring of activities towards achieving the plan, and evaluation of the intervention.

The intervention phase should begin with the development of an intervention plan that builds on a comprehensive assessment of the service user's situation and addresses the statutory obligations of the service provider. In statutory social work, it is vital that the service provider and service user develop a shared understanding of the intervention goals and outcomes. This is imperative because of the significant personal, practical and legal consequences of the failure to achieve agreed intervention goals. These outcomes can include serious harm to service users or others around them; for example, the failure of a parent to address their drug use may lead to harm to their children, or the failure of a person who uses violence to address this tendency may lead to others around them being subject to violence. There is also the likelihood that, as a statutory service worker, you may be forced to act in more coercive ways than you may see as desirable should you and the service user not achieve agreed intervention goals. For example, in child protection services, it may be necessary to remove children from their parents' care, or in mental health services, you may need to involuntarily admit a service user to a psychiatric inpatient facility.

The process of developing an intervention plan is, itself, part of the intervention and should reflect your values and responsibilities as a statutory social worker. Consistent with the values of self-determination and respect, it is important that the service user is involved in the process of developing the plan (Healy and Darlington, 2009). This involvement can help to ensure the development of a plan that is relevant and meaningful to the service user and one that they are likely to commit to achieving. For the service user to be meaningfully involved, it is important that plain, jargon-free language is used, focusing on identifying change goals and methods of achieving them. Goals and outcomes need to be expressed in ways that help both service provider and service user to monitor their achievement. In the 'signs of safety' approach (Turnell and Edwards, 1999; Turnell and Parker, 2009), which draws on strengths-based and solution-focused theory, it is suggested that a series of questions can guide the development of an intervention plan. While originally designed for child protection practice, these questions are relevant to guiding intervention planning in other practice contexts. The questions are given in Table 4.1, with some suggestions for how we might complete this table when working with Jed.

Table 4.1   Questions to ask to guide the
development of an intervention plan

What is our goal?	What needs to change?	How will we achieve this change?	How will we know this goal has been achieved?
For Jed to re-engage with work and friendships.	Jed needs to loosen the grip of depression on his life.	Social worker will speak to the medical team about short-term use of antidepressant drugs to help Jed overcome current bout of depression. Jed will work with social worker to identify ways of managing stress so as to avoid depression. Jed and social worker to develop a plan for helping Jed return to work.	Jed feels more control over his mood or 'state of mind'. Jed knows how to stop depression before it gets a hold on him. Jed has returned to work, perhaps initially on a part-time basis.

In this intervention plan, we work with the service user to develop a clear picture of our goals and what needs to happen to achieve those goals. In this example, we have used a narrative therapy approach by referring to the depressive episodes he experiences as 'depression' (White, 1995). We have presented his increased control over depression as a goal and we have identified a number of ways he can loosen its hold on him.

The process of developing the intervention plan must, at a minimum, involve the statutory caseworker and service user. It can often involve others as well, such as other professionals and family members. In some fields of statutory work, case conferences and family meetings are well-established methods of involving a broad network of professionals and the service user's family network in developing an intervention plan. One of the major challenges in group conferences is that of ensuring that the service user has a fair say in determining their goals and the ways of achieving those goals. Regrettably, several observational studies of these meetings have demonstrated that they are often biased towards the professionals' views as a result of the numerical dominance of professionals and their tendency to dominate the interactions at these meetings (Hall and Slembrouck, 2001). In contexts where group meetings, such as case conferences, are held to develop intervention plans, there are some practical strategies you can use to ensure that service users' voices are heard in developing these plans:

- spend time prior to the meeting helping the service user clarify what they want in the intervention plan

- ensure that the service user has a support person present who can advocate for their voice to be heard if needed

- seek to ensure that there are equal or greater numbers of service users and their supporters present

- seek to ensure that equal or greater time is spent engaging with the service user's views at the meeting

- where possible, begin the meeting with the service user's views rather than the professional view of the circumstance.

In statutory social work, it is usually important that the intervention plan is written down, with both the social worker and service user having a copy. A written plan helps to create transparency and accountability in the intervention process. It is vital that the plan is written in plain, jargon-free language. Also, the plan should be a 'living document', by which we mean that the plan is frequently discussed and adapted, with the permission of the worker and the service user, as required throughout the intervention.

Process

In the intervention phase, meetings with the service user should be focused on the implementation and monitoring of the plan. Implementation involves identifying and acting on the activities and tasks that need to be completed to achieve the agreed goals. The social worker can assist the service user to implement the agreed plan by:

- Breaking down the goal into step-by-step activities and tasks that will enable the service user and the worker to achieve agreed goals. For example, in working with Jed, we might consider what we need to do at each of our meetings in order to work towards the goal of his return to paid employment.

- Problem-solving with the service user how to address barriers to the achievement of goals. For example, Jed may decide that a meditation course would assist him to manage stress and we may work with Jed to identify how to access such a course.

- Rehearsing with the service user tasks that must be completed to achieve goals. For example, we might rehearse with Jed the skills required for a job interview.

- Case management often forms part of statutory casework as it is likely that the social worker will need to coordinate and monitor the involvement of other service providers, such as health professionals, in achieving service goals with the service user. For example, in the case of Jed, the social worker may play a role in coordinating medical interventions with Jed.

In using the statutory social work method, the social worker must pay attention to ensuring that the process of intervention reflects and reinforces goals, values and legal responsibilities. Trotter (2004) refers to the importance of statutory social workers adopting a prosocial stance, by which he means that the social worker should reinforce behaviours and attitudes that are consistent with the practice goals (see Chapter 2). This involves modelling the behaviours that are consistent with your practice goals and responsibilities. A prosocial perspective also means being alert to, and challenging, the client's engagement in antisocial comments and behaviour, especially those that contravene your statutory responsibilities.

Evaluation

In statutory practice, like all forms of social work, we should aim to continually improve our practice. We can do this by evaluating the outcomes and process of our involvement with the service user. In a statutory practice context, the capacity to evaluate the outcomes of our practice is often complicated by:

- **The involuntary nature of the relationship:** The compulsory nature of the relationship may, of itself, contribute to lower levels of service user satisfaction and poorer levels of engagement with the achievement of agreed goals than might be the case for social work practice with individuals in voluntary settings.

- **The legal context and implications of the relationship:** In some cases, it will be necessary for statutory social workers to take coercive action, such as removing children from their families or compelling a service user to enter a mental health facility. These outcomes may lead both the worker and the service user to assume that their intervention has failed; however, such outcomes may be unavoidable in order to avert other negative outcomes, such as the death of a child or self-harming behaviour.

- **The complex range of factors contributing to the involvement of statutory services:** Statutory social work can bring social workers into contact with complex situations where previous less coercive forms of intervention have failed. We need to be clear about what social work intervention can achieve if we are to develop meaningful evaluation measures of our practice. For example, in a mental health context, we may focus on evaluating whether the service user has developed strategies for managing the impact of their illness on areas of their life that matter to them, such as family relationships and employment opportunities.

There are three dimensions that need to be considered in evaluating statutory social work practice. They are the extent to which the intervention has:

- achieved the goals agreed with the service user

- realized our legally defined obligations, such as keeping children safe, supporting families, assisting a person with a severe mental illness to remain safe within their community, or assisting a young person who has committed crimes to resist further involvement in crime

- contributed to service user satisfaction with the process and outcomes of service provision.

In many contexts of statutory casework, external review bodies exist to examine negative case outcomes, such as child deaths from child abuse and neglect. Yet it is not sufficient to rely only on these mechanisms to review our practice, given that external reviews tend to focus on negative case outcomes (Healy and Oltedal, 2010). In the interests of the continuous improvement of our practice, it is important that we take responsibility for assessing our progress, or otherwise, in achieving goals, our professional responsibilities and service user satisfaction. There are several ways we can evaluate our practice with service users. These include, first, reviewing our goals and progress towards the achievement of those goals with the service user as an integral part of our case practice. This discussion should occur regularly in our meetings with service users and it should be documented. The review and its documentation can help the worker and the service user to identify progress that is being made in the process of intervention. This helps to recognize practice outcomes over the entire period of engagement, not only at key points. This ongoing evaluation can be important for working towards lasting change with the service user. For example, in a mental health practice context, a social worker and service user may work together to re-engage a service user with employment opportunities. So even if the goal of keeping the service user out of hospital is not achieved, the fact that substantial progress towards other life goals has been realized needs to be considered in evaluating our work.

A second way we can review our practice is through a case record review. The review involves examining case practice and outcomes of our practice over time. The review should focus on whether we are achieving agreed goals with the service user, which should include the realization of our professional and legal responsibilities. For example, a child protection worker has a responsibility to review whether their interventions have contributed to keeping children safe and, where possible, with their families. It is important that the review is undertaken systematically and at regular time periods, such as at three-monthly intervals, to avoid too much focus on specific incidents or unusual events. It may be helpful to involve a peer or supervisor in the review so as to assist us in reviewing the patterns in our practice, the range of factors contributing to these patterns, and to consider options for improving our practice and for achieving change in the environmental factors contributing to negative outcomes for service users.

A third approach is the collection of information from service users and other service providers about their perceptions of the effectiveness and their satisfaction with the service outcome (Trotter, 2006, Ch. 8). We can use surveys or interviews to collect this information, although the data should be collected by someone other than the person who provided the service in order to reduce bias in how the service user reports on their experiences and perceptions. Ideally, this survey or interview should involve the collection of quantitative and qualitative data. The quantitative data can involve such things as service users' ranking, on a scale of 1–5, whether the service provision has achieved agreed goals and the level of service user satisfaction with service provision. The inclusion of quantitative data makes it possible to compare scores over time both with individual service users and across the group of service users with whom you practise. The inclusion of qualitative data, such as service users' reasons for the scores they have provided, can give insights into service users' perceptions and can also be used as a basis for improving our work.

A fourth approach is the review of critical incidents in our work. This approach is useful for evaluating our work and for ongoing development of our practice. The use of the critical incident technique as a basis for critical reflection in practice involves learning through the regular review of practice incidents that we have experienced as challenging (Fook and Gardner, 2007). This technique involves identifying an incident that has challenged us, for example responding to a service user who has resisted our invitations for collaboration. The critical review of the incident involves exploring our assumptions and expectations that may have contributed to the incident being experienced as challenging and reviewing our practice assumptions in the light of this challenge so as to move forward to manage these circumstances more constructively in future. Like the case record review, having peer or supervisor involvement in the review can help us more fully consider our practice assumptions and ways of moving forward based on the learning that has occurred (see Fook and Gardner, 2007).

Conclusion

In this chapter, I have introduced statutory casework as a method of practice. I have outlined the specific challenges associated with statutory casework practice, much of which centres on the dual nature of the social worker's role. I have also considered the importance of statutory practice as a method of social work, specifically the need to bring social work values to this form of practice. I have outlined practical strategies for implementing the four phases of social work practice in the statutory casework method. In essence, statutory social work is an important method of social work practice and it is important that social workers understand and are able to work constructively within this complex field of practice.

Review Questions

1. What issues do statutory caseworkers need to be aware of when they express empathy with service users?

2. Why is it important for statutory social workers to help service users understand that the statutory role involves both helping and social control elements?

3. What are the arguments for and against the use of structured decision-making tools in statutory casework?

4. How would you collaboratively involve service users in the development and implementation of an intervention plan in statutory casework?

Critical Reflection Question

1. In this chapter, we have argued that it is important for social workers to engage in statutory work. What do you see as the arguments for and against social workers involvement in this method of practice?

Practice Exercise

Imagine you are a social worker working in a statutory child protection service where one of your responsibilities involves work with families where children may be at a significant risk of abuse and neglect. You are just about to meet Doug and Sally O'Rourke, who are parents to three young children under five years of age. Doug is 26 and Sally is 25. Their children are Jack (4), Samantha (2) and Breanna (6 months). They have lived in a public housing apartment in the inner city for two years. Both Doug and Sally are unemployed. Doug hurt his back in a motorcycle accident just before Breanna was born and has been unable to return to his job as a cleaner since then. Sally has remained at home since her first child was born, although before that she worked in various retail jobs.

Neighbours on the estate have raised concerns about Doug and Sally's heavy use of alcohol. It is reported that the parents appear to be drunk sometimes early in the morning. A neighbour reports that last Tuesday (six days ago), Jack went to a neighbour's apartment at 8am in the morning in a state of distress because his mother and father were unconscious on the lounge and his baby sister was screaming uncontrollably. The neighbour comforted the child and his siblings, gave them breakfast at her apartment and waited for the parents to wake up. The neighbour reported that Doug and Sally's apartment was 'littered with empty beer cans'. Doug and Sally explained the incident away to the neighbour as a 'one-off' event, and said that they had been celebrating a compensation payout Doug had just received after the accident. Over the last week, the neighbour has not seen the family but has heard the children crying for long periods on several occasions. The neighbour is concerned about the ability of Doug and Sally to care for their children.

Imagine you are just about to meet Doug and Sally.

1. What would you see as the elements of your role?

2. How would you explain these elements of your role to them?

3. How would you raise the concerns with Doug and Sally?

4. What about the children, how would you engage them?

5. What would your assessment of their situation focus on?

Further Reading

● Trotter, C. (2006) *Working with Involuntary Clients: A Guide to Practice*. Crows Nest, Sydney: Allen & Unwin.

Focuses on effective practice with mandated service users. Presents an evidence-based approach to working with mandated service users in a variety of practice contexts, with a strong focus on work with offenders and families involved with child welfare and child protection services. This accessible book is essential reading for anyone considering working with mandated service users.

- Berg, I.K. and Kelly, S. (2000) *Building Solutions in Child Protection Services.* New York: W.W. Norton.

Insoo Kim Berg, a pioneer of solution-focused therapy, and Susan Kelly, a senior child protection practitioner, outline a solution-focused approach to child protection. A major strength of this book is that it demonstrates how to practically apply strengths-based and solution-focused ideas with mandated service users. Although set in a child protection context, it has significant relevance to other statutory social work practice contexts.

- Turnell, A. and Edwards, S. (1999) *Signs of Safety: A Solution and Safety Oriented Approach to Child Protection Casework.* New York: Norton.

Turnell, A. (2005) *Introduction to the Signs of Safety* (DVD). Perth: Resolutions Consultancy.

- Turnell, A. (2010) *Effective Safety Planning in Child Protection Casework* (DVD and workbook). Perth: Resolutions Consultancy, www.signsofsafety.net.

Andrew Turnell and Steve Edwards developed an approach to working with vulnerable families titled the 'signs of safety' approach. Originally developed in a statutory child protection context, it has great relevance for all forms of social work practice where the worker must manage the dual role of addressing safety issues and helping individuals and families. I have found these works helpful, and a great deal of material is available on the 'signs of safety' approach at www.signsofsafety.net.

Part 3

Working with Families and Groups

Part 3 focuses on social work methods and skills with families and groups. These methods of practice are also known as 'mezzo' practice methods. Social work with families and groups draws on the many of the skills discussed in Parts 1 and 2 of this book.

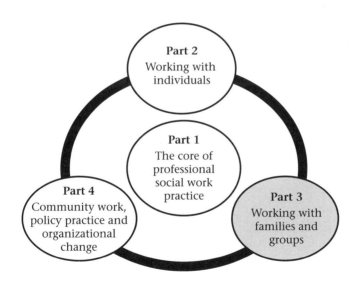

In contrast to social work practice with individuals, in practice with families and groups, social workers need to achieve a shared understanding among a group of people about the nature of the problem to be solved and foster their participation in working together to achieve change. There are many challenges common to family and groupwork practice such as recognizing different viewpoints of the challenge facing the family or group and building people's commitment and capacity to work together for change.

Part 3 comprises two chapters. Chapter 5 focuses on social work practice with families. In this chapter I define, and provide justifications for, social workers' involvement in practice with families. I outline different methods of social work with families, such as family casework, family group conferences and family therapy. In Chapter 6, I introduce social work practice with groups. I define a variety of types of groupwork and then discuss the practical strategies social workers use to enable groups to be vehicles for change. In Chapters 5 and 6, I show how the four phases of social work practice, introduced in Chapter 1, can be applied to practice with families and groups.

5

Working with Families

Social workers work with families in a range of contexts. In fields as diverse as child protection, care of the elderly, mental health, disability support, the prison service and youth justice, social workers engage with families in the course of their work. Families are important in the lives of many service users and community members with whom social workers practise. Social workers work with families in a variety of ways including assessing and building the capacity of families to provide support to address individual service users' needs, and intervening to address family dynamics that may be harmful or troubling for family members.

In this chapter, I introduce family work methods in social work practice. I begin with a definition of the term 'family' and discuss why and how social workers practise with families. I also outline some of the challenges in social work practice with families. Drawing on theoretical ideas from systems theory, strengths approaches and critical social work traditions, I discuss core skills in working with families. The skills I focus on are engaging families, assessment with families, intervention with families, and working with families to evaluate practice processes and outcomes.

What is a Family?

Social workers need to be aware of diverse family structures. In many wealthy, 'advanced' societies, the term 'family' is often used to refer to two parents and dependent children living in the same household, sometimes referred to as the 'nuclear family' (Blieszner, 2009). Even within this narrow notion of the family, variations exist, such as the presence of one or two parents, married or cohabiting relationships and whether the partnership between the parents is a same-sex or heterosexual relationship. This narrow definition of family does not take account of kinship relationships, that is, extended family relationships, that in many cultures are central to caring within families. These extended family relationships may include grandparents, aunts and uncles, and cousins. The important point here is that fami-

113

lies vary in their structure, membership and roles. Recognition of this diversity is essential for effective work with families (Crichton-Hill, 2009).

Family relationships are an important source of informal care and support for many people. In a range of practice contexts, such as care of the elderly, disability and mental health services, social workers are involved in assessing the nature and extent of informal care available to service users (Blieszner, 2009). The availability of caring relationships can make substantial differences to service users' and community members' quality of life and also to practical outcomes for them. For example, the availability of informal support can mean the difference between a person with age-related impairments having the option to live in their own home rather than in a care home.

Social workers often are involved in assessing matters related to the 'family of origin' and the current family context of the service user. The term 'family of origin' is used to refer to the family in which one was raised as a child and which, from a psychosocial viewpoint, is often regarded as formative in our identity development (Woods and Hollis, 1990), while the term 'current family context' refers to those whom the service user considers as members of their family in their life now. As social workers, we need to understand how the service user sees their family, that is, who they regard as a family member. The service user's definition of family may include but need not be limited to biological relationships, such as the relationship between a birth parent and a child, or legally recognized relationships, such as marital relationships. In some circumstances, service users may regard members of their community as family. For example, members of a homeless community may regard those with whom they share experiences of homelessness as their family.

Why Work with Families?

Social workers work with families in a wide range of practice contexts and for a variety of purposes. Indeed, in multidisciplinary teams, social workers may be called upon to provide expertise in engaging families in case plans and in the analysis of family dynamics. For example, in courts of law, social workers are one of the professional groups asked to provide family reports. In these reports, social workers may provide an analysis of the family structure and dynamics in ways that will help legal decision-makers to determine outcomes for families, such as custody and access arrangements between parents and children (Seymour and Seymour, 2007). In health settings, social workers may have responsibility for working with the families of patients in order to help explain healthcare needs and to assess the capacity of the patient's family to support those needs.

While many other professions recognize working with families as a core part of social work practice, there are several reasons why the profession itself needs to embrace working with families. A focus on the family is consistent with the systems approach, which has provided a key theoretical foundation for social work practice. Systems perspectives require the social worker to consider the service user in their family, community and broader societal contexts (see Germain and Gitterman, 1996). From this perspective, practice with families is an important adjunct to other methods, such as casework and policy work, in enhancing the interaction between the person and their environment.

Focusing on families in our work is also important because service users' challenges and opportunities for responding to those challenges may be shaped by their family context. Problems in the family, such as families where parents struggle with alcohol or drug issues or with mental illness, can contribute to vulnerability for children and young people. Tensions among family members can also bring families into contact with social workers. For example, social workers may offer counselling services to help families manage developmental transitions, such as the transition from childhood to adolescence. Social workers also have a responsibility to support and build the capacity of families to provide support and care. For example, in mental health services, social workers can provide families with access to education and peer support for families living with mental illness and, in so doing, help them to better understand how they can support a family member who is experiencing mental health problems.

Types of Family Work Practice

Social workers can be involved in a range of approaches to working with families. In this section, we outline some of the methods of working with families in which social workers are involved. These are family casework, family therapy, family group meetings, and family support work. The following is a summary of the approaches to working with families I will discuss.

The term 'family casework', sometimes referred to as 'family work' or 'family social work', applies to approaches where the social worker works with the family of the service user in order to 'better the welfare of one of its members' (Coulshed and Orme, 2006, p. 205). The service user's definition of their family should be used to guide the social worker in determining who should be invited to participate in family casework practice. Family casework practice may involve the nuclear family or may extend to involve kinship and other caring networks (Crichton-Hill, 2009). For example, a young person in care may consider their parents, extended family members and foster carers as part of their family and, accordingly, the social worker should involve these family members in family work practice with the young person. In many practice contexts, social workers meet the family in order to gain an understanding of family members' perspectives on the nature of the strengths and issues facing the family. For example, in youth justice settings, the social worker may meet the family of the young person involved in crime in order to clarify what support the family can offer in assisting to reduce the offending behaviour of the young person.

'Family therapy' refers to a set of practice approaches that take the family as the context of change. There are a variety of family therapy traditions including structural, strategic, solution-focused, and narrative approaches to family therapy (Rasheed et al., 2011). These diverse approaches to family therapy are united by a common view that problems and challenges facing a family member are influenced, and may be produced, by family dynamics. Family therapists seek to understand and transform family dynamics that are unhelpful or troubling for an individual or a family. Generally, family therapy involves the therapist meeting several members of a family. However, a family therapy approach can be used in practice with individuals when the practitioner seeks to assist the individual service user to understand and intervene in family dynamics that may be contributing to the challenges facing them. For example, a family therapist may assist a person who is experiencing debilitating anxiety to consider how the dynamics in their family of origin and in their current family context may be contributing to these anxiety states. The worker may then assist the individual to challenge the ways of thinking that emerged from their family of origin or to challenge patterns of behaviour in the client's current family context that contribute to the individual's anxiety. Thus the worker may intervene in the family dynamics by helping one family member to better understand and resist existing family norms and dynamics. While family therapy may be incorporated into professional social work practice, it is commonly viewed as a specialty area of psychotherapy or clinical social work practice (Crago, 2008). Family therapy methods are also deployed by several other professional groups such as psychiatrists and psychologists.

Another form of practice with families is the 'family group meeting', designed primarily for assessment and decision-making purposes, such as to develop an intervention plan. Family meetings are not intended primarily as a form of intervention, although of course such meetings may affect family dynamics. A key purpose of family meetings is to develop a shared understanding both within the family and between the family and professionals about the family's concerns and to develop a plan of action to address these concerns. There are many models of family meetings (Healy et al., 2011), and one of the best known is the family group conference (FGC). The FGC approach first emerged in New Zealand and was introduced in the Children, Young Persons and Their Families Act in 1989. This model has been widely influential in both child protection and youth justice practice contexts. Arising from Maori cultural origins and consistent with social work values (Doolan, 2004), FGCs offer a 'narrative over a rational' solution-based approach to decision-making (Hall and Slembrouck, 2001, p. 159). FGCs can support collaborative decision-making and the sharing of power and responsibility between professionals and the child's or young person's family, including the extended family and members of their community circle significant to the child's or young person's life (Holland and O'Neill, 2006). In a child protection context, the core principles of FGCs include preparation and planning time, where professionals provide families with information and support required to clarify the purpose of the meeting and to enable the family to actively participate in it; and private family time where families privately deliberate to resolve the child's safety and support needs (Morris and Connolly, 2010). There is a great deal of debate in the research literature about the uses and limits of the FGC approach, and related family decision-making models, for increasing family inclusion in decision-making and promoting the safety of vulnerable children (Healy et al., 2011; Shlonsky et al., 2009; Sundell and Vinnerljung, 2004).

The term 'family support' refers to services that seek to benefit families by improving their capacity to care for family members and to strengthen family relationships (Australian Institute of Health and Welfare, 2001). While much of the research on family support practice focuses on building families' capacities to care for children and young people, family support work is also relevant to building families' capacities in a range of service contexts, such as care of the elderly, mental health and disability support services (see Qualls and Zarit, 2009). For example, social workers in mental health services may provide support to families to manage the emotional challenges associated with the experience of a family member having a severe mental illness and in demystifying mental illness.

In family support work with families with children, three levels of intervention (primary, secondary and tertiary levels) are often identified and may also be relevant to other fields where family support work is undertaken (see Healy and Darlington, 1999). Primary intervention refers to those forms of intervention that are universally, or widely, available to the community regardless of level of vulnerability. For example, in some countries, maternal and child health nursing services are available to parents and newborn children in the first weeks or months of the child's life to ensure that parents have access to information about caring for a newborn and medical care, such as the provision of vaccinations. Secondary intervention refers to those forms of intervention targeted at families who are considered to be at elevated risk of abuse or neglect or families who because of some form of vulnerability may not receive mainstream health services. For example, a family support service may be developed to reach teenage parents because these parents may be less likely to use mainstream health and welfare services. Tertiary intervention services are those services targeted at families where an adverse outcome such as abuse and neglect has occurred and where, without ongoing intervention, further adverse outcomes are likely. For example, intensive family support interventions involving the provision of in-home support services, such as parenting skills advice and practical home maintenance, may be provided on a short-term basis to families to enhance their capacity to care for their children independently.

There are a wide variety of ways in which social workers work with families. Despite this diversity, there are some commonalities in the challenges and skills in working with families in social work practice. I turn now to a consideration of those challenges.

The Challenges and Cautions in Working with Families

A key challenge in social work practice with families pertains to the temporary nature of social workers' involvement in the family; this contrasts with family members' own longstanding, and usually enduring, relationships with each other. When working with families, we are challenged to gain sufficient understanding of the family's circumstance, norms and dynamics to be helpful to the family. Of course, in social work practice, one must always be aware and respectful of the service user's knowledge of their circumstances, but the difference in family work is that the social worker is meeting a group that has a shared knowledge of the concern, even if their views of the concern differ, and established patterns of relationship with each other. Coulshed and Orme (2006, p. 199) succinctly point to these challenges of engaging with families in their observation that:

> Trying to understand a family is like jumping on to a moving bus: you have the disadvantage of being a temporary passenger on their journey through a stage in their life, with people leaving and joining along the way.

When working with families, the social worker needs to take time to get to know the family and to understand through observation and exploration the dynamics of the family environment. Seeking to understand the family environment is important for engaging with all family members and to ensure that all family members participate in developing solutions they will be responsible for implementing.

A second challenge is that the social worker will often have a complx role with the family. In some contexts, the social worker's role may involve both helping and surveillance. This complexity is most obvious in child protection contexts, where the social worker will be professionally and, perhaps, legally bound to act, even against the wishes of the family they are helping, in the event that they become aware of harm to the child. Miller (2009, p. 115) observes that:

> Family work in a statutory context is not 'soft'; it is intellectually rigorous and interpersonally challenging, as there are multiple agendas and multiple layers of experience and 'truth'.

In essence, when working with families, the social worker may have many roles, which may include responsibility for the assessment of child protection risk, building family capacity to respond to provide a safe and caring environment, and assessing and addressing practical support needs of families. In establishing relationships with families, social workers need to make clear the nature of their role and any binding professional, legal or organizational responsibilities they bear (Trotter, 2004). For example, in some organizations working with vulnerable families, proto-cols exist about the reporting of child abuse and neglect and, consistent with a respectful and transparent approach to our practice, we need to ensure that service users are aware of these protocols. Trotter (2004) points out that being transparent about responsibilities demands more than an initial statement about these responsibilities; he suggests that social workers need to engage in frequent and honest conversations about the nature of their role and their responsibilities, including external reporting responsibilities.

Feminist and anti-racist social workers have raised concerns that social work with families can reinforce sexist and Eurocentric assumptions about families (Orme, 2001). For example, feminist authors have exten-sively criticized both social workers and family social workers for their acceptance of patriarchal norms in their practice with families (Orme, 2001). Anti-racist social workers have criticized those forms of social work practice that fail to recognize cultural diversity, such as diversities in family structures and norms, and in so doing perpetuated racist assump-tions about families from culturally and linguistically diverse communi-ties. Maiter (2009) contends that a culturally competent approach to working with families involves respecting the diversity of family struc-tures in culturally diverse communities and challenging the broader social structures that exclude these families from full participation in society. In short, critically informed approaches to family social work demand that the social worker works not only with the family directly but also challenges institutional practices within social service agencies and educational institutions that rest on sexist or racist assumptions about families. For example, an anti-racist social worker would seek to ensure that a broad range of family relationships are recognized and included in family group meeting processes. This may involve ensuring that meeting rooms are available to accommodate members of kinship networks and that meeting processes are responsive to cultural norms, such as protocols for welcoming family members to a meeting and closing a meeting (see Crichton-Hill, 2009).

A fourth issue that has significant implications for how and, indeed, whether work with the family occurs is the presence of violence, such as child abuse and neglect, or domestic violence. According to Douglas and Walsh (2010, p. 491):

> Domestic violence refers broadly to violence, whether physical or emotional, between intimates (including spouses) and is understood to have complex power dynamics whereby the abuser seeks to control the victim.

The critical issue is that in circumstances where one party has coercive control over another, the capacity of family members to participate in any form of family work will be constrained and may risk further violence. We should avoid conducting family meetings in circumstances where family violence is present if the meeting would expose participants to further violence or where participation will be constrained by the threat of violence. If a meeting is unavoidable, protocols for ensuring the safety of family members must be established (Johnson et al., 2005).

Working with Families

In the remainder of the chapter, I will outline the skills required for social workers to engage in family work, also known as family casework. Drawing on the four phases of social work practice outlined in Chapter 1, I will discuss how social workers can engage families in meetings, in assessing needs, in creating change, and evaluating outcomes. Throughout, I will discuss the importance of sensitivity to cultural differences in the definitions and dynamics of working with families. My focus in the remainder of this chapter will be primarily on working with vulnerable families where child protection concerns and risks may be present. I acknowledged earlier that social workers work with families in a wide variety of contexts. However, for the purposes of demonstrating the application of specific knowledge and skills in family work practice, it is necessary to locate the discussion with reference to a specific type of practice context.

Engaging Families

I turn first to the knowledge and skills involved in engaging families. Like all forms of social work practice, it is important to build a purposeful and constructive relationship with the service user from the outset. One way in which social work with families differs from casework practice is that the primary client is not an individual but rather a group of individuals, that is, the family.

In our initial engagement with families, three matters are important. As in all forms of social work practice, the first is clarification with the family about your role and your understanding of the nature and scope of your work with the family (Trotter, 2004). For example, a hospital social worker will have different obligations when they engage with a family compared with the process and content of engagement if the worker is a family therapist or a child protection social worker. Of course, our purpose can be conveyed directly with a clear statement, such as: 'I am a social worker from the children's hospital. I am here because the doctor is concerned about your son's health. I want to find out from you how your son Jonathan came to be so dehydrated and to ask what we can do to help you and your family.'

The second element is developing an understanding of the family's definition of family. While the nuclear family (two parents and their children) might be considered the 'norm' in many wealthy nations, in social work we will encounter a wide constellation of family types. Members of kinship networks beyond the nuclear family, such as grandparents, aunties, uncles and cousins, may consider themselves to be the immediate family of the primary service user. Indeed, while the terms 'immediate' and 'extended' family are commonly used in social work, these terms may not make sense for families where relatives other than biological parents and their children have direct caring responsibilities for each other. Thus, in organizing a family meeting, it is important to begin with who the individual client or family regards as 'family'.

A third element is creating an environment that is welcoming, appropriate and safe to the family meeting context and helps to build a constructive relationship with them. As Crago (2008, p. 71) observes, the skills we 'most often call upon in the early stages of family work are skills of "starting small", safeguarding each individual's right to talk, managing conflict, and diffusing or postponing potential "accidents and accusations"'. In terms of 'safeguarding each individual's right to talk', the worker needs to ensure that the meeting space is not threatening to family members and easily accommodates all those regarded as family. For example, for families with previous negative experiences of statutory child protection services, it may be helpful to hold a meeting in a community hall or the meeting space of a nongovernment service agency rather than in the statutory agency (Healy et al., 2011). The physical layout of the room, such as circular rather than hierarchical seating arrangements, can also assist in building an inclusive environment. The provision of refreshments, which may seem an incidental consideration, has been shown in some family meeting contexts to further help in creating a welcoming environment (see Crichton-Hill, 2009; Healy et al., 2011). It can also be helpful to have a visual aid, such as a whiteboard, so that family members can see (as well as hear) issues, assessments and agreed actions that are emerging from the family meeting together. The use of a visual support can help reduce misunderstandings as family members can challenge or correct information that emerges during the meeting.

Another aspect of creating a welcoming environment is ensuring that everyone present at the family meeting is formally introduced, that clear communication ground rules are set with participants and that expectations about the duration and frequency of meetings (if there is to be more than one meeting) are clear. Formal introductions are especially important where people other than family members are present, such as support workers, advocates or legal representatives. But even when it is a meeting of only family members and worker, formal introductions can help to ensure that the worker has an accurate understanding of each participant's role in the family. The family meeting should always begin with a clear statement of who is at the meeting, including the convenor. Absent family members who are relevant to the family issues being discussed, such as children, should be acknowledged or represented in some way, such as the presence of toys or photographs of the children in empty chairs. In some contexts, such as where a decision directly affects the child and there is good reason for the child not to represent themselves at a meeting, a separate representative of the child may represent the child's views to the meeting. A key point here is that we should not assume that other family members or professionals can act as a proxy for the child unless they have specifically assumed the role of being the child's advocate or representative and can credibly distinguish their professional or personal interests from the interests of the child.

Following an introduction, the social worker should clarify the communication ground rules, that is, the expectations of how people will communicate at the meeting. The ground rules can help to ensure equitable participation of family members in the meeting and that participants feel safe in expressing their views. To facilitate this, the social worker may ask family members to identify what rules or principles need to be agreed in order for all family members to participate in discussing the issues and these principles should apply to all members. As social workers, we should contribute to the formation of principles for communication at the meeting, drawing on our expertise about what helps and hinders communication in the context of family meetings. Our contribution is important because the family is likely to have little experience of a formal family meeting environment and may also have developed communication practices that are unhelpful to problem-solving, such as people talking over each other. In developing ground rules for communication, the social worker should demonstrate sensitivity to communication protocols within the family. For example, in many cultures, protocols exist about who is regarded as a senior member or head of the family. If we fail to recognize these protocols, we risk alienating the family as a whole and causing discomfort to individual members. For example, in a spirit of egalitarianism, we may wish to begin the family meeting with the views of the youngest person in the room, yet in a family context where elders are regarded as the 'head' of the household, such a process may be uncomfortable, both for the young person and the older members of the family. It may also limit your credibility as someone who can help the family.

Depending on the purpose of the family meeting, it may be necessary to meet family members individually, prior to the meeting. Preparatory meetings with individual members are important in situations where there are significant decisions, particularly decisions with legal implications, arising from the meetings and where the meeting is part of a legal process. For example, preparatory meetings with individual family members can be important in family meetings in child protection and family law matters (Healy et al., 2011). This pre-meeting preparation is important for reducing power differentials in contexts where the family is meeting others, such as child protection workers, who may have a great deal more experience of the meeting context than the family. In other contexts, such as a family meeting held for the purpose of helping the family themselves to explore an issue or to make decisions about a family meeting, it may be sufficient to establish the purpose and the ground rules at the beginning of the meeting, rather than prior to it; for example, if a family is meeting a counsellor to discuss how to manage the sale of the family home as the parents are moving into a nursing home. Even in these situations, the family worker needs to be aware of power differentials within the family, which may in some contexts necessitate a pre-meeting interview with individual family members to ensure that power differences are acknowledged. A pre-meeting interview with individual family members is especially important in circumstances where the social worker has reason to suspect that there is abuse or violence, such as domestic violence, occurring. If it is established that violence is present, the meeting should be deferred until the safety needs of the person subject to the abuse or violence are addressed.

Over to you ...

Imagine you are a social worker in a support service for people who have grown up in institutional care. One of the clients you work with is Jane Sleeman who is 38 years old. Jane has a 14-year-old daughter Rhiannon and a 10-year-old son Sam. Jane is divorced from Craig Sleeman (42), the father of Rhiannon and Sam. Jane's partner of two years is David Cochrane (38), who lives with Jane and her children.

Jane grew up in foster care where she experienced abuse. David experiences depression, which requires ongoing medical treatment and he is sometimes hospitalized for depression. He was last hospitalized for six weeks about a year ago. Due to depression, David is unable to work full time but does have ongoing part-time work at the local supermarket. Jane has participated in the support services for people who have grown up in care for five years and she is now a peer worker offering support to others who have grown up in care. Jane has a well-established and trusting relationship with your service. Your service also has strong relationship with Jane's children, who have participated in a range of the service's activities, such as arts programmes.

Jane has come to you in a state of distress about the conflict she is having with her children. Jane feels that Rhiannon is abusive towards her, such as swearing at her and calling her offensive names. According to Jane, Sam seems to be following Rhiannon's lead and has also started swearing at Jane. Jane says she feels out of control and is worried she might starting hitting out at Rhiannon and Sam. Jane says that David does nothing when the children are abusive towards her.

1. What might a family meeting with this family achieve?

2. If you were try to organize a family meeting, what would you do? Who should participate in the meeting?

3. How would you begin the meeting and how would you ensure that you are safeguarding each individual's right to talk and managing conflict in a constructive way?

Assessment with and for Families

A key issue in the assessment is to develop an understanding of the nature of the challenges facing the family and their capacities to resolve those challenges. Often, when professionals are talking about assessment of families, we are talking about the professional's view of what is going wrong with the family (Turnell and Parker, 2009). Ideally, in working with families, we aim to develop an understanding with them of the nature of the problem *and* their strengths and capacities in the social context of their lives.

Social work assessment is characterized by a focus on understanding the person in their social environment. As mentioned in Chapter 3, the term 'psychosocial' assessment is often used for assessment that is focused on understanding the interaction between the individual and their social environment. The genogram is a tool often used by social workers, and other helping professionals, to gain insight into the psychosocial dynamics of the individual and their family. The genogram is a pictorial representation of family relationships, issues and dynamics over at least two (and usually more) generations of a family. The relationships that are signified in a genogram include, but are not limited to, parental relationships, intimate relationships, separations, divorces and losses, such as the death of a child or a parent. The issues and dynamics that are considered include family members' perceptions of attachment, distance and tension among family members.

Genograms are often used in family casework to develop and communicate a shared understanding of the family context and dynamics. The genogram is often developed by the social worker in collaboration with the family and may also be shared with other professionals working with the family. Indeed, in many settings, it is common for genograms to be included in the case notes. While genograms are widely used in health and welfare service settings, there are few universal rules about the presentation of genograms and even widely recognized conventions may change over time. For example, two decades ago, cohabiting relationships were commonly denoted in genograms with a dotted line, whereas married relationships were depicted with a single unbroken line. Today, both types of relationships may be depicted with a single unbroken line. One of the conventions that does appear to be widely recognized is that the relationships between different generations are always presented hierarchically, starting with the oldest generation and finishing with the youngest. The genogram is usually read from left to right, so the older members of a single generation are represented on the left-hand side, while the younger members are on the right. Because of the lack of universal rules beyond some widely recognized conventions, it is important to get to know the conventions that are used in the context in which your genogram is likely to be read, and it can helpful to the reader if you provide a 'key' or definition of the symbols used in your genogram. Figure 5.1 contains some of the conventions commonly found in genograms, although please note that these conventions are likely to vary in different disciplinary contexts.

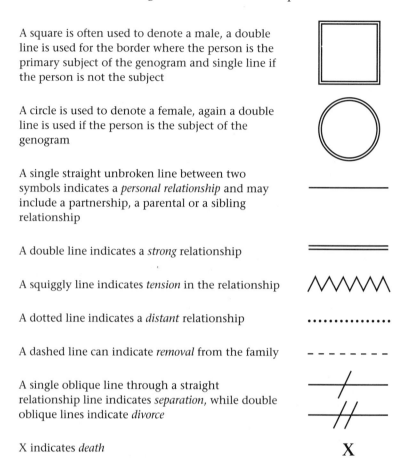

A square is often used to denote a male, a double line is used for the border where the person is the primary subject of the genogram and single line if the person is not the subject

A circle is used to denote a female, again a double line is used if the person is the subject of the genogram

A single straight unbroken line between two symbols indicates a *personal relationship* and may include a partnership, a parental or a sibling relationship

A double line indicates a *strong* relationship

A squiggly line indicates *tension* in the relationship

A dotted line indicates a *distant* relationship

A dashed line can indicate *removal* from the family

A single oblique line through a straight relationship line indicates *separation*, while double oblique lines indicate *divorce*

X indicates *death*

Figure 5.1   Some commonly used genogram conventions
Source: Adapted from McGoldrick et al., 2008

As an example, Figure 5.2 is a genogram of the family situation involving Jane, David, Rhiannon and Sam, as presented in the case study above, with some extra information about Jane's parents.

The genogram in Figure 5.2 provides a pictorial illustration of relationships across three generations of the case study family presented earlier. Jane is at the centre of this genogram, represented by a double line because she is the primary client in this case study. The genogram shows a dashed line with her parents to indicate that she was removed from their care. A genogram could also include information about Jane's siblings and David's parents and siblings. The genogram also includes Jane's husband Craig and her current partner David. With regard to family 'events', this genogram shows that Jane's father has died and also gives some information about his age and the year of his death. The squiggly lines between Lorraine and Jane and Jane and her children indicate tension in these relationships.

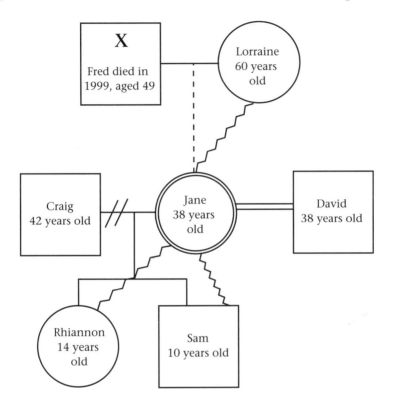

Figure 5.2 Genogram of the case study family

A genogram can be helpful for organizing a great deal of information in a way that is readily accessible to workers and the families with whom they work and also to colleagues who may later view case notes of the family meeting. One advantage of the genogram is that it helps the worker and family members to gain a shared view of the family structure and dynamics. Another advantage is that it may bring to the attention of the worker and the family information about family dynamics that may be useful to explore. For example, the genogram in Figure 5.2 shows that tensions exist in relationships across two generations of the family. It might be useful for the worker and family to explore the nature of those tensions and whether they reflect common themes in the family, such as a need for the development of conflict resolution skills. A further advantage is that the genogram can be used to explore the meaning of events for the family. For example, we see that Fred (Jane's father) died not long after Rhiannon's birth and before Sam's birth. We might explore, for example, what the children know of their grandfather. We might also explore the nature of the children's relationship with their father Craig, who, we can see from the genogram, is divorced from their mother Jane. If we were working with Jane as an individual, we might explore her perceptions of the nature and impact of her removal from her parents' care on her relationship with her parents and now on her experience as a mother. We might also explore her relationship breakdown with Craig and its impact on her as a parent and as a partner to David. These issues are likely to be inappropriate to explore in the presence of her children.

Over to you ...

Draw your own genogram

Draw a genogram of three generations of your family of origin. Include information about significant events, such as deaths, divorces and separations and about family dynamics, such as tension or estrangement among family members.

Once you have completed the genogram, consider the following:

1. What seem to be the most significant relationships for you in your family?

2. Are there any common dynamics across the generations represented here?

3. What impact have events in your family, such as losses, had on the dynamics within your family, for example, has it brought people closer together?

4. Are there events or dynamics within your family you would like to know more about as a result of completing this genogram?

While the genogram is a widely used tool in social work practice with families, we need also to recognize the limitations of this tool. A genogram can be difficult, time-consuming and confusing to use in large extended families where there are complex family dynamics. For example, even in the genogram presented in Figure 5.2, some information about Jane's family of origin has been omitted, because to include information about Jane's siblings, for example, would risk making the genogram confusing to the reader. It is also possible that some service users will identify several families of origin such as where a family member has had several foster care placements. This information is difficult to represent in a genogram.

An added problem is that various readers may interpret the genogram in a different way from that intended by the social worker or service user, in part because of the lack of a common interdisciplinary language for the symbols used in genograms. For this reason, when the genogram is incorporated into case notes or reports, it should always be accompanied by a written interpretation.

A genogram can help the worker develop a common view with the family of the family structure and dynamics. But it is unlikely this information, alone, is sufficient to address the problem or challenge that the social worker is seeking to address with the family. Ultimately, in the assessment phase, we are seeking to gain a clear and shared understanding with the family of the nature of the problem or challenges facing the family that has brought them into contact with you, and the capacities that already exist in the family and their environment for resolving these problems. In some contexts of practice, such as child protection, you may also need to make an assessment of the signs of risk and safety in this family's environment (Turnell and Parker, 2009). Our assessment, preferably developed with the family, forms the basis of our intervention plan. In order to promote family participation in the development and understanding of the assessment, it is important that the assessment of the family is balanced, that is, there is recognition of both problems and capacities, and also that the assessment is succinctly stated in clear and jargon-free terms. A shared understanding of the assessment maximizes the possibility for the family to participate in defining goals and developing a plan of action.

I want to turn now to some strategies you as a social worker can use to maximize family involvement in the development of an assessment of the challenges and capacities of families. Visual aids to assist all those present at the assessment process to view the assessment that is emerging are important for including families in assessment processes. Writing each element of the assessment on a whiteboard or butcher's paper that is clearly visible to all participants is one way of achieving a shared understanding of the emerging assessment. It is important to note that while whiteboards are commonly used as a visual support at family meetings, they can risk creating a classroom-like atmosphere. Additionally, if using visual supports such as whiteboards, consideration needs to be given for supporting those with visual impairments or limited literacy to read the material.

Creative approaches can help with involving families in the assessment process. The use of visual images, such as photographs and drawings, can help family members to voice those different elements of the family's strengths, concerns and goals that might be difficult to put into words. Let's take the example of how a social worker might use photographic images to work with Jane, David and their children Rhiannon and Sam in discussing what is strong about their family, what concerns they each have and what goals they might work towards. In this situation, photographic images (such as images of the built and natural environment or single words) may be used to stimulate discussion about emotions and perceptions held by each family member of their situation. For example, a single word like 'happy' may be used to explore with the family what brings them most happiness in their family situation. In short, visual images can be used to help stimulate discussion that can assist social workers and the families with whom we work to gain a clearer and shared understanding of families' needs, strengths and goals.

Interventions with Families

I will now consider how we can use the information gained in the assessment with the family to involve them in developing goals for change and strategies for achieving those goals. I will discuss the challenges in setting goals and in managing setbacks towards achieving those goals.

The intervention process must focus on the achievement of shared and agreed goals. These goals should emerge from our shared assessment and guide our work with the family. Crichton-Hill (2009, p. 197) observes: 'Goals define what the family is striving for and how they are going to get there.' While families should be encouraged to define the goals and strategies for achieving goals, in some contexts of practice, the worker may be required by law to contribute to the definition of goals (see Chapter 4).

In many contexts of health and welfare practice, the worker must be sensitive to the pressures on families to comply with the intervention planning process. These pressures may lead to intervention plans that are unrealistic and may worsen the family's situation or have significant legal ramifications. For example, in the UK and Australia, families in the child protection system are often involved through case conferences and family group meetings in developing intervention plans for ensuring the safety of vulnerable children (Healy et al., 2011). The successful achievement of case planning goals may determine whether or not a child is returned to the family. Under these circumstances, families may feel under considerable pressure to agree to goals and time frames they perceive to be required by the child protection agency. For example, a family may agree to simultaneously address a series of significant life challenges, associated with joblessness, drug or alcohol use and mental health issues, so as to appease what they perceive to the requirements of the child protection authority. In any context where family members experience pressure, including pressure from statutory authorities and institutions or even from within their own family to participate in a family intervention process, it is important that the social worker is aware of, and seeks to minimize, these pressures so that a useful and realistic intervention plan can be achieved. In helping the family to develop a case plan, the worker has an obligation to ensure that the goals and time frames are reasonable and the resources are adequate to address the issues raised in the assessment process.

Goals form the basis of our intervention with the plan. The goals need to be stated in specific terms, with clear tasks for their achievement, the resources needed must be identified and accessed, and the goals must be measurable (Crichton-Hill, 2009). While specificity of goals is always important in intervention plans, in working with families it is vital that a shared understanding of the goals and how they are to be achieved is developed among family members. For example, a goal stated in general terms such as 'improving communication' may mean something quite different to Jane than to her partner David or her children, Rhiannon and Sam. A more specific statement of this goal could be: to stop swearing at each other and for each family member to find at least 30 minutes on two occasions over the next two weeks to listen to each family member.

Once goals are identified, specific actions for achieving those goals need to be identified and responsibility for those actions should be allocated. For example, for family members to achieve the goal of not swearing at each other and to listen better to each other, each may need to identify what causes them to become verbally aggressive and to address how they can learn more assertive communication. Actions may involve taking a course in assertive or nonviolent communication or to rehearse more assertive forms of communication in the family meeting. The worker may have some responsibility for the achievement of goal-related tasks. For example, the family may identify that their overcrowded housing situation has contributed to family conflict and that a goal may be to find more suitable housing. The worker may undertake the task of finding out about low-cost community housing options for the family.

Experiential strategies may be useful for assisting family members to gain insights into each other's perceptions and to rehearse tasks that are consistent with their goals. For example, we might ask the family to role-play a recent situation when a conflict emerged and then, in the safety of the family meeting, explore what caused the situation to escalate. The worker may then assist the family to consider or 'brainstorm' alternative approaches that could prevent the conflict from emerging. We might then encourage the family to role-play the conflict situation again using the strategies they have identified.

Discussion of the resources required to achieve goals can help to ensure that goals are realistic and achievable for the family. For example, Rhiannon may have the goal of gaining entry to a hairdressing apprenticeship but a barrier to this goal may be a poor school attendance record. In a family meeting, the worker should engage the family in identifying factors in the family environment that prevent Rhiannon from being able to achieve full school attendance and what practical resources, such as access to transport, might be needed to improve her attendance. Like all other parts of the intervention plan, the worker should help the family to clarify how the resources will be attained and the time frame within which they will be attained. For instance, Rhiannon may have responsibility for investigating how other young people in her area travel to school and what it costs them and the worker may be responsible for investigating the financial support available to assist in covering Rhiannon's transport cost.

Intervention goals also need to be measurable so that the family can assess their progress as well as observe and address any setbacks that may occur. We may agree that each family member will keep a diary of their attempts to listen better to one another and that they fill in the diary on two days of each week. The diary entries may, for instance, include a rating on a scale of 1–5 of their individual views of how well they listened to each family member in the previous three days and a similar scale of the extent to which they felt they were listened to. Family members may agree to share their ratings at the next family meeting. The worker might then help the family to explore successes, such as times when family members felt they were listened to, and setbacks, such as times where family members felt that either they were not being listened to or they were not listening themselves. Insights from these reflections may help the family better understand what gets in the way of them achieving their goal, of improving how they listen to one another, and what they can do to achieve it.

Evaluation

Like all forms of social work practice, our practice is enhanced by evaluation of the outcomes of our work. The intervention process we have described incorporates an evaluation dimension in that the social worker and the family are encouraged to monitor progress and address setbacks as the intervention plan is implemented.

In evaluating our practice with families, it is important that we systematically collect and review reliable information about practice outcomes. At a minimum, this should include the perceptions of all family members about the extent to which goals were achieved and their satisfaction with the process and achievement of outcomes. Because family workers are likely to be involved with family members across several generations, consideration should be given to developmentally appropriate strategies for involving family members in the evaluation of service outcomes and processes. For example, one should develop evaluation forms for children and young people as well as adults using a service. An evaluation form for children may incorporate visual images, such as images of different facial expressions, to help children to articulate their experience of the intervention process. The material collected from families needs to be systematically analysed and recommendations developed to improve one's practice with families.

In some contexts of family work practice, it may be appropriate to seek feedback about the medium and long-term outcomes of interventions from multiple stakeholders. Stakeholders, like schools and members of multidisciplinary teams, may provide us with important feedback about the extent to which family work interventions have contributed to positive outcomes for families. In some cases, this feedback may occur at team meetings, such as when a multidisciplinary health team member reports back on the progress of a client. In cases where we plan to actively seek out external stakeholders' views of the family's progress, the family should be aware of, and consent to, our seeking this information.

To date, there has been limited research on the medium and long-term impact of family interventions. However, of some concern is the evidence suggesting that some forms of family intervention may be less productive for achieving positive outcomes for service users than promised. For example, two substantial reviews of family decision-making practices in child protection contexts have concluded that the family involvement in decision-making increases service user satisfaction but the benefits in terms of reducing the risk of harm to children remain unproven (see Shlonsky et al., 2009; Sundell and Vinnerljung, 2004). The findings of these studies do not suggest that we should abandon the goal of involving families in decision-making, but they do indicate that, as profession, we need to differentiate between what these processes can achieve, such as improved client satisfaction with social work interventions, and to recognize their limitations in their current form to achieve other important outcomes, such as enhancing child safety. These insights drawn from the rigorous evaluation of one form of family practice have the potential to contribute to improvements in our understanding, and the practice of, family group decision-making.

Conclusion

Social workers work with families in a range of contexts to achieve a variety of outcomes. Families are an important part of the context of individual service user's lives. Families may contribute to the problems or challenges facing service users or they may be part of the solution. Moreover, in a multidisciplinary context, social workers are often considered to have expertise working with families and hence we may carry responsibility in these teams for working with families. In this chapter, I have provided an introduction to the foundations of working with families in social work. I hope this introduction will assist you to work productively with families in the many contexts where family work is a vital and integral part of the social worker's role.

Review Questions

1. What are the four types of social work practice with families?

2. Why do service users feel pressure to agree to unrealistic intervention goals and time frames? What can you, as a social worker, do to help families to develop useful and realistic intervention plans despite these pressures?

Critical Reflection Questions

1. What would you see at the greatest challenge you would face in working with families? How would you address this challenge?

2. I have suggested that social work with families is an important method of practice in a variety of health and welfare settings. To what extent do you agree (or disagree) with the claim that social work with families is a core method of social work practice?

Practice Exercise

Consider the following case study and in pairs or small groups discuss your answers to the questions. Imagine you work in a family support service providing a range of family work interventions. Binh Ho, a 15-year-old young man, and his family have been referred to your service by the school counsellor at Binh's school because of conflict between Binh and his parents. Binh and his family are of Vietnamese origin. Binh's parents, An (mother) and De (father), were born in Vietnam. Binh's extended family, including An's parents and De's mother, also live with them. Binh has a younger brother, Thuc (12) and two younger sisters, Mai (8) and Dung (4).

Binh's parents are worried about Binh's poor performance at school and are concerned that he is getting involved with a 'bad crowd' of young men. Binh has been in trouble at school because of his failure to complete assessments and he is at risk of failing school.

This is a big change for Binh, who until last year was one of the highest performing students in the school. On meeting the school counsellor, at the insistence of one of his teachers, Binh became distressed. He said that he felt like a failure and that he could not live up to his family's high expectations of him. He said that his once close relationship with his father was now distant and tense and that his mother is often angry with him, saying that he presents a bad example to his younger brother and sisters. Binh says he has a lot of respect for his parents and he is sad that he has disappointed them. Binh says that his parents' view of his friends as a bad influence is wrong and that the real reason for his poor school performance is his own inability to live up to his parents' expectations.

1. What do you see as the key issues in this case study for you as a family support worker?

2. What benefits and limitations would you see to involving Binh's family in a discussion of the situation confronting Binh?

3. If you were to involve Binh's family in a meeting, who do you think it would be most appropriate to involve and why?

4. Imagine you were meeting Binh and his parents, how would start the meeting and what processes would you see as important for creating a welcoming, safe and effective working relationship with the family?

Further Reading

● American Humane Association (2010) *Guidelines for Family Group Decision Making in Child Welfare*. Englewood, CO: American Humane Association.

These guidelines provide an excellent overview of the evidence for achieving family involvement in decision-making. Although primarily intended for child welfare and child protection service settings, the principles for coordinating family involvement are relevant for many contexts of family decision-making.

● Qualls, S.H. and Zarit, S.H. (eds) (2009) *Aging Families and Caregiving*. Hoboken, NJ: John Wiley & Sons.

Addresses various aspects of social work practice with ageing families. Includes chapters on therapeutic work with ageing families and policy and practice responses to carers in ageing families.

● Rasheed, J., Rasheed, M. and Marley, J. (2011) *Family Therapy: Models and Techniques*. Thousand Oaks, CA: Sage.

Presents a history of family therapy and outlines contemporary approaches to therapeutic work with families, including narrative, strengths-based and solution-focused approaches. Excellent introduction to family therapy practice.

● Trotter, C. (2004) *Helping Abused Children and their Families: Towards Evidence Based Practice*. Crows Nest, Sydney: Allen & Unwin.

Outlines the evidence for what works for enhancing outcomes in social work practice with vulnerable families. Focuses on how to build effective relationships based on clarity of roles and a shared commitment between workers and service users to an agreed intervention plan. Provides an excellent introduction to evidence-based practice in child protection work with families.

6

Working with Groups

Social workers are often involved with groups, as a method of intervention and as a context of practice, such as when working in interdisciplinary teams. Our focus in this chapter is on working with groups as a method of intervention. Groupwork is the practice of bringing together a group of people to achieve a shared purpose. Groupwork is widely used in a variety of social work service contexts such as health services, child welfare and neighbourhood centres. In this chapter, I will define groupwork and consider the uses and limitations of groupwork. I will outline practical strategies for engaging people in groupwork and for promoting change in, and with, groups.

What is Working with Groups?

A group refers to a collection of at least three people who identify as part of a group, share a common purpose or task related to that group, and who relate to each other to achieve this common purpose. There are a range of possible objectives for groups; some of the more common objectives of groupwork include achieving person change, reducing isolation or promoting social change. The social worker's role in groupwork is a facilitative role, which can range from a formal leadership role in which the social worker is responsible for establishing the structure and content of the group, to a nondirective role, where the social worker plays a largely 'behind the scenes' role in managing aspects of the group process. For example, a social worker may support a self-help or peer support group by assisting group members to develop group leadership skills, manage conflicts or to address the practical needs of the groups, such as transport and childcare, that are essential to ensuring that the group runs smoothly.

While a group of 3 is possible, in many contexts of social work practice, a minimum of 5 participants is preferred in order to achieve the benefits associated with groupwork, such as collaborative problem-solving. Similarly, the group facilitator may set an upper limit on the number of people participating in a group. This is because the benefits associated with group-work, such as the opportunity to gain feedback from members, become difficult to achieve once the group exceeds a certain size. The preferred number of group participants varies depending on the topic to be covered. For example, a psychotherapeutic group focused on analysis of deeply personal issues is likely to benefit from a smaller number of participants, possibly 5–8 members, compared to a community education group, such as a programme on healthy ageing, where more than 20 people might partici-pate in a group. Indeed, a larger group may maximize opportunities for 'spin-off' activities, such as social groups, to emerge. Most behaviour change and support groups, a common part of social work practice, have between 5 and 15 members (Tuckman, 1965). An important decision early in the life of the group is how many participants are required to enable the group to achieve its purpose.

Groups may vary in duration, with some groups being limited to a specific number of meetings, while others are open-ended and may continue as long as members find the group a useful forum for them. Time-limited groups tend to be focused on addressing specific issues, such as behavioural change and psychoeducational groups. By contrast, open-ended groups are more often focused on the provision of support and self-help among partici-pants or to achieve social change goals. Because of their longer duration, open-ended groups are often characterized by an increasing transition of group responsibilities from the groupworker to the group members. Another dimension of duration is the length and regularity of group meetings. The duration of individual meetings needs to be of sufficient length to ensure that each group member has the opportunity to participate in group activi-ties but not so long as to be experienced as burdensome for participants. Most groupwork meetings in social work practice are between 1.5 and 2 hours' duration, with 3 hours being the outer limit for most regular group-work meetings. With regard to regularity, group meetings need to be suffi-ciently frequent for group members to maintain a connection with the content of the group or other group members. Yet there needs to be suffi-cient space between group meetings to allow members to consolidate learning from the group, such as practising new skills, and to ensure that group members can sustain their participation in a group. For groups focused on behaviour change or skill development, weekly group meetings are typical, while for some other groups, such as social action groups, less frequent meetings, such as fortnightly or monthly, may occur.

Groups may be open or closed to newcomers. Open groups are those that allow new participants to join the group after the initial formation stage. Most open groups allow newcomers to join at any time, while some allow new members to join only at specific time points, such as new members being accepted every three months. Many support, self-help and social action groups are open to new members. One of the challenges for groupworkers is to ensure that open groups are truly open to newcomers, given that existing group members may have formed alliances. The establishment of a buddy system for newcomers or a formal welcoming process can be a way of engaging newcomers. Closed groups are those that do not allow newcomers after the formation phase of the group. Key rationales for having a closed group are that such groups allow for the formation of trust among group members and ensure that participants have a shared basis of knowledge and skill as the group proceeds. This means that group members are able to achieve more advanced learning than may be possible if the group has to return to earlier learning for new members. Examples of closed groups may include behaviour change or skill development groups developed around sequenced groupwork programmes and some psychotherapeutic groups.

Why Work with Groups?

Groups are the most appropriate method for achieving some of our purposes as social workers. Groups are especially relevant in situations where social workers aim to provide education (such as health education groups), reduce isolation, build support, or promote social action around a common concern for service users. In addition, groups can be an efficient and effective mode of practice for a number of reasons. Groups can be efficient because they allow the facilitator(s) to engage with a greater number of people within a given time period than is possible through one-to-one casework. Groups can be effective when:

● They provide an opportunity for participants to gain support and learn from the experiences and insights of others facing a similar issue. The knowledge provided by other participants has credibility because it is based on lived experienced. For example, a person facing a life-threatening illness may gain individual support from a counsellor, but the group context also provides opportunities for the individual to learn from others with similar experiences.

● They offer participants a forum for practising new skills and feedback that can provide a motivation and direction for change. For example, an assertiveness group may provide members with the opportunity to test out new skills and encourage the utilization of these skills in participants' lives outside the group.

● The group context itself helps to address the problems facing the individual (Coulshed and Orme, 2006). For example, participation in groups may, of itself, address social isolation. In addition, the group provides a forum for individuals to engage in collaborative problem-solving. For example, parents unable to afford the cost of a babysitter might be able to work together to offer childcare to each other, or share the costs of a babysitter, or perhaps raise funds to develop more responsive childcare services.

Despite their many advantages, there are some situations in which groupwork may be inappropriate. These include situations where:

● Individuals are overwhelmed by their life circumstances in ways that limit their capacity to engage in the learning and support needs of others. For example, in the immediate aftermath of challenging news, such as diagnosis with a terminal illness, an individual may benefit from individual support rather than group intervention. In these circumstances, individual support may be a precursor to groupwork.

● An individual has had negative previous group experiences. Groups should provide a constructive context for individuals to gain support and/or to learn from each other. For some individuals, their previous experience of groups may provide particular challenges to them experiencing groups as a constructive environment. For example, individuals who have experienced bullying or other forms of abuse in groups may be reluctant to participate or participate in ways that limit the effectiveness of the group for them. Should these individuals choose to participate in a group, it may be important that they have the opportunity for individual support outside the group.

● Significant confidentiality issues exist. These could include the disclosure of information that participants regard as embarrassing or compromising. It is important for group facilitators to remember that information revealed in the group may be shared outside the group, regardless of the ground rules established within them. This has the potential to embarrass participants and may, in some circumstances, threaten their physical or emotional safety.

The Range of Group Types

Groups are used in social work for a wide variety of purposes. Groups are usually oriented towards achieving change, but the specific nature of the change sought varies from personal change to social action. Regardless of the type of group, social workers' approach to working with groups should continue to reflect their value base, including promoting service user capacity for self-determination, equality and respect for difference. These are the key types of groups in which social workers and health and welfare service professionals may be involved:

- **Group psychotherapy:** This is focused on promoting personal change in the participants' understanding of themselves. Group psychotherapy is usually offered as a complement to individual counselling, with the group context providing opportunities for insights generated through engagement with others on a similar journey of personal change and through learning about the self in the group process. For example, participants in the group may be encouraged to reflect upon their response to certain issues and processes as they arise in the group; this process of self-reflection is, of itself, intended to create insight and personal change. Group facilitators typically work from a specific school of psychotherapy, such as Gestalt or Jungian therapy, and this school of thought provides a framework for the group structure and process.

- **Group counselling:** This is focused on members exploring and learning about experiences they have in common, such as experiences of living with infertility, being recently separated from partners or experiencing a life-threatening illness. While these groups involve elements of peer support, the group leader will have an overt role focused on facilitating group members through a process of personal and group exploration of the shared concern on which the group is focused.

- **Behaviour change groups:** These are groups conducted with the specific purpose of enabling members to explore and address a behaviour that has become a problem for them. Some examples of behavioural groups include groups focused on building members' skills to manage behaviours such as aggression and violence or emotional states such as anger, anxiety or depression. In many, although not all cases, behaviour change and skill development groups are structured around a standardized groupwork programme – the programme will be similar regardless of the national or institutional context in which it is implemented or the population with whom it is implemented.

- **Psychoeducational groups:** These groups are intended to develop members' knowledge and skills to address an opportunity or challenge they may be facing. Unlike behavioural change groups, which tend to focus on addressing a deficit or problem in group members' behaviours, skill development groups focus on building on the existing skills of group members. Group members tend to be motivated less to address a problem and more to develop a higher level of knowledge and skill in relation to a particular opportunity or challenge in their lives. Many parenting skills groups aim to provide parents and carers with the knowledge and skills to enhance members' existing parenting skills, rather than correct a problem in parenting. Similarly, some community service organizations run leadership programmes for community members to enable those members to more effectively participate in community activities such as public meetings.

● **Support groups:** In these groups, the groupworker aims to enhance members' capacities to provide support to one another in the face of a common challenge. Support groups have become increasingly common in social work and in many fields of health and social care provision, as it is recognized that peer knowledge and assistance can enable members to manage and hopefully thrive as they support one another through a shared challenge or issue. For example, young parents support groups can enable young parents to experience acceptance of their youth and parenting status as well as benefit from the social engagement such groups may offer. Similarly, in the health field, support groups have been established to enable people sharing common health challenges, such as living with a life-limiting illness, to benefit from others with the lived experience of the specific health challenge.

● **Self-help groups:** Like support groups, self-help groups aim to build members' capacity to respond to a shared challenge, but here group members also take on a leadership role in managing the group process. In self-help groups, the authority and credibility of group leaders and group members are based on the lived experience of a common concern, such as living with a mental illness or having a family member living with such an illness. Very often these groups have emerged in the context of members experiencing a long-term problem or challenge and also having experienced some disillusionment in the formal social care or healthcare system in responding to their experience. The role of social workers, or other paid workers, in these groups is focused on building and supporting the capacities of group members to lead the group themselves. So, for example, the social worker may be involved in providing information, skill development and support opportunities to group members in relation to issues such as how to manage conflict and how to write funding applications to support the essential work of the group.

● **Social action groups:** These groups bring together people with a shared concern or challenge with the intention of creating change in the broader community or society. Social action groups may focus on challenging stigma and discrimination, attracting resources to their community, or on protesting against a policy or proposal that is likely to disadvantage their group or community. Some social action groups may be short-term groups formed for the purpose of addressing a specific issue, for example a community faced with the imposition of pollutants within their community, such as building a vent for an underground transport tunnel. In the social care and health fields, there are many examples of ongoing social action groups. These groups tend to emerge where a group is likely to experience discrimination or disadvantage in a range of contexts, or where the problem facing the group is complex and ongoing. For example, in many countries, citizens living with disabilities have formed social action groups to campaign against the discrimination they face in a range of service contexts from social care and health contexts through to public transportation and employment. Social action groups usually do involve some form of personal change as group members develop a collective and critical awareness of the problems they face not only as personal problems but also as problems shared by others, which may have their origins in unjust social structures. However, the main focus of group activity is creating social change.

Some groups may involve a combination of group types, for example a counselling group may also involve group support. Also, groups may change their focus over time, for example a support group may become a social action group as group members develop a shared and critical consciousness of the matters that are of concern to them. For example, young parents may form an education and employment action group to address the discrimination they face in gaining access to education and employment opportunities available to other young people.

Stage Theories of Groups

There are a wide variety of theories on the stages of group development (see Toseland and Rivas, 2009). These theories draw attention to the changing dynamics of groups that may occur at different stages in the life of the group and the differing responsibilities of group leaders across these stages. In various ways, many of these theories highlight differences in the beginning, middle and ending phases of groups. One of the most influential stage theories of groups is that initially articulated by Tuckman (1965), and later elaborated by Tuckman and Jensen (1977) to a five-stage model of group development. These stages are forming, storming, norming, performing, and adjourning. It is difficult to overstate the influence of Tuckman and Jensen's model (1977; see also Tuckman, 1965) on the groupwork literature in health and welfare services and social work, where the five-stage model, or elements of it, are expounded (see Coulshed and Orme, 2006; McMaster, 2009). While there are a variety of stage theories of group dynamics, most are founded on the idea that the group dynamic varies over the life course of the group. Recognizing the different challenges that are likely to emerge over the life course of a group can help the groupworker prepare for these challenges and maximize the opportunity of responding to them in a constructive way for group members.

The beginning phase of the group refers to the preforming and forming phases of the group. In the *preforming phase*, decisions must be made about the initial purpose and task of the group, who is part of the group and, where necessary, how to recruit people to a group. These decisions also have secondary implications, regarding the resources required to conduct the group, such as location of the group meetings, and to meet other needs, such as travel, provision of refreshments and childcare. In some situations, such as if a group forms from an existing network, the members may be able to take responsibility for addressing the tasks in the preforming and forming phases of the group. However, if the group is a new initiative, it is necessary for the social worker to take a more formal and active leadership role in the tasks of the preforming and forming phases. In this phase, the key tasks that the social worker must ensure are addressed are that potential group members are made aware of the group including its purpose and duration, and to ensure that the resources needed to facilitate access to the group are in place, which may involve acquisition of funding or other forms of support, such as access to meeting locations. The practical tasks of ensuring that potential participants are aware of the group and are provided with the necessary resources to facilitate attendance are critical, yet often hidden, determinants of group success.

The *forming stage* begins as group members engage with the group. The key tasks to be achieved in this stage are the development of relationships among group members and with the group leader and a orientation towards the group task (Tuckman, 1965). Key questions for participants in this phase are: What is the purpose of this group? Do I belong to this group? The social worker must ensure that group members have the opportunity to understand and develop the purpose of the group and the goals to be achieved and that there is sufficient commonality and confidence among participants to achieve the group tasks. A number of strategies are used by group leaders to assist group members to achieve the tasks of the forming stage. These include:

● **The development of 'ground rules' for the group:** At the first point of engagement, it is important that group members develop a set of principles or rules by which the group will function. It is important that these rules are established at the outset to promote members' clarity about group expectations and also to prevent members viewing any of the principles as a personal attack on them. Typical principles are that the group members maintain confidentiality and that people listen respectfully to group members. It is important that these rules are achievable and appropriate to the group context. For example, in some contexts, such as tutorial groups, it might be appropriate to have a privacy policy where participants are discouraged from sharing a great deal of personal information, yet such a principle might be inappropriate in a therapy group. It is also important that the group agrees on strategies for ensuring the group principles are adhered to and this may involve, in the first instance, encouraging group members to review how the group principles are operating at the initial meetings of the group.

- **The use of icebreakers:** This refers to the exercises used to introduce group members and establish rapport among them, which may also help to form the foundations for the emergence of a group identity. These exercises are not usually focused on the specific tasks of the group. For example, group members might be asked to form pairs and then in pairs, discuss something about themselves, such as their favourite colour, to the group. It is important that group members are made aware of the purpose of icebreakers in terms of group formation and ensure that they do not extend for too long, lest they interfere with the achievement of group tasks.

- **Facilitating group involvement** in determining the purpose of the group, and the goals and strategies for achieving them: At the outset of the group, it is important for the social worker to ensure that the group members have a clear sense of the group's purpose and, as far as possible, participate in shaping that purpose. It may be necessary to continue having open conversations with the group, and the role of the social worker in it, as the group evolves. Establishing a shared sense of purpose can be difficult when participants are in some way compelled to attend, but especially in these circumstances, it is important to develop a shared sense of purpose, although that purpose might differ in some respects from the formal purpose of the group. For instance, the formal purpose of the group might be anger management but the 'real' purpose for the participants might be to keep a partner who is threatening to leave. By understanding the participants' true motivations, the groupworker can maximize opportunities for participants to reflect on the links between the formal and other purposes of the group.

In the middle phase of the group, the main work of the group towards achieving goals occurs, yet this phase is often characterized by conflict. In Tuckman and Jensen's (1977) stage theory of groups, the middle phases are referred to as the storming, norming and performing stages of groupwork. In the *storming phase*, conflict emerges as differences among group members become apparent and group members begin to test out the relationships within the group and, in some instances, seek dominance within the group. One of the dangers in this phase is that a particular group member may be held responsible, or made a scapegoat, for the conflict emerging in the group. If such scapegoating is allowed to continue, the participant is likely to experience distress and may exit the group; the group may also fail to develop its capacity to deal with conflict because it is widely assumed that an individual is at fault. Yet conflict can be productive if handled well, and it is here that the groupworker has an important role to play in normalizing conflict and in assisting the group to understand the sources of the conflict and strategies for addressing the conflict in the interests of the group.

The norming and performing stages of groupwork are complementary. *Norming* refers to the development of expectations about the roles and behaviours of group members. Often group norms allow the group to focus on the task of achieving the group's aims, confident in the knowledge that group expectations will be respected by participants. However, norms can also be unhelpful if they discourage group members from testing out new behaviours or attitudes that are relevant to achieving the group's purpose. For example, in an assertiveness training group, it may be unhelpful for a norm to develop in which some members are labelled as the 'quiet' members. The groupworker has an important role to play in challenging those group norms that block the achievement of group goals. Challenging these norms need not be overt but can involve initiating activities that disrupt unhelpful group norms. For example, to create a more equitable flow of conversation within a group, the groupworker might introduce an activity whereby the group members 'mark' the amount of time each person speaks in the first part of the session. One way of marking the flow would be to ask group members to collect a token from the centre of the group each time they talk in the group. After a specified period, such as 30 minutes, the groupworker could ask participants to count the number of tokens collected and to invite the group members to reflect on norms around speaking roles in the group. The groupworker could then encourage members to spend the next speci-fied period of the group, such as 30 minutes, reversing the 'expected' roles within the group by encouraging those who talked less to contribute more and visa versa. Again, reflection on how these different conversation flows affected the group could increase members' awareness of conversational norms within the group and, if necessary, the group could engage in a process of transformation of those norms in order to enable the group to achieve its purpose.

Performing refers to the focused stage of working in the group in which participants work on achieving the purposes of the group. This phase is characterized by shared clarity of purpose and clarity about roles and responsibilities (McMaster, 2009). In many groups, members may be able to take more responsibility for leadership roles, such as preparing activities focused on achieving group goals and actively contributing to the learning of others in the group. The role of the groupworker in this phase is to provide sufficient focus and structure for the group to achieve its purposes, while also encouraging members to take increasing responsibility for the group process. In this phase, the groupworker may face the challenge of developing stimulating activities that match the growing capacities of the group.

The final phase is referred to as the *adjourning, termination* or *closure phase* of the group (McMaster, 2009; Tuckman and Jensen, 1977). This usually occurs when the group has achieved its purpose, although sometimes closure can be imposed on the group due to external events, such as the loss of funding for the programme in which the group is embedded. Regardless of the reason for closure, this phase provides an opportunity for group members to consolidate learning from the group and to have a positive experience of transition out of the group. The groupworker has an important role to play in planning for this final phase. Activities carried out in this phase include a formal evaluation of the group process and achievements, as well as opportunities for members to provide constructive feedback to others about progress they have observed. Often this phase is marked by a celebration of the group's existence and conclusion. These closure activities are more than 'feel good' events, they can lay the foundation for members to retain or maintain that which they have learned in the group and to consider involvement in future groupwork or transition to another group that can help them maintain or build upon their learning from the group that is now ending. For example, an individual who has participated in a behaviour change group may, on conclusion of a groupwork programme, decide to transition to a self-help group in order to continue to build on advances they have made.

Group Leadership

There are a range of approaches to group leadership. At one end of the continuum, there is expert-centred leadership, where the group facilitator is positioned as an expert in relation to the topic area of the group. For example, in some health education groups, the health professional may seek to impart their expert knowledge to the group. An illustration of this would be a psychiatric education group for families of people experiencing mental illness, where the focus was on educating group members about the nature of the illness. At the other end of the spectrum is service user-led groups, where the participants are recognized as the experts in the topic area of the group and play a substantial role in group facilitation and leadership. Figure 6.1 provides an illustration of the continuum of groupwork leadership and examples of groups.

Facilitator led		Service user led
←		→
Psychotherapy groups	Community education groups	Self-help
Behaviour change groups	Peer support groups	Citizen action groups

Figure 6.1 The continuum of groupwork leadership from facilitator led to service user led

In Figure 6.1, I suggest that some forms of groupwork, such as psychotherapy or behaviour change groups are likely to be facilitator led. This is especially evident where the group facilitator is recognized by the group or the organization in which the groupworker is employed as having expertise or a knowledge base that is relevant to achieving the group's objective. One illustration of this is where the groupworker has responsibility for implementing pre-existing structured groupwork programmes. These standardized programmes exist in relation to a wide range of issues including parenting programmes, assertiveness training, and anger management training.

At the other end of the leadership spectrum are groups led by their members. Some of these have a focus on the provision of support to their members, such as groups established to support people with a relative or friend experiencing a mental illness. Others have a strong social action focus, such as groups established to achieve recognition and compensation for adults who were abused as children by members of faith or health and welfare service institutions (see Commission to Inquire into Child Abuse, 2009; Hutchins and McLucas, 2004). Many of these groups have professional support and some have sufficient funding to employ workers, but the critical feature is that they are run by and for their members.

Many groups in social work practice fall between either end of the leadership spectrum. Such groups may involve professionals working in collaboration with service users to determine the focus, structure and content of groups. These groups differ from service user-led groups in some key ways. These differences include that the worker has responsibilities to an employing agency or a funding body, as well as to group members, which may impact of the nature and focus of groups. The group may be established by the worker prior to members being recruited to the group. For example, many community services offer a range of peer support groups that are initiated and supported by workers. Finally, group members might not be in a position to assume responsibilities for group leadership. For example, a young parent may be interested initially in joining a support group rather than taking on the more onerous task of running a group. Even while recognizing our responsibilities to members, employers, funders and our professional role, we can still maximize opportunities for group ownership of the process. Indeed, many community education groups are based on this form of collaboration (Healy, 2006).

Many social work texts promote a democratic and inclusive approach to leadership. This approach emphasizes the facilitator's responsibility to encourage collaboration through developing shared responsibility for agenda-setting, group decision-making and group action (see McDermott, 2002; McMaster, 2009; Preston-Shoot, 2007). Mullender and Ward (1991, p. 128) summarize this position well:

> Workers must want to work with people and not direct intervention 'to' or 'at' them. The group worker should find their most effective contribution in facilitation rather than in leadership in the traditional sense.

Social workers tend to emphasize a collaborative approach to groupwork, as collaboration is, of itself, viewed as productive for achieving our purposes, that is, developing members' skills and confidence in their capacities.

The collaborative approach to group leadership involves a fine balance between having sufficient authority and credibility within the group to facilitate the group's achievement of their goals, while encouraging shared responsibility for processes and outcomes. A collaborative approach to leadership is necessarily dynamic, in that the responsibilities of the group facilitator are likely to change over time in response to the changing needs and capacities of the group. For example, at the outset, the group facilitator may adopt a more formal role in establishing ground rules and providing the group structure. As the group's capacities grow, it is often possible for the facilitator to share many of these responsibilities with group members. With the development of group members' capacities, it may be necessary for the facilitator to renegotiate their role with the group.

Reflecting on the Self as Leader

A reflective approach to groupwork requires that the groupworker understands, and is able to articulate, their position within the group. This involves transparency about roles, responsibilities and agendas. In addition, the group leader needs to decide their position as an 'insider/outsider' to the group. Preston-Shoot (2007, p. 109) reminds us that: 'Being group-workers requires practitioners to be able to tolerate a degree of separateness from the group in order to fulfil their roles.' Yet maintaining this separation is particularly challenging (and important) when the group leader shares an aspect of identity that is important to the group. For example, if the group concerns recovery from sexual assault and the group convenor has experienced sexual assault, they need to consider whether they will share this 'insider' status with the group. There are a number of issues to consider here. Sharing 'insider' status may confer credibility on the leader, it may also help to normalize an experience for group members and provide them with the motivation to address the issue on which the group is focused.

However, the insider status can also be problematic. Because of the symbolic power of the group leader, discussion of their experiences may lead to a focus on the leader's experiences and the minimization among group members (including the leader) of important differences between the group leader's and the other members' experiences and progress in relation to that experience. For example, it is likely that the group leader will have had previous opportunities to reflect on their experiences and this may lead others within the group to negatively evaluate their own 'progress' compared the apparent progress of the facilitator. Similarly, the group leader may have greater resources as a result of financial status, education or professional networks to manage their experience, and sharing their experience may be unhelpful for group members in determining their own pathway for managing their experience. In the event that the group leader decides to share their insider status with the group, they must avoid implying that their experience or management of it is in any way superior to that of group members. This can be achieved by ensuring that the focus remains on the members' experience and management of their experiences.

Further issues to consider are the extent to which sharing an insider status may interfere with the worker's capacity to undertake key roles. For example, a focus on the worker's experience and strategies for managing that experience may limit their capacity to facilitate discussion and equal evaluation of group members' experiences and responses. In addition, sharing personal information has the potential to damage the worker's professional identity or reputation. Although group members may recognize the importance of confidentiality of matters discussed in the group, there can be no guarantee that confidences will be kept. Of course, all group members need to be aware of the limits to confidentiality, but there are specific challenges for group-workers in relation to issues of confidentiality, arising from the fact that they are conducting a group in their work environment as part of their professional role. In some work contexts, there may be considerably more risks for a worker to discuss matters of personal nature with group members. For example, were a worker in a mental health support group to discuss personal experiences of mental health problems, they would need to be aware that this may raise questions about their professional 'objectivity' and capacity for some within the group and, perhaps, also with their colleagues. As a rule of thumb, groupworkers should be aware that the groupwork environment is a public environment. In deciding whether or not to share one's personal experiences, the worker should take into account the pros and cons for sharing such information with the group and the possible costs to them should the information become more publicly known.

Over to you ...

To share or not to share?

1. Thinking of the wide range of groups that social workers are involved in, what groups would you consider yourself an 'insider' in?

2. What aspects, if any, of your experience as an insider might it be helpful to share in a group? How might this information be helpful to group members?

3. What aspects, if any, of your experiences would be unhelpful to share in a group? How might this information be unhelpful to group members?

4. What aspects, if any, of your experiences could be harmful to you, should this information become public knowledge? How might this information harm you?

Creating an Environment for Change: Groupworker Responsibilities

We turn now to the process of creating change in and with groups. We will use ideas from critical social work and from the strengths-based approach to create change in groups. I outline the four elements of creating change in, and through, groups that will be discussed. These elements are building trust, building a positive group identity, promoting group ownership, and creating direction for change.

Establishing Trust

The effectiveness of groupwork depends on the quality of the relationships among its members. McDermott (2002, p. 62) observes that: 'Once group members have begun to trust each other, the work of the group can take place.' The groupworker has a vital role to play in ensuring that sufficient trust is established among members to enable the group to reach its goals, whether these be personal goals such as behavioural change, social support goals, or social action goals. Groupworkers can sometimes break trust by failing to recognize the important role they play in the creating trust in the group process. For example, being habitually late for the group, failing to facilitate ground rules for ensuring personal safety, failing to model the established rules, and failing to intervene to address emerging problems are all issues of significance.

There are a number of tasks and processes in which a groupworker can engage to promote trust:

● **Establishing ground rules** about the expected behaviours within the group at the outset is vital to creating a safe environment. It is important that this happens at the outset before a problem emerges, as the early development of ground rules will build participants' sense of engagement with the group.

● **Modelling behaviours** that are expected in the group. For example, it is important that groupworkers demonstrate reliability, confidentiality, listening, attentiveness, and effective communication if they want to help members do the same. Modelling behaviours is important because group members are likely to look to the leader, at least initially, to understand the implicit rules of the group. Thus the leader has an important role to play in establishing the culture, or the norms, of the group. By modelling behaviours, the group leader may also provide members with opportunities to learn new skills or new ways of looking at their world. For example, McDermott (2002, p. 71) observes that: 'In groups for men who are violent or sexual abusers, male and female co-leadership has been seen as providing opportunities for the leaders to model non-stereotypic gender relationships.' If a man and a woman facilitator work together as equals, the group process may challenge assumptions held by some participants and encourage them to interact more constructively with people of the opposite gender.

● **Creating a safe group environment**. This entails consistently showing acceptance of the person but not their poor behaviour. Sometimes it is necessary to discuss behavioural problems with a person outside the group.

● **Addressing and managing conflict**. In the 'storming' phase of the group, conflict is likely and it is important that the group facilitator demonstrates the capacity to manage this conflict in ways that are constructive and inclusive for all group members. If conflict is managed well, this can enable group members to develop greater trust in the group and also an enhanced sense of confidence in their capacity to manage difficult situations.

Building a Positive Group Identity

The groupworker should aim to facilitate the development of a positive group identity. The term 'positive' refers to creating pride among participants in being part of the group. Having a sense of pride in the group identity is important to building commitment to the group process and can, of itself, contribute to achieving the purposes of the group. For example, groups for people who grew up the 'care' of the state can create a positive identity among participants by acknowledging the knowledge, skills and capacities of this group of survivors. Indeed, in several countries, these groups have been important participants in creating political change and achieving compensation for those who suffered abuse in institutional care.

McMaster (2009) observes that groups often become problem saturated. This can occur because the group is focused on a shared challenge or perceived deficit. However, if the group becomes problem oriented, participants may not have confidence in the capacity of the group to contribute to change. There are several ways in which the groupworker can contribute to building pride in a common identity. One is for the groupworker to identify common strengths and exceptions to the problem. McMaster (2009) also suggested reframing problems to solutions. For example, in a group of young parents, the participants may be discussing the frustrations of dealing with their children's tantrums; the groupworker could encourage participants to share successful strategies they have developed for managing these frustrations. Encouraging participants to develop a name for the group that reflects the strengths or aspirations of the group can also help to create a positive identity both within the group and externally.

A key challenge for the groupworker is to support the development of a group identity that recognizes what members share in common while also respecting diversity within the group. One way of achieving this is to encourage the respectful discussion of difference among group members and for members to develop strategies for managing and valuing these differences. For example, in a group of people from diverse ethnic backgrounds, the groupworker may encourage members to learn about each others' culture through non-threatening activities such as participation in preparing shared meals that reflect different cultural origins. In the context of participating in these activities, participants could be encouraged to consider how the group processes and activities could further reflect respect for the cultural differences of the members.

Promoting Group Ownership

Promoting group ownership refers to encouraging group members to share responsibility with each other and, as appropriate, with the group leader for the group process and outcomes. This principle is important for reducing dependence on the group leader and for recognizing that all members have an important role to play in sustaining the group. Paradoxically, promoting group ownership is likely to involve considerable skill and effort on the part of the groupworker, who needs to assess and build members' capacities to extend their responsibilities in the group.

A potential pitfall is that the groupworker hands over responsibility before members have the capacity or the commitment needed to share this responsibility. For example, if the groupworker asks members to share responsibility by preparing an activity for the group and members fail to do so, this can have a negative impact on group commitment. Hence, it is important for the groupworker to assess the capacities of the group to share responsibility as they seek to build members' sense of shared ownership of the process.

The groupworker can build the willingness, confidence and the capacity of the group to share ownership of the group process in a number of ways. It is important that the groupworker facilitates conversations with the group about the group's purpose and role expectations. Members will be more likely to extend their role when they perceive the groupworker is willing to share aspects of the leadership role and that there are advantages for members to take on new roles. Some advantages of assuming new roles include that members will develop skills that may be transferable to other areas of their life or that help to address the challenges they face. For example, members attending a group to help them to deal with anxiety may find that assuming some responsibilities in the group, such as preparation of a groupwork activity, can help them deal with an anxiety-provoking event in the safe environment of the group. Using a strengths-based approach, the groupworker could also highlight to the group evidence of their relevant knowledge and skills as these emerge. For example, the worker could focus on evidence of organizational skills among group members. In the event that the groupworker becomes aware of knowledge or skill deficits within the group relevant to their capacity to take ownership of the group process, the worker may also consider offering group training to build the group's capacity to assume increasing responsibility within the group.

Creating Direction for Change

Many people engage in a group with an expectation of change; this can be personal change, as is usually the case for participants in psychotherapeutic groups, or broader social change, as is the case for participants in social action groups. The groupworker has a role to play in ensuring that group activities achieve the change purpose. This involves helping the group clarify its purpose, particularly the forms of change that are desired. It is important to establish clarity about change aspirations at the beginning of the group and it is often helpful to return regularly to the aspirations of the group in order to assess group members' progress towards those goals.

In many groups, the worker plays a pivotal role in ensuring that the group structure is appropriate to achieving the change goals as efficiently and effectively as possible. In many types of groups, the groupworker has responsibility for coordinating the groupwork programme in order to ensure that group time is used most efficiently to achieve the group's purpose. This involves the groupworker being aware of the likely duration of the group. In some types of groups, such as many behaviour modification groups, the group may be structured according to a standardized groupwork programme, in which the duration of sessions and the overall programme is predetermined. However, even in relatively open-ended, unstructured groups, it is important that group members are aware of and, where possible, participate in determining the nature and type of group structure that is appropriate to the change purposes. For example, a groupworker conducting a psychoeducational programme for families and carers of people with mental illness would need to take into account the amount of time members had to commit to the group and their expectation of change from the group. A group is likely to fail to meet participants' expectations of change where it is inappropriately structured, because of too little or too much formal structure, to meet the change goals in the time available.

Once the change goals and group structure are established, there is much the worker can do to facilitate change among or through the group. Many groups encourage participants to reflect on their behaviour and attitudes within and outside the group. Group members may, for example, provide stimulus materials, such as photographs or video excerpts, to ask participants to reflect on their feelings or attitudes towards a particular issue being considered in the group. Exercises intended to enable members to test out newly developing skills, such as role-plays, can also help to facilitate learning and reflection. The use of 'homework' exercises is a common strategy for encouraging members to test out new skills and consolidate group learning. As McMaster (2009, p. 223) observes: 'Strengths-based approaches are clearly targeted at changes in behaviour, so the person should always be able to leave the group session with something to try out or do differently.'

From a strengths-based perspective, the groupworker has an important role to play in ensuring that the group avoids becoming problem focused. The strengths-based groupworker seeks to challenge problem-oriented stories and highlight the group's capacities and potential to address the issues facing them. One way the groupworker can do this is to observe exceptions to the problems facing the group. For example, in a support group for people experiencing depression and anxiety, the groupworker may regularly ask participants to reflect on the times in the previous week where they have had a victory over the depression or anxiety that affects their life.

From a critical and anti-oppressive perspective, the groupworker aims to encourage members to critically analyse the challenges they face individually in order to reduce a sense of individual blame and to create the foundations for collective action against the injustices faced by the group. Critical groupwork involves facilitating participants' recognition of the extent to which their private troubles are shared concerns among the group and that these concerns arise not from personal failing but from social injustices (Mullender and Ward, 1991). For example, a critical approach to supportive groupwork with people experiencing mental illness may include consideration of how the public negative stereotypes of mental illness adversely affect the lived experience of mental illness among group members (Crossley and Crossley, 2001). Drawing on this reflection, group members might consider collective strategies for contesting the negative public images of people experiencing mental illness. The focus on critical analysis and creating capacity for collective action in critical or anti-oppressive social work means that groupwork from this perspective may involve an element of social action even where the group has other purposes, such as the provision of social support.

Group Facilitation Techniques

As I have emphasized, groupwork practice involves the establishment of a shared identity and purpose among members and the implementation of activities to assist the group in achieving its change goals. If you are new to groupwork, it can be difficult to know where to start in facilitating a groupwork process. We turn now to a few practical strategies you can use to facilitate group participation. There is a large body of literature on groupwork exercises focused on facilitating group involvement that can help to stimulate you to maximize members' involvement (Doel, 2006; Garvin et al., 2004). Of course, the groupworker needs a clear sense of the group's purpose, particularly its change goals, before deciding on which exercises will facilitate achievement of the group's purpose. Groupwork exercises can facilitate achievement of our goals but they cannot make up for lack of preparation, clarity of purpose and understanding of group dynamics.

Getting to know you exercises, also referred to as *icebreakers*, are intended to facilitate opportunities for members to get to know one another in a way that is nonthreatening and relevant to the group's purpose. Icebreakers occur at the formation phases of groups and go beyond asking members about their purpose for attending; they encourage members to get to know one another in a more holistic way than might be revealed just through a discussion of their reasons for attending. The icebreaker should not ask participants to reveal personal information or engage in activities that are in any way potentially embarrassing before an appropriate level of trust has been established in the group. For example, to ask participants to discuss information about abuse or relationship breakdown in an icebreaker exercise may be experienced as personally threatening. At the same time, icebreaker exercises need to be relevant to the group's purpose, otherwise some members may view the exercise, and possibly the group, as a waste of time. For example, at a support group for young parents, it may be helpful to start with an exercise about their favourite activity with and without their children. By contrast, an icebreaker exercise where participants are asked to discuss a seemingly trivial matter, such as the origins of their name, may frustrate some participants. These are two examples of icebreaker activities:

● Ask the group to break into pairs and to discuss a pastime, an ideal holiday destination, or their child's favourite meal.

● Ask group members to focus on shared stimulus material, such as a set of photographs, and discuss what the images mean to them. For example, in a parenting support group, you might present a series of images about parents, children and families and ask members to discuss these.

Brainstorming refers to participants articulating the range of ideas that arise for them in relation to a particular issue. Brainstorming is used to free up the group to consider a wide range of perspectives or possibilities. The key rule in brainstorming is that there is 'no wrong answer' and participants are encouraged to put forward ideas regardless of how relevant these may first appear. Brainstorming is intended to facilitate creative thinking among group members and to promote a sense of group ownership in developing responses to the issues under consideration. Brainstorming can be used for a wide variety of group issues such as establishing the group programme or developing solutions to a challenge facing the group. Brainstorming activities may be introduced by the groupworker who should explain the 'no wrong answer' principle. The groupworker, or a group member, should then take responsibility for writing up each of the ideas that emerge from the brainstorm. Immediacy is important in this activity and so it is important that documentation of ideas occurs as they are articulated and preferably in a way that can be viewed or understood by all members of the group. Brainstorming usually occurs at a relatively fast pace with discussion focused on identifying ideas not evaluating them. Once the full set of ideas arising from the brainstorm is documented, the groupworker can then facilitate a group review of those ideas. For example, group members may be asked to consider the pros and cons of each idea for achieving resolution of the issue to which the brainstorm was addressed.

Stimulus materials refer to a range of items used to encourage group reflection or discussion. Stimulus materials can include images, such as photographs or paintings, words or phrases, DVD excerpts or sound recording excerpts. Most often this material is provided by the groupworker, although in some instances group members might be asked to provide this material as part of a group exercise. For example, group members might be asked to bring a photograph or object from their home that represents some aspect of their life. The choice of stimulus material should be clearly linked to the purpose of the group. For example, strengths-based workers have developed strengths cards, which focus on particular capacities or emotions. One way these cards are used is to encourage group members to use the images to focus on their hopes and dreams for the future. The stimulus material encourages all group members to focus on a common set of stimuli and as such can be helpful for promoting group reflection. Stimulus material can be helpful for promoting the participation of group members who find it difficult to quickly articulate their responses or feelings about a specific issue.

Role-plays can be used to facilitate the group's active engagement in developing skills. Role-plays involve the use of scenarios in which participants play a role or character. Role-plays may represent a 'real-life' issue being experienced by members or may be constructed to give the members the opportunity to develop skills. For example, in an assertiveness skill development group, members might be asked to role-play a particular challenge a member is experiencing with demonstrating assertiveness in their life. The other members can provide the member with an opportunity to demonstrate these skills in the role-play and to see others demonstrating these skills. Role-plays may be followed by a 'debriefing', wherein group members have the opportunity to consolidate their learning through the role-play by providing feedback about the experience of, and learning from, being in different roles. If role-plays have stimulated emotionally intense feelings among participants, debriefing can also be used to return participants to an emotional state where they can engage in other group activities.

Continuums involve the group in the physical representation of responses to a concern. When using continuums, the groupworker asks group members to imagine that a line runs across the middle of the meeting room and this line represents the different positions on a particular issue, with extreme views at each end. For example, a groupworker in a social action group might ask the group to consider their attitudes towards the use of public protest to address an issue by asking the members to place themselves along a continuum in which one end represents the view 'I feel entirely comfortable with engaging in public protest to address this issue', while the other end represents the view 'I feel entirely uncomfortable with engaging in public protest to address this issue.' The groupworker could then facilitate a discussion among group members about the reasons they have placed themselves at different points in the continuum and to consider then as a group what this means for future action by the group. Continuums can be an excellent strategy for enabling group members to recognize, and understand, the diversity of opinions within a group. However, continuums can also be threatening because they can so clearly expose differences and this can lead to conflict. Because of these possible problems with continuums, they should be used with caution, if at all, to explore issues of substantial conflict in the group. Like continuums, group sculptures are a method for physically representing viewpoints within the group.

Finally, the groupworker can make use of *different group formations* within the group to facilitate different types of interactions during the group meeting. Breaking the whole group up into pairs or small groups of three or four can help to break the dominance of a small number of members over the large group discussion, enable focused reflection on an issue or to practise a skill. Particularly in the early stages of the group, some members may be more willing to actively participate in pairs or small groups or larger groups. The groupworker can also facilitate each pair or small group to report their learning from small group exercises to the larger group. One problem with breaking the group into smaller groups is that cliques may form within the group. To minimize the chances of this, the groupworker may consider ways of ensuring variation in the small groups and pairs to ensure that all participants have the opportunity to engage in small group discussion with one another. One way to achieve this is to randomly assign participants to pairs or encourage participants to join with members with whom they have not previously worked. The groupworker also needs to consider that the format of the meeting room is conducive to group discussion relevant to the purposes of the group and also to reflect our aspiration as social work groupworkers to create a democratic and inclusive environment with service users and colleagues. Often a circle or semi-circle is used to facilitate group discussion; in large meetings, it may be helpful to arrange the seating in a number of small round table formations.

Tips for Success in Groupwork Interventions

The following checklist is intended to assist you in planning for groupwork. Groupworkers should ensure that:

● Group members share responsibility for the success of the group in achieving the group goals. This can be achieved by regular opportunities for the group to discuss group and individual goals and to reflect on the group's progress in reaching these goals.

● At the outset there is opportunity to discuss expectations of workers and group participants and that there are opportunities to return to these discussions as the group progresses.

● The practical tasks needed to enable participants to access the group and create an effective working environment for the group are addressed. This can include addressing issues such as transport access, disability access, availability of childcare, and availability of refreshments.

● There is sufficient structure to enable the group to work towards the achievement of shared goals. The level of structure required can change according the focus of the group and group members' experience of participating in groups; the level of structure required to facilitate participation can also change over the life of the group.

● Issues and conflict are addressed as soon as possible and in ways that maximize the inclusion of all group members.

● There are opportunities for individuals to exit the group and the group to terminate when the goals have been achieved.

Evaluation and Termination in Groupwork

Finally, I turn to the evaluation and termination of groupwork. Like all methods of social work practice, it is important that we evaluate groupwork practice. Evaluating our practice assists us to gain insight into what works for achieving group satisfaction and ensuring that groups achieve the objectives for which they were established. Evaluation is also important for ensuring that we minimize potential harm for participants, that is, being aware if our intervention is creating unintended, negative consequences for service users. For example, an evaluation may reveal high levels of dissatisfaction among participants about the group process that members for various reasons feel unable to voice in the group. By gaining these insights, we can reorient the groupwork to better achieve intended outcomes.

Again, like other forms of social work evaluation, we need to be clear about the purpose of our evaluation and from that purpose we need to clarify the focus of our evaluation. While the purpose of all evaluation should be to improve our practice, in undertaking our evaluation we need to further clarify what elements of our practice we seek to improve. Consistent with our concern with quality service delivery and respect for group members, we are also likely to be interested in group members' satisfaction with their experience of the groupwork intervention. When assessing the effectiveness of groupwork, we will seek to understand the impact of the intervention on outcomes for members. To assess outcome, we need to be clear in our unit of analysis, that is, what is the change outcome being sought in the group. The kinds of change we may be interested in measuring include changes in behaviours, attitudes, emotional statements, perceptions, and changes in the social environment of the group members. For example, in an assertiveness skill development group, we may wish to evaluate the extent to which group members have been able to exercise assertiveness skills in their home and community environments and what impact their use of these skills has had on their quality of life.

Evaluation of groupwork practice is complex because, like other forms of social work practice, it is difficult to separate the impact of the groupwork from other factors in a group member's life. For instance, an improvement in assertiveness skills may be linked as much to a group member getting a new job or leaving an unhappy relationship as it is to the skills actively learned in the group. For a variety of ethical and practical reasons, randomized control trials are rarely conducted in social work practice and this makes it difficult to establish the impact of groupwork practice (Gant, 2004). Yet other approaches to evaluation can be helpful in assessing and developing our groupwork practice, as long as we are aware of the limitations of the various evaluation methods available to us and we do what is possible to address these limitations (Gant, 2004).

To enhance the value of our evaluation for providing insight into group members' satisfaction with groupwork interventions and whether the groupwork methods have contributed to desirable changes (individually or in the social environment of the group member), it is vital that we draw on several types of information and certainly not rely only on group members' accounts within the group. Groupwork evaluation is vulnerable to 'attractiveness bias', where group members' reports on the group process and outcomes can be influenced by a desire to conform to group norms and expectations. For example, in a group on recovery from abuse, members may be reluctant to share setbacks in recovery for fear of being seen as a failure in the group. We also need to consider how evaluations can be conducted so as to enable us to assess whether the groupwork intervention helped the client achieve their change goals.

There are several types of information we may use in our evaluation:

- **Seeking input from group participants** about their perceptions of, and satisfaction with, group processes. We can gain this information in several forms, such as written surveys or interviews with group members. We can also gain this information through participants reporting on information they have collected themselves, such as in reflective diaries, about the impact of the groupwork intervention on change goals (Magen, 2004).

- **Using standardized instruments to measure changes** over time related to the change objectives of the group. A wide range of standardized instruments are available for assessing change in individual behaviours, attitudes and social environments and we may decide to use these to assess change (Magen, 2004). One advantage of standardized measurement instruments is that they have been tested in a range of contexts and can help to ensure that the worker takes into account a range of relevant indicators when assessing the extent to which interventions have enabled members to achieve change goals.

- **Observation of group members** is another way of evaluating outcomes and members' satisfaction with the groupwork intervention. Observational data can be particularly vulnerable to the biases of the observer, as we may notice those behaviours and attitudes that coincide with our assumptions about the group outcomes and processes. If we wish to use observational data as a basis for evaluation, it is important that we are systematic about what we are observing and make sure that we collect that data in a systematic way. For example, if we want to assess participation in a group, we should be clear about what the concept means and what behaviours or speech actions we would consider to be indicators of participation.

- **Insights from others (nonparticipants)** whose lives might be changed by transformations brought about by the groupwork. For example, in conducting a group with vulnerable parents, one may evaluate the impact of support not only the parents who attended the group, but their children who may also have benefited from the support provided to their parents.

The process of evaluating groupwork need not be complex but it should be systematic (Magen, 2004). This means that information about group outcomes and processes are regularly reviewed. Because most groupwork interventions occur over time, sometimes over months and even years, it is important that the evaluation also occurs over time so at to capture changes and to allow for a reorientation of groupwork practice where unanticipated negative outcomes are emerging.

The termination phase of groupwork requires attention to the ending of the group as an entity, although relationships among group members may continue. Termination of group processes may happen in two ways. In ongoing groups, that is, groups without a clear time limit, it is likely that some members will exit the group along the way. The decision to exit may be the decision of the individual or may be determined by others. For example, some groups may have an age limit and maintaining this limit may be important to sustaining the identity of the group. In the case where the individual leaves a continuing group, it is important to mark this occasion so that the group can acknowledge a change in its membership and also so that the individual can have the opportunity to recognize their achievements in, and contributions to, the group. For example, a celebratory activity such as afternoon tea might be held to mark the occasion and group members, including the member who is leaving, have the opportunity to reflect with the group on the contribution and achievements of the individual and the group.

Another type of group termination is when the group disbands. The group may disband for many reasons, including that the agreed time span of the group has been reached (this is common in skills-based groups, which often involve a structured programme over an agreed number of sessions), the group's goals have been achieved, members have decided that the group is no longer viable because they are not sufficiently committed to its continuance, or a loss of resources for the group, as when an external funding source is withdrawn. A well-handled termination phase can enable members to acknowledge their contributions to, and achievements within, the group. The termination phase can enable members to look back positively on their group experience and this is important for building on the gains made through groupwork and for encouraging members to engage in groupwork should an opportunity arise in future. Group members may choose to mark the conclusion of their group in a variety of ways, such as through celebrations or participation in the creation of a shared symbol, such as planting a tree, to recognize what the group has achieved together. In this termination phase, it is important that group members have the opportunity to participate in planning how the group should terminate and that there are opportunities for members to respectfully share with group members their reflection on the group experience.

Conclusion

In this chapter, I have outlined groupwork as a method of social work practice. I have argued that groupwork has advantages over some other methods, including that the group itself provides a context for change and group members can learn from each other. Of course, groupwork also has limitations and may be unsuitable for some people and for some types of change activity. I have also argued that social work practice with groups is often characterized by a democratic and inclusive approach to leadership. I have introduced skills and strategies social workers can use at each phase of groupwork practice to promote members' participation in the identification and achievement of change goals. Social workers often use groupwork as a complement to other methods of practice. My intention in this chapter has been to provide you with a foundational understanding of the use and practice of groupwork so that you may feel confident in using groupwork methods whatever your context of social work practice.

Review Questions

1. What does the term 'storming' mean in groupwork theory and what is the purpose of this stage for the group? What can a groupworker do to ensure that the storming phase is managed in a constructive way for group members?

2. Why might some participants be reluctant to participate in a behaviour change group? How can groupworkers encourage group members' participation in groupwork?

3. What is a democratic and inclusive approach to groupwork? How can groupworkers demonstrate their commitment to this approach in their leadership of a group?

Critical Reflection Questions

1. What experiences do you have of participating in a group? From your experiences, what are your reflections on what contributes to success and failure in groups achieving their goals?

2. Identify one theoretical framework that is important to your social work practice and discuss how this theory would inform your approach to working with groups.

Practice Exercise

Imagine you have been employed to conduct a group with 12 young people leaving state care. These young people are 17–18 years old and all were removed from their families because of concerns about abuse and neglect. Most were placed in state care before

▶

they were 10 years old and have lived in a combination of foster families and residential care services. They are all now living in residential care homes in your geographical region and they cannot remain in these placements long term.

One of the common challenges they face is the move to independent living, and so your organization has funded the group to operate for up to six months to support young people as they move to independent living. Apart from their shared experience of living in out-of-home care, the young people have a variety of employment and education statuses. Six of the young people have left school, with four being employed in casual work either in the retail or building sector, while the remaining six are currently studying full time, either completing school or undertaking further study.

1. What do you see as the key purpose(s) of the group?
2. What type of group do you think is appropriate for these young people, given their needs and the duration of the group?
3. What do you see as the opportunities and challenges for effective groupwork for these young people?
4. How would you create an environment for change with this group?

Further Reading

- Doel, M. (2006) *Using Groupwork*. London: Routledge.

  Practical guide to groupwork that provides an overview of commonalities and differences in groupwork practice in a range of settings. Excellent guide to practical activities over the life course of a group, with tips for dealing with common problems encountered in groupwork practice.

- Garvin, C.D., Gutierrez, L.M. and Galinksy, M.J. (eds) (2004) *Handbook of Social Work with Groups*. London: Guilford Press.

  Comprehensive overview of theory and practice of working with groups in a range of practice contexts, including child welfare, older people, people with mental health concerns, and voluntary and involuntary clients and social action groups. Includes chapters on evaluation of groupwork practice.

- Preston-Shoot, M. (2007) *Effective Groupwork*, 2nd edn. Basingstoke: Palgrave Macmillan.

  Detailed guide to groupwork using an anti-oppressive perspective. Presents practical strategies for planning and leading groups.

Part 4

Community Work, Policy Practice and Organizational Change

In this final part, I turn to the areas of practice often referred to as 'macro practice'. In the final three chapters, I outline the rationale for social workers involvement in creating systemic change. I argue that working to build community, create more just policies and organizational arrangements are consistent with our theoretical and value frameworks.

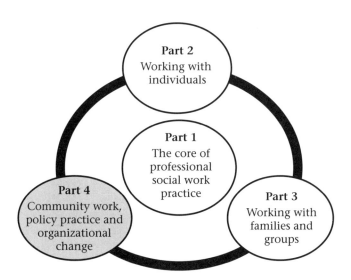

The three methods of practice I discuss in the final part of this book are highlighted in the figure. In Chapter 7, I discuss the history, rationale for and skills involved in community work practice. In Chapter 8, I focus on policy practice, differentiating between a policy specialist arena of work and policy practice as part of professional social work practice, that is, a method in which social workers involved in direct practice might engage. In Chapter 9, I look back over the themes in this book and discuss how social workers can contribute to organizational change to create more humane and responsive social work organizations.

7

Community Work

Community work refers to a set of approaches focused on understanding individuals as part of a community and on building the capacity of that community to address the social, economic or political challenges facing its members. Twelvetrees (2008, p. 1) defines community work as 'the process of assisting people to improve their own communities by undertaking autonomous collective action'. Debate exists about whether or not community work should be considered a method of social work practice or as a separate field of practice (Tesoriero, 2010). I refer to community work as a method a social worker may undertake either as their primary activity, such as when they are employed as a community development worker, or as part of their social work role, such as when they apply community work methods alongside other practice methods.

I begin by defining the term 'community' and five types of community work practice. I discuss the history of community work practice in social work and tensions from within, and outside, the profession of social work about the place of community work as a method of social work practice. I will introduce the community work practice skills required to engage communities, assess community strengths and needs, promote participation, and evaluate practice.

Community Work Practice: Defining the Terms

Community workers build the capacity of communities to recognize and utilize their strengths and assets and to address the challenges facing their members. The worker's approach to community work will vary according to factors such as the strengths and needs of the community, the agency or funding body's expectations and requirements of their role, and their own theoretical orientation and practice skills. The term 'community' has a diversity of meaning, as Turunen (2009, p. 49) asserts:

> In community work, the concept of community has at least three references: a
> geographical area (a district, village, suburb, neighbourhood, etc.), a unit of social

169

system and interaction (an association, an organization, working place, network, and so on), and a symbolic unit of identify and feelings of togetherness (shared values, traditions, problems, interests, forms of behaviour and lifestyles, etc.).

In essence, most community work practice is focused on one, or a combination, of three types of community – geographical communities, communities of association and identity-based communities:

● **geographical communities:** where people share common concerns and interests based on their residential locality. The local community work tradition, particularly when practised in urban contexts, is often referred to as 'neighbourhood' work (Henderson and Thomas, 2002).

● **communities of association:** people who share common interests or concerns based on their involvement in formal associations such as religious organizations, trade unions or workplaces. So, for example, a national network of people committed to supporting public broadcasting or food cooperatives or trade union activity may be referred to as a community of association.

● **identity-based communities:** where a common identity, characteristic or experience binds a community. For example, care-leavers or people living with a mental illness or disability may form an identity-based community. This type of community is associated with the emergence of new social movements in many fields of health and social welfare such as the disability rights movement and the mental health consumers' movement (Healy, 2005). In some situations, it is difficult to differentiate between locality and identity-based communities. For example, community work with indigenous people living in remote areas may involve both identity and local community-building aspects.

There are a wide variety of types of community work practice and there have been numerous attempts to develop community work typologies (see Rothman, 2001; Weil and Gamble, 2005). In practice, the types of community work rarely exist as ideal or distinct types and a combination of the different approaches is common (Hoatson, 2003; Rothman, 2001). For example, a community development worker might assist a group of community members to develop a social action campaign, or a community service worker might use community education methods.

I refer here to five commonly acknowledged types of community work practice used both within, and sometimes outside, social work practice. These are community service, community development, community planning, community organizing, and community education There is much debate among researchers or practitioners about the exact meaning of terms such as community development or community work (Twelvetrees, 2008), and this contributes to some conceptual confusion and much debate about terminology (Tesoriero, 2010). Despite the challenges, it is important to try to distinguish between commonly used terms in the field.

Community service refers to a form of community work focused on enhancing the interaction between service users and the service system. This is achieved by improving service users' access to the service system and also by seeking to build the capacity of the service system to respond to the diverse needs of specific service user groups. This approach is also referred to as 'community social work' and 'community care work' (see Twelvetrees, 2008) and, of the approaches discussed in this chapter, is most closely aligned to a traditional or treatment model of social work. As an illustration of community service work, consider the community outreach undertaken by a mental health social worker when they work with people hospitalized with mental health conditions to locate and sustain housing in the community, work with community housing providers to ensure the quality and responsiveness to people with mental health needs, and assist people with mental health conditions to develop self-help support networks that help to sustain them in the community. Community social work activities can complement other modes of health and welfare intervention by ensuring that service users' needs are better met within their community.

Community development involves facilitating the participation of citizens in identifying shared change goals and working collaboratively towards achieving these goals. Community development is characterized by practice with small groups, often, although not always, working within specific localities. Community development often focuses on building the social or economic capacities of a community (see Midgley and Livermore, 2005). Community development practitioners seek to build the capacity of the community to recognize their shared concerns and to identify and realize common goals (Twelvetrees, 2008). Focusing on locality-based forms of community development, Rothman (2001, p. 30) asserts that:

> locality development fosters community building by promoting process goals: community competency (the ability to solve programs on a self-help basis) and social integration (harmonious interrelationships among different racial, ethnic and social-class groups – indeed among all people).

The theme of promoting citizen or community participation is emphasized throughout the community development literature and a diversity of strategies are used to achieve community members' participation. There is also a strong emphasis on building the capacities, such as knowledge and skills, of community members to help themselves.

Community planning, also referred to as 'social planning', 'emphasizes a technical process of problem-solving regarding substantive social problems, such as delinquency, housing and mental health' (Rothman, 2001, p. 31). This approach focuses on the involvement of experts, such as social planners and social and health workers, in defining community needs and developing responses to those needs. The role of the experts is to assemble and analyse data, such as evidence of community needs, and to provide solutions to those problems (Rothman, 2001). The participation of community members tends to be limited to consultation. Social workers' roles in community planning may involve several activities including liaison among professional groups and promoting community input into the community planning process. According to Twelvetrees (2008, p. 3), a community worker's involvement in social planning may include: 'initiating projects, liaising and working directly with service providers to sensitise them to the needs of specific communities, assisting them to improve services or alter policies'.

Community organizing, also referred to as 'community activism', is associated with an activist approach to community building and advocacy (Bunyan, 2008). Drawing on critical social science theoretical perspectives, community organizers seek to redress the imbalance of social and economic power in society. As Rothman (2001, p. 33) states:

> This approach presupposes the existence of an aggrieved or disadvantaged segment of the population that needs to be organized in order to make demands on the larger community for increased resources for equal treatment.

Community organizers seek to mobilize disadvantaged citizens to recognize their shared oppression and take joint action to achieve a better deal for their communities. Activities in which community organizers are involved include consciousness raising, a process through which oppressed citizens are encouraged to reject individualistic explanations of the challenges they face and instead gain greater awareness of the contribution of social processes, such as those associated with classism, sexism and racism, to their oppression, and the coordination of collective activities, which often include overtly political activities such as public protest (Ronnby, 2009).

Some commentators question whether community organizing is a viable mode of practice for workers engaged in community work as a professional activity (Rothman, 2001). There are two reasons this approach can be problematic for professional social workers and community workers. First, it can be difficult for the worker to generate and sustain an income when the primary focus of their activity involves critiquing those agencies that also fund community work practice. Second, community organization relies on leadership from within the community and professional social workers or community workers are likely to be outsiders in some way from the community they serve. For example, even if the community worker resides in the same geographical community, they are unlikely to share the lived experience of disadvantage, disability or illness experienced by the oppressed community. Despite the difficulties of engaging in community organizing as a primary mode of professional social work or community work practice, there may be situations in which professional workers may promote or support community organizing activities. For example, in circumstances where other forms of community work have failed to achieve outcomes for the group, it may be necessary for the community to engage in more overt forms of struggle to have their voices heard and acknowledged by powerful groups, such as policy-makers and politicians.

Community education, also known as 'popular education' or 'informal education', aims to 'recognise and build the knowledge of a community by engaging community members as peer learners and teachers' (Healy, 2006, p. 259). Community education has been incorporated into community development activities in both developed and developing countries (Kane, 2010). The work of Paulo Freire, a literacy educator from Brazil, provides a theoretical and practical foundation for community education practice (Kane, 2010). Freire (1997) criticized traditional modes of education because, in his view, these rely on a 'banking' model, wherein the teacher deposits knowledge on the student. Instead, Freire (1997, p. 64) argues for a problem-posing approach that involves the development of critical understanding and encouraging community members to engage in social action based on that critical awareness:

> In problem-posing education people develop their power to perceive critically the way they exist in the world with which and in which they find themselves; they come to see the world not as a static reality, but as a reality in process, in transformation.

Because of its focus on building community members' capacity for social action, this approach is often linked to progressive forms of community development and community organizing (Kane, 2010).

Consensus versus Conflict Models

Alongside the typologies of community work, some commentators distinguish between consensus and conflict-based models of community work (Rothman, 2001). Consensus-based approaches involve enhancing the capacity of the community to meet identified social and economic needs. Proponents of consensus approaches seek to build partnerships across different groups and sectors within, and beyond, communities. Ohmer and DeMasi (2009, p. 13) assert that: 'Consensus organizers believe that power can be created, shared, and harnessed for the mutual benefit of communities and external power structures.'

The asset-based community development (ABCD) model incorporates many elements of a consensus-based approach to community development. A key principle of ABCD is that in order for change to be sustainable, it must be 'relationship-driven' (Kretzmann and McKnight, 1993, p. 3). At its core, ABCD promotes the development of cross-sectoral relationships within communities, such as relationships between local neighbourhood associations, schools and businesses (Mathie and Cunningham, 2003).

Conflict-based models proceed from the assumptions that society can be understood as divided between the privileged and marginalized, there is an inherent conflict between the interests of the more powerful (the haves) and those with less power (the have-nots), and that 'the powerful are unlikely to change their position unless intense pressure is applied' (Hoatson, 2003, p. 27). Essentially, conflict-based models emphasize differences in power and influence within communities and across society. Critical traditions place power and conflict at the centre of analysis and action, and, as such, are deeply critical of notions such as empowerment and partnership for failing to acknowledge the interests of the powerful and elites in maintaining the status quo. For example, when reflecting on the ideas underpinning the community organizing tradition, Bunyan (2008, p. 125) states that:

> in the contested arena of public action, the interests of the poor and those who lack power are best served when power is developed to the extent that the potential and possibility for conflict exists. Without the potential for conflict and the necessary tension this involves, existing power relations remain unchallenged and the possibilities of developing a more radical and transformative agenda remain dormant.

Proponents of conflict-based approaches seek to achieve broad social transformation in order to address the root causes of the oppression facing many disadvantaged or excluded communities.

Some types of community work can be categorized as either consensus or conflict based. For example, community service is usually consensus oriented, while community organizing tends to be conflict based. However, in community development and community education traditions, there is evidence of both consensus and conflict-based approaches. Rothman (2001) describes locality-based community development as a consensus mode of community work. On the other hand, radical and feminist community development models are aligned with the conflict tradition (see Dominelli, 2006; Stepney and Popple, 2008).

The History of Community Work in Social Work

The use of community work methods as part of a purposeful effort by concerned citizens to enhance the life opportunities for the most disadvantaged can be traced to the late 1800s (Fisher, 2005; Weil and Gamble, 2005). The settlement movement emerged during this period as an alternative to the individualistic helping ethos that dominated the emerging Charity Organization Societies in the USA in the 1870s (Fisher, 2005). The settlement movement has had an enduring influence on social work through the work of Jane Addams (1860–1935), who wrote about her experiences in establishing a settlement house known as 'Hull-House' in Chicago during this time (Addams, 1910). Members of the settlement house movement adopted a multidimensional approach to personal helping and community building as: 'Aiding individuals, building community, and changing society were all integral parts of the community organization practice pyramid' (Berry, cited in Fisher, 2005, p. 39). The influence of the settlement house movement in social welfare work generally, and on the emerging profession of social work in particular, declined in the postwar period, when psychological treatment methods gained an increasing hold on the profession.

In the postwar period, Rothman (2001, p. 91) observed that there was a remarkable 'growth spurt' worldwide in community development practice and in state support for this work. Several authors have observed that governments' renewed interest in community development activities was inspired, at least in part, by a concern with reducing the threat of social unrest in the context of increasing awareness of social and economic inequality within countries, such as between urban and rural areas, and internationally, between economically affluent and economically disadvantaged countries (see Midgley and Livermore, 2005; Rothman, 2001).

During the 1960s and 70s, a variety of radical approaches to community work emerged. According to Eriksson (2010, p. 10), the 'radical dimension' that grew in this period 'contained ideas about self-organization among the marginalized in society … There was an ambition to create a "better" society that can take a clearer stand on human rights etc.' These aspirations continue to influence community work, particularly community organizing, community development and community education approaches (see Bunyan, 2008; Tesoriero, 2010). Of course, the radical orientation was not entirely new and is seen by some as a reassertion of the overtly political approach of the settlement movement (Rothman, 2001). Yet, the re-emergence of this orientation was also possible because of political activism of the time. According to Midgley and Livermore (2005, p. 160): 'As community development became more radicalized, it was increasingly associated with wider progressive movements.' These movements include the informal education movement inspired by Paulo Friere (1997), the pacifist movement of Mahatma Gandhi, the radical activism of Saul Alinsky (1971) and feminism (Dominelli, 2006).

By the 1980s, in many 'advanced nations', community was increasingly recognized by the state as a legitimate mode of intervention. Indeed, in England, several major government reports, such as the Seebohm Report (1968) and the Barclay Report (1982), had emphasized the need for community-based, preventive and holistic forms of intervention (Stepney and Popple, 2008). Similarly, in many 'advanced nations' such as Australia, Canada and the Nordic countries, governments supported a range of community work interventions alongside individualistic approaches to service delivery (Hutchinson, 2009).

Since the 1990s, community development has been reshaped by the changing political context. Governments in many countries have supported community work initiatives, particularly those that build the capacities of disadvantaged communities to address social and economic exclusion. Community work is, in some respects, well integrated into the state-sponsored responses to disadvantaged communities. For example, the Sure Start programme in Britain fostered partnerships between local communities and service agencies to create a better start to life for vulnerable children and their families (Stepney and Popple, 2008). Yet the legitimization of community work practice has occurred as neoliberal ideologies adopted by the state have created a more constrained environment for all forms of social work and community work practice (McDonald, 2006). Community development workers now face increased pressure to demonstrate that their practice builds the capacities of communities and that these capacities produce social and financial benefits for governments and the broader community (Stepney and Popple, 2008). The more constrained political environment has reduced opportunities for community workers to engage in more overtly political advocacy such as campaigning.

While community workers seek to involve community members in building a better quality of life on their own terms, it is also important to recognize that this method can, like the other methods discussed in this book, have negative effects. Reflecting on the British context, Stepney and Popple (2008, p. 50) warn that the state's interest in community:

> is driven by a need for containment, management and surveillance of difficult and disruptive areas and their residents. The state's role to enhance the well-being of its people is based on the premise that the market should be protected and extended ... So community, which could be seen as offering a much needed identity and refuge from relentless economic growth, is also a site of friction and unhappiness.

Social workers involved in community work practice must critically reflect on the potential for community work practice to serve oppressive agendas such as facilitating the reduction of state support for vulnerable communities (Mowbray, 2005). Notwithstanding the challenges facing community workers today, community work continues to be regarded by many social workers as a key method or field of practice for breaking isolation, building the capacity to address social and economic challenges and transforming society (see Hutchinson, 2009; Stepney and Popple, 2008; Tesoriero, 2010).

Community Work and Social Work: Points of Commonality and Tension

Among professional social workers and community workers, there are different views about whether community work can be considered a method of social work practice. While in this book I write about community work practice as a method of professional social work, I acknowledge that community work can be seen as a method of social work and as a specialist field undertaken by a broad range of practitioners and thus not exclusive to social workers (for a discussion, see Rothman, 2001).

There are several reasons why social workers should recognize community work methods as integral to the discipline and the profession. First, the ecosystems perspective, a core framework for social work practice (Healy, 2005), highlights the importance of the community system in shaping service users' lives (Stepney and Popple, 2008). In addition, there is substantial research evidence to suggest that many of the problems facing service users have social, rather than individual, origins and therefore demand community responses (see Vinson, 2007). Furthermore, research evidence suggests that community work can help to create better health, educational and social inclusion outcomes for service users. As Twelvetrees (2008, p. 200) observes: 'Organised communities tend to be healthy communities, in every sense of the phrase … It is also clear that community workers help create organised communities.'

Yet despite social workers' extensive involvement in the development and practice of community work, tensions exist between the profession of social work and some within the field of community work about the recognition of community work as a social work method. Indeed, some question whether community work is compatible with an individualistic treatment approach that is said to dominate professional social work (see Reisch, 2005; Turunen, 2009). This tension between professional social work and community work has a historical foundation in that, during the 1960 and 70s, a radical movement emerged within the social work profession (see Bailey and Brake, 1975) and within the community work field. Within social work, radicals critiqued the profession's reliance on psychodynamic perspectives, which had dominated the profession for the preceding five decades, for failing to recognize or address the social injustices experienced by service users (Healy, 2005). At the same time, many within the radical community work tradition sought to distance themselves from professional social work on the basis that the psychodynamic frame, so dominant at the time, failed to address issues of social injustice and oppression (Mayo, 1975). Hence, from within the profession of social work and the community work field, some came to define community work as alternative to social work generally and psychodynamic modes of practice in particular. There are also clear tensions between a view of community work as a vocation, as advocated by some (see Westoby and Dowling, 2009), and the view of social work as a profession and an occupation (Fisher, 2005).

While these tensions around the view of community work as a method of social work and as a distinct field remain unresolved, claims that community work is incompatible with professional social work can be challenged on several grounds:

1. The treatment orientation of some forms of social work practice may complement community work practice.

2. Today, the social work profession cannot be defined as being only individualistically or psychodynamically oriented. While it is true that some social workers adopt an individualistic approach to their practice, it is inaccurate to present the profession as entirely or even primarily focused on interpersonal work. Social workers have extensive involvement in community work as researchers and practitioners (Stepney and Poppple, 2008) and community work methods are endorsed by the International Federation of Social Workers (IFSW, 2000) as part of the suite of methods used by practitioners.

3. The distinction between community work as a vocation and social work as an occupation or profession can be critiqued from several angles. Indeed, the distinction is questionable, given that, like social workers, many community workers also draw an income from the state for their work and are required to fulfil certain policy objectives determined, at least in part, by the state.

4. However, perhaps the most problematic aspect of the attempt to distinguish community work as a vocation is the gender equity issues raised by this position. Indeed, feminist writers in community work, and in community services more generally, have challenged the state's contin-

uing reliance on the unpaid, or underpaid, work of women in the community (Dominelli, 2006). To embrace poor (or no) financial remuneration or the lack of occupation recognition as a distinguishing feature of community work is unjust for women workers who constitute the majority of social and community work practitioners; it is also unsustainable for those who lack an alternative independent income source.

Community Work Skills

I turn now to a discussion of practical skills in community development practice. Social workers, particularly those working in nongovernment agencies, are often involved in community development to achieve goals such as breaking down isolation, creating opportunities for communities to articulate their shared strengths, needs and goals, and facilitating the participation of community members in shaping policies and practices that affect them. There is an enormous range of skills and techniques that community development workers use in their work and we are limited in the range we can offer here. Readers interested in community work practice to should consult the Further Reading at the end of this chapter. In this discussion, I outline how the four-phase model of social work practice, introduced in Chapter 1, of engagement, assessment, intervention and evaluation applies to community development practice. The skills we discuss are relevant to both consensus and conflict-based modes of community development.

Engaging the Community

The process of engaging communities differs from interpersonal forms of practice in several ways. Most significantly, the community worker must actively reach out to the community and must foster a voluntary and purposeful working relationship between themselves and the community. This outreach focus differs from interpersonal forms of social work (see Chapters 3 and 4), where the service user may seek out casework services or receive them as a part of a suite of health and welfare service or, as is the case in statutory social work, the service user is compelled to receive the services. The community worker may also take an active role in constructing a common identity among community members, that is, members of a locality or people with common interests may not perceive themselves as part of a community. Also, the worker needs to engage the community in ways that facilitate community participation in identifying needs and strengths as well as a capacity for action. Henderson and Thomas (2002, p.

145) assert that the community worker should 'resist temptations and pressures to take on a major leadership role which should be filled by a member of the group, despite the difficulties at times of doing so'. I separate the process of engaging with the community into two phases: preplanning and meeting the community.

Phase 1: preplanning

Preplanning is the phase of getting to know about the community as a precursor to meeting community members. In this phase, we build a knowledge base that can enhance our credibility in our initial meetings with community members and also help to ensure that you understand issues and subgroups within the community. There are two important dimensions to orienting ourselves to the community before meeting community members:

● Getting to know the features of the community. This involves investigating the past and current circumstances of the community.

● Getting to know the role of the community worker. The community worker needs to understand how their role has developed, and the expectations of employers, funding bodies and community members of the role.

There are several strategies the community worker can use to orient themselves to the community and their role, including:

● **Observation of the community**. We can observe features of the community including physical infrastructure, such as buildings, shops, and recreational facilities, social networks, such as the presence of subgroups and networks between them, service infrastructure, such as schools and health facilities, and socioeconomic differentials, such as the presence of pockets of affluence or disadvantage.

● **Meeting people who have a historical perspective on the community**. For example, if we are working with an identity- or association-based community, it can help to meet some people who have had a previous link to the community, such as in the formation of the community.

● **Reviewing agency documentation**, such as the minutes of committee meetings, annual reports, and other agency publications, such as the funding application for your position.

● **Media scan**. A media analysis can yield information about what issues are most significant to community members. This analysis can also reveal much about how the community is understood by stakeholders and outsiders.

Phase 2: meeting the community

This initial phase of meeting community members and developing a working relationship with them can be referred to as 'negotiating entry' to the community (Henderson and Thomas, 2002, p. 42). The worker aims to meet community members so that they can establish a working relationship based on the worker's understanding of the community's strengths, challenges and goals and the community's understanding of the worker's role as a community worker. This role involves facilitating community members' identification of, and participation in, community development activities aimed at improving the quality of life of community members (Twelvetrees, 2008).

A core goal of the negotiating phase is for the community worker to begin to establish purposeful relationships with a broad cross-section of the community, not only those groups with whom we have an immediate affinity or who are already engaged with our agency. There are several ways the community worker can meet community members for the purpose of initiating a working relationship with them and all these strategies involve active outreach to the community. One way of achieving this is by being present in places where community members congregate. For example, the neighbourhood worker might attend senior citizens' meetings, parents' support groups and the skatepark as a way of meeting up with community members. Second, the worker can distribute information about themselves and their role in the local media, institutions and websites used by the community. For example, a neighbourhood worker might provide a media release about themselves and their role for school newsletters and the local newspapers (see Healy and Mulholland, 2007, Ch. 7). The worker may also use agency and community websites and newsletters to distribute this information. The distribution of information through websites and newsletters can be used to complement other activities, such as the community worker attending face-to-face meetings with the community.

Initiating a formal meeting with the community is an important strategy for engaging the community, but it can be a difficult one. If the community has a strong sense of identity and good existing relationships with our agency, then an event to introduce the community work practitioner can be an effective way to begin a purposeful working relationship with the community. This strategy can be problematic where there is a weak sense of community or if there is hostility in the community. In these cases, it may be necessary initially to meet subgroups within the community in order to build their trust in our capacity to work constructively with them. Some community workers have also found it useful to hold low-key events such as picnics in open spaces as a way of engaging communities in a friendly and welcoming atmosphere (see Compass, 2002). There are several strategies a community worker can use to encourage engagement of community members in an initial meeting with them:

● Ensuring the meeting is in a neutral venue rather than in an area regarded as owned by a particular group in the community. For example, young people are unlikely to attend an event held in the senior citizens' hall.

● Providing food and refreshments as a way of demonstrating our goodwill to community members.

● Having a clear, but low-key focus on understanding members' views of their community and our role in the community. Our preplanning work in understanding the community is important here by showing that we have some insight into the history of, and current strengths and issues for, the community.

● Making sure that a broad cross-section of the community is aware of the event.

● Addressing support needs for community members to attend the meeting. For example, parents will be more likely to attend if childcare is available, while some people may require transport to the event. Ensuring these resources are available is a gesture of goodwill and, even more importantly, can support the involvement of people who would otherwise remain marginalized.

Community Assessment: Developing a Community Profile

The development of a community profile is a well-established technique for assessing community capacities and needs. Hawtin and Percy-Smith (2007, p. 5) define a community profile as:

> A comprehensive description of the *needs* of a population that is defined, or defines itself, as a *community*, and the *resources* that exist within that community, carried out with the *active involvement of the community* itself, for the purpose of developing an *action plan* or other means of improving the quality of life of the community itself.

In this definition, we see that the community profile is a representation of the needs, strengths and resources of the community and provides a foundation for community-building activity (see also Kretzmann and McKnight, 1993). The term 'needs' can refer to a range of deficits, such as personal, social, financial or physical capital, that prevent the community achieving a better quality of life. For example, low levels of social capital may contribute to isolation and fear among community members, while in other communities, the absence of financial resources, such as businesses, may limit employment or service options for community members. 'Resources' refer to those capacities or forms of capital that exist in the community and that contribute to improving the quality of life in the community. These resources can include human and social capital, such as schools and community associations, as well as businesses and physical infrastructure, such as buildings. In developing a profile, the community worker looks for resources currently in use but also currently underutilized resources, such as abandoned buildings or areas for social network development (Hawtin and Percy-Smith, 2007).

A community worker can use the community profile to achieve several goals, including:

- Building community through facilitating members' recognition of shared concerns and participation in building a response to those concerns.

- Advocacy with, and on behalf of, the community. The community profile can be used to advocate to policy-makers and funding bodies for an increased share of resources for the community.

- Helping the community to understand and prioritize collective action based on an understanding of strengths and needs.

A community profile should be comprehensive. This means that a broad range of needs and resources should be considered. Areas of assessment can include:

- **Human capital**, that is, the personal capacities and interests of community members

- **Social capital**, such as the social networks that members of the community have within and beyond their local community

- **Physical capital**, this includes physical infrastructure

- **Environmental capital**, particularly the natural environment of an area

- **Financial capital**, the participation of businesses in the area and the capacity of community members to access finances to engage in business activities

- **Political capital**, the active participation of community members in electoral politics and members' networks with elected MPs and representatives of political institutions.

Just as in interpersonal methods of social work practice, where the involvement of the individual in defining their own needs and strengths is an important dimension of the process, involving the community in developing their own profile is also an important dimension of community development practice. As Hawtin and Percy-Smith (2007, p. 8) emphasize:

> A profile that is undertaken with the full co-operation and involvement of the community is likely to result in a fuller, more comprehensive and accurate description of that community and, as such, form a better basis on which to build an action plan.

Citizen participation in developing a community profile contributes to a more accurate assessment but can also contribute to community engagement insofar as it builds trust among community members and between the worker and community members.

A range of information sources should be used to build the community profile (Hawtin and Percy-Smith, 2007) and, consistent with the community work principle of promoting citizen engagement, it is important that community members are also involved in knowledge development. In planning the community profile, the community worker should separate what data can be accessed from existing sources, such as national and local government statistical databases, and what should be accessed from the community. It is important not to waste time and effort in gathering data when accessible, high-quality information already exists.

Existing data sources relating to the community can provide an important foundation for building knowledge about the community. Information available from national population statistics related to a range of social indicators, such as housing, health, education, child protection and wellbeing, education and imprisonment, can help to create an understanding of how the community you are working with is faring compared to other communities. This information is vital for policy-makers and should form an important part of your community profile. A comparison of national and local data statistics can help build a picture of your community that is compelling to policy-makers, as well as highlighting to the community areas that may need action. For example, rates of certain health conditions (such as smoking-related respiratory conditions) and social indicators (such as rates of imprisonment) tend to be higher in disadvantaged communities. By creating a community profile, the community worker may facilitate the community to critically question why the rates of certain health and social indicators are different to other, more advantaged communities and this may lead to an action plan, such as a better health plan or a community prevention plan for young people at risk of imprisonment.

The types of statistics that are likely to be helpful in building a community profile include:

- National health and social statistics such as national census data and data on health, education and welfare needs. In all advanced nations, governments collect this data and much of this data is publicly available.

- Service statistics from relevant health, educational and social welfare agencies. Government departments collect data on the level of service provision and expenditure on services. This data may be available at national and regional level.

- Local government statistics on the range and extent of service delivery, local area population profiles, emerging health, educational and social trends.

- Specific information on disadvantage. Governments and some nongovernment special interest or advocacy groups collect data on indicators of disadvantage, which can include information about matters such as mortgage default rates, disconnection of power supply, and income levels, including the proportion of the population reliant on government benefits as a primary income source.

Some national and local government population and service data is available to the general public, for example annual reports of government agencies will report on levels of service provision and expenditure. However, some government data must be purchased either by libraries or your organization. Therefore it is important that you have access to a comprehensive library in order to examine a range of data sources. Librarians can help to guide you through the range of statistical data sources available to you.

Data collected with the community can also inform the profile. There are certain kinds of data that should be drawn directly from the community rather than relying on secondary information sources, including:

- Data about community members' perceptions of their needs, strengths and capacities

- Data about quality of life and service access for members of the community

- Qualitative information such as narratives of the lived experience of community members.

There are several ways of collecting this information:

- **Community surveys**, such as the capacity inventory, social audit or community survey

- **Observational research**, such as observing subgroups' use of different community resources, such as who is more likely to use libraries and recreational resources in the community

- **Focus groups** within specific groups in the community

- **Community forums**, such as public meetings.

The advantage of a community survey is that it allows you to gather a substantial amount of information from a cross-section of the community. Observational research allows the worker or researcher to gain information with, or about, practices or activities that community members are unaware of, or about which inaccurate perceptions exist. For example, some community members may have a perception that young people 'hang around the shopping mall all day and harass shoppers', but an observational study of the shopping mall may show that there are a small number of young people in the mall who are present at certain times of the day. Focus groups and public meetings provide excellent opportunities for community members to share their perceptions and lived experiences with community members.

The box below provides a brief example of questions that might be included in a community survey (adapted from Ohmer and DeMasi, 2009).

We would like to know about your views on the community you live in.

1. How long have you lived in the area?

2. Do you own or rent the home you live in? If other, please specify _____

3. What do you like about the area? What do think are the community's major strengths and/or assets?

4. What do you dislike about the area? What do you think are the community's major weaknesses or issues?

5. What local associations, if any, are you are member of?

6. How active are you in these associations?

7. Indicate on a scale of 1 to 5, with 1 strongly disagree and 5 strongly agree, the extent to which you agree or disagree with the following statement: In five years' time, I would like to still be living in this area.

1_____2_____3_____4_____5

Strongly   Strongly
disagree   agree

Please comment on the reasons for the rating you have provided here

_____

_____

8. Demographic questions (such as age or year of birth, individual and household income and source of income, number of people in household, number of children and young people in household)

The questions asked in this short example could generate information about respondents' perceptions of the strengths and the weaknesses of their community, level of community involvement, and their commitment to remaining within the community. When coupled with statistical information about the population characteristics, and the health, social and educational needs of the community, this information can help us to build a comprehensive picture of the community's capacities and challenges.

Community participation in data collection is important both because participation is a core principle of community development but also because one aim of a community profile is build a knowledge base for community action (Hawtin and Percy-Smith, 2007). The community can be involved in the design of data collection instruments (such as surveys, focus groups and forums), and in data collection and analysis. The community worker will need to be proactive in facilitating community involvement and may need to undertake activities such as facilitating meetings to design data collection instruments, offer, or facilitate the provision of, training in survey administration and data entry, and coordinate community involvement in reviewing data.

There are a variety of ways you can collect data, such as by mail, the internet, telephone or in person. Each data collection method has its strengths and weaknesses; extensive information on these is outlined in the community research and general social research literature (see Hawtin and Percy-Smith, 2007; Rubin and Babbie, 2007). For example, mail surveys tend to have low response rates, while internet and telephone surveys often miss those members of the community who do not have access to these technologies. In-person survey collection can be time-consuming but if the worker can involve the community in data collection, the process of conducting in-person survey interviews can be part of the community-building process. In deciding about modes of data collection, it is important that the worker seek opportunities for community involvement and participation, while using collection methods that best reach a cross-section of the community they seek to profile.

The following points are important to bear in mind when collecting data about your community:

● Be clear about the purpose of your data collection. Consider what your profile will be used for and ensure that the data collected will meet that purpose.

● Ensure that the data collected helps to empower the community by, for example, ensuring that information collected about needs is balanced with information collected about strengths.

● Ensure that community members have the opportunity to participate in the data collection process.

● Be sensitive to the time demands placed on community members who participate in building the community profile. Seek to balance community participation with choosing the least intrusive and most time efficient means of data collection and analysis.

● Provide a range of ways community members can contribute to the development of the profile. For example, providing different data collection formats, incorporating written, spoken and visual methods, can help to maximize the participation of community members who may vary in literacy skills, available time and personal preference in modes of participation.

● Demonstrate respect for participants' contribution to data collection by limiting demands on their time and by providing timely feedback from the data collection process.

Once the data is collected, it is necessary to analyse and present the information. The strategies for analysing data will depend on the data collected. Readers seeking detailed information on how to analyse quantitative and qualitative data collected in the process of building a community profile should consult the applied social science research literature and also detailed practical guides on developing community profiles and community inventories (see Hawtin and Percy-Smith, 2007; Kretzmann and McKnight, 1993). The use of simple data analysis methods ensures the relevance of the profile to a cross-section of community members and stakeholders; the profile is primarily a tool for community engagement, assessment and advocacy rather than an exercise in social science research. As Hawtin and Percy-Smith (2007, p. 107) assert:

Most community profiles can be produced using only frequencies and some cross-tabulations and perhaps some verbatim comments drawn from interviews or groups discussions and some well-chosen photographs. Analysing data if done manually need not be too daunting and can prove interesting and enlightening and, if done collectively, can be enjoyable.

In analysing community data, it is important to focus on the purpose of building a picture of the community that is easily understood by a range of stakeholders. Furthermore, the analysis process can yield new insights into the community and can also be a collaborative activity that, of itself, builds community. Here we will provide some brief points on data analysis for developing community profiles.

In the main, quantitative material will be analysed using descriptive and comparative approaches; while inferential analysis may be possible, the use of these techniques also risks alienating readers who do not have a grounding in statistics. The types of descriptive statistics that should be presented in a community profile include information on the overall size and characteristics of the community and its subgroups. For example, the profile may include:

- information on the proportion of citizens in different age subgroups, such as children and young people and/or those in the retirement age bracket
- indicators of socioeconomic status, particularly income levels and sources
- indicators of community stability, such as the proportion of homeowners and/or long-term residents of an area
- information on housing types, such as the proportions of public and private housing.

It can be useful to highlight community population characteristics that are different from those found in the broader society, such as a high proportion of young people, or higher burden of disease. It is especially important to highlight these differences if you are seeking to have an impact on policy-makers or politicians.

There are two forms of qualitative data analysis that are most relevant to community profiles. The first is thematic analysis, wherein the community worker incorporates themes from across the body of data. For example, we may identify themes in community members' perceptions of the strengths of their community. These themes may be represented in order of frequency with which they emerge from the data. The second form of qualitative data analysis is the identification and presentation of case studies. Case studies can help to illustrate concepts or themes that have emerged in the data analysis. For example, if respondents' talk about feeling welcomed into the area as a motivation for staying there, you may include a case study of one person's experience of arriving in the community. Case studies can be a powerful tool for illustrating to external stakeholders the experiences of community members.

Finally, we turn to the presentation the community profile. The profile must be presented in ways that will engage the audiences you seek to reach. One of the challenges is that these audiences may have different knowledge bases and interests; consider, for example, the different interests of policy-makers, who may want to know how the specific community you profile compares with other communities in their region or nation, and the interests of local community members, who may have an interest in action for improving local services and levels of community engagement. Given these differences, you may consider making the report available in a number of ways, for example in written forms as well as a spoken form, such as a presentation at a community forum.

In presenting the community profile, it is important to maximize its accessibility to a range of community members. Some strategies that can help include:

- **Use clear, simple, jargon-free language.** If you need to use acronyms or any other terms that might be specific to certain groups of stakeholders, such as policy-makers, consider including a glossary of terms in your report (Hawtin and Percy-Smith, 2007).

- **Provide a short executive summary** that highlights key messages.

- **Summarize the messages and findings** from the profile and include suggestions for next steps for different stakeholders, such as policy-makers, practitioners and community members.

- **Provide a clear and easy to follow structure**, for example including a table of contents and section headings.

- **Incorporate a mix of quantitative and qualitative material**, as a report based only on one form of data may alienate some of your audiences. For instance, a highly quantitative report may be perceived as 'dry' by community stakeholders, while a report focused only on qualitative data may be perceived as too local by policy-makers or politicians.

- **Make use of case studies** that demonstrate those elements of the community you are profiling. For example, if your profile is focused on areas of capacity and strength in the community, you might showcase case studies of these strengths and capacities.

- **Include visual images**, such as maps of the community or photographic images. However, ensure that you have the permission of community members to use any photographic images of them and their community and that they fully understand the implications, such as they will be publicly identified with their community possibly for years to come.

- If possible, **engage a professional graphic designer and printing service** to ensure that the final product is one that you, and the community you work with, can feel proud to use within the community and in advocating to other stakeholders, such as governments or private funding agencies.

Promoting Participation

Community developers aim to maximize community members' participation in building and achieving a plan for change. According to Twelvetrees (2008, p. 3): 'Community development workers operate as facilitators with people in relation to what those people decide to become involved with, helping them realize their collective goals.' This emphasis on facilitating community participation in change, rather than relying on experts, is a feature of all phases of community development practice from initial engagement through to intervention and evaluation. Here we will focus on strategies for facilitating participation in the intervention phase of community work.

Once the community profile has been developed, the next phase is to create an action plan with community members. There are at least two ways the community worker can maximize community members' participation in developing an action plan. The first is to facilitate a public meeting involving as many subgroups within the community as possible to develop an action plan. This strategy can be helpful for creating links between members of different subgroups within the community and to assist them to recognize their shared interests. A public forum of this nature demands considerable planning to promote community involvement in facilitating the meeting and in ensuring the facilitation methods are relevant to different subgroups within the community. This strategy is most likely to work when different subgroups in the community can readily identify shared concerns that go beyond their differences. For example, in some communities, social isolation due to poor public transportation and a stigmatized public image can provide a shared focus for action across subgroups within a community.

Another way the community worker can promote the involvement of a cross-section of the community is by facilitating action meetings with subgroups within the community. The advantage of this strategy is that the community worker can better match the facilitation process to specific subgroups. For example, the community worker may use a graffiti artist to facilitate the participation of young people in determining an action plan for the community, while using other techniques to involve older people. The disadvantage of this approach is that it can reinforce existing divisions within the community. Hence, if the community worker initially engages subgroups to develop a community action plan, consideration should be given to providing strategies for promoting collaboration between the subgroups.

While a public meeting is extensively used as a strategy for bringing the community together, this forum may seem unappealing to groups who perceive that they do not have voice within their community. Creative approaches to community meetings can help to engage a broad range of community members. Some creative approaches include:

- Holding an 'ideas festival' or 'think tank' in the community, where community members come together to share ideas rather than participate in a traditional meeting format

- Using community arts approaches to facilitate community involvement

- Facilitating field visits to other communities to observe strategies used in those communities for achieving change.

Creative approaches require community members to engage in new ways and with new mediums and this can disrupt established power relations within a community.

Community work practice manuals provide ideas for facilitating community members' involvement in developing a collective action plan (see Ohmer and DeMasi, 2009). The SWOT (strengths, weaknesses, opportunities and threats) analysis, frequently used in organizational reform, can also provide a framework for facilitating community members' participation in developing an action plan. This framework can used to enable community members to reflect on evidence of:

- **Strengths within the community:** for example, the community profile may reveal that many people in the community feel committed to staying in the area and are willing to participate in community-building activities

- **Weaknesses or challenges within the community:** for example, the community profile may reveal high levels of health issues or educational exclusion

- **Opportunities for the community:** for instance, the community profile might reveal business opportunities arising from high demand for specific services that are either nonexistent or not well developed in the local area

- **Threats for the community:** for instance, the community profile might show that the community is stigmatized as a result of media reporting.

An action plan is more likely to be a useful foundation for community work practice if:

- it is 'owned' by a broad cross-section of the community, rather than captured by specific interest groups
- all community members who have an interest in implementing the plan have a role to play in its realization
- it includes short- and long-term goals
- action goals are prioritized, so that community members feel challenged but not overwhelmed by the plan, and the goals that community members are most motivated to address are given priority.

Once an action plan is developed, the community worker seeks to facilitate community members' participation in the implementation of the plan. On some occasions, groups within the community may initiate action, and in other situations, the community worker may need to take an active role in bringing community members together. Regardless of whether action is initiated by community members or the worker, it is important again to ensure that a broad cross-section of the community are aware of, and encouraged to participate in, the action plan. This can be achieved by the use of a variety of formats for informing the community of activities, including word of mouth, web-based information, and the distribution of information through schools and other places where community members congregate, such as shopping centres and senior citizens' halls.

A lack of confidence or a perceived mismatch between the capacities of community members and the action plan can provide obstacles to community participation in the implementation of the plan. These barriers may be pronounced in communities where citizens experience exclusion, including exclusion from education and employment opportunities. The community worker should ensure that the community development process is one that builds confidence among community members to achieve their goals. For this reason, it can be helpful to start with relatively small, achievable goals. Ohmer and DeMasi (2009, p. 254) observe that: 'Competence breeds confidence. As small projects are completed, the resident group may begin to dream bigger.'

The community worker can facilitate training and education opportunities for community members to address a perceived mismatch between community capacities and action goals. For example, community members may identify that they lack the literacy skills needed to achieve community goals such as representing themselves in the media and to policy-makers. A community worker may involve a literacy educator and media expert in working with community members to build skills in identified areas of need. Consistent with community education principles, it is vital that education and training processes are respectful of the lived experience of community members and responsive to different learning styles among community members (Healy, 2006; Twelvetrees, 2008).

Finally, a lack of resources, such as access to childcare or transport, can also present a barrier to community members' participation in an action plan. Community members may be hesitant to raise resource issues because this may stigmatize them or they may not consider they are entitled to support or because they are frustrated that these self-evident needs have not been considered. While the community worker should consult with the community about the resources and supports they require to participate, the community worker should also consider the details of what would enable community members to participate. Other considerations for maximizing participation include the time and place of community activities. For example, some groups in the community, such as people in paid employment, may not be able to participate in community activities held in working hours, while parents may find it difficult to participate in meetings outside school hours.

Evaluating Community Work

Evaluation in community work involves a well-designed and systematic approach to inquire into, and draw conclusions about, the effectiveness and efficiency of community work practice in realizing identified processes, outcomes and outputs (Wadsworth, 2011). Evaluation needs to occur from the outset as well as at the end of intervention if it is to contribute to ongoing improvement of our work. Evaluation has become an increasingly important part of all social work practice, including community work activities, and there is a burgeoning literature on this topic (see Ohmer and DeMasi, 2009; Twelvetrees, 2008). In this section, we will briefly cover some key issues in evaluating community work.

In planning the evaluation, one needs to clarify what is being evaluated. This can be difficult because some of the objectives of community work practice such as increasing citizen participation or empowerment can seem large scale and thus difficult to assess. The evaluation may focus on process, outcome and/or output objectives. Process objectives refer to indicators of how community members are engaged in a project, such as the extent of citizen participation in determining project goals. Outcome objectives refer to the extent to which community work practice contributed to changes within individuals or the community, such as 'changes in knowledge, attitudes, and behaviours of the individuals' or 'economic, social, and/or physical changes in the targeted community' (Ohmer and DeMasi, 2009, p. 330). Output objectives refer to products arising from community work activities, such as tenant participation manuals, DVDs, and local community guides.

The next step in evaluation is operationalizing the objectives. This means identifying indicators of the objectives. Indicators are measures for assessing the extent to which the activities, such as community development work, help to achieve particular objectives. Ideally, a combination of quantitative and qualitative approaches should be used to assess our practice (Mitchell and Correa-Velez, 2010). The combination of quantitative and qualitative data can sharpen your understanding of the reasons behind the progress, or lack of progress, towards achieving community goals. For example, data about attendance numbers at groups and public events combined with qualitative feedback of participation or nonparticipation by community members can help us understand how to better engage community members in specific activities. Because evaluation should inform our practice as we proceed, it can also help to differentiate between short-, medium- and long-term indicators of progress. The time frames for what counts as short, medium or long term will vary according the nature of the community work in which you are involved. For example, in the context of a community work project as part of a four-month student field placement, short term might refer to a two-week period, medium term to the midway point of the placement and long term as the four-month point. The importance of defining and collecting data at different points in the practice implementation process is that this information can assist you to build on success, if the material demonstrates that you are on track towards meeting project objectives, or to redirect your practice if your evaluation data reveals problems in your progress towards objectives.

Table 7.1 includes possible indicators for process, outcome and output objectives in a community development project. I have included indicators for short-, medium- and long-term progress towards the achievement of community development goals.

Once we have clarified the 'what' of evaluation, we also need to identify who the evaluation is for. There are at least three audiences for community work evaluation: the funding agency; the agency employing the community worker; and community members. The funding agency may require a formal evaluation as a condition of funding and often provides a format for the evaluation. The employing agency may also seek evaluations to ensure ongoing improvement of the agency's work (Henderson and Thomas, 2002). Ohmer and DeMasi (2009, p. 321) assert that: 'Evaluation helps organizers and residents clarify and set more realistic and achievable goals. Successes can

Table 7.1   Indicators for process, outcome and output
objectives in a community development project

Objective	Examples of short-term indicators of progress	Examples of medium-term indicators of progress	Examples of long-term indicators of progress
Process objective: community members will participate in community-building projects.	Numbers of community members involved in working groups related to the action plan. Community members' expression of satisfaction with the process of developing an action plan.	Increase in numbers and range of community members observed participating in community projects. The majority of community members' surveyed express satisfaction with the community development process.	Evidence of sustained community involvement in projects, such as that at least 50% have been involved in community projects for more than three months.
Outcome objective: increased literacy skills among community members.	Working group formed with community members and literacy educator to plan community literacy programme. A baseline of current literacy levels has been established.	Literacy programme is established and attended by a specified minimum number of community members.	The majority of participants who complete the programme demonstrate increased literacy skills.
Output objective: community members will have accessible information about health and community services.	Establishment of working party of community members and other stakeholders, such as health and community services providers for the project. A baseline of current knowledge within community is established.	Community members and service providers continue to meet regularly to develop project.	A local health and community services manual has been produced by community members and has been distributed to relevant stakeholders.

be documented ... Setbacks can be caught earlier.' Consistent with the community work principle of participation, the evaluation should also involve community members. In addition, the involvement of community members can ensure that the evaluation itself contributes to building community members' understanding of the challenges and strengths of the community and to act on this knowledge. One way of involving community members in practice evaluation is through the establishment of a critical reference group. A critical reference group is a group comprising community members, particularly excluded or disadvantaged members of the community, who can assist in providing feedback and guidance from the perspective of their lived experiences as a community member (Wadsworth, 2011).

We turn next to how to evaluate community work practice. The complex environment of community work practice, where a variety of personal and community factors can impact on outcomes, creates a barrier to some forms of 'scientific' evaluation. For example, while the randomized control design is widely regarded as the 'gold standard' of evidence-based evaluation, there are ethical and methodological difficulties in separating control and intervention groups in community work practice. More naturalistic forms of inquiry are often used in community practice evaluation. In reflecting on evaluation in community practice contexts, Wadsworth (2011, p. 38) observes that:

> We set about finding out about the meanings that are real to people in the same way we do in ordinary life ... We 'engage' with life, becoming immersed in it on an 'up close and personal' basis, more like an empathetic anthropologist than a laboratory scientist looking down a microscope.

Naturalistic forms of evaluation involve the community worker in collecting information with, and about, community members and other stakeholders' perceptions of the processes, outcomes and outputs of community work activities. The collection of information about community members' experiences should not be limited to only those directly participating in the community work activities. Information from other stakeholders in the community indirectly impacted on by community work activities should be collected.

Evaluation data collection processes should be minimally intrusive and efficient. The purpose of community work, to assist community members to work together to achieve changes at the community level, should remain our focus. Evaluation should improve, not replace, our focus on direct community work practice. To reduce the intrusiveness of evaluation in direct practice, the community worker should make use of existing data as a source of evaluation information. Existing data can include agency records, such as records of community involvement in existing projects, and baseline data about service users' knowledge and skills.

Where it is necessary to gather evaluation data directly from community members, it is important to use data collection approaches that are appropriate to the community. In disadvantaged communities, some members may be reluctant to use written forms of data collection for a range of reasons, including low literacy levels or a preference for oral communication. For example, in some indigenous communities, the use of oral rather than written forms of communication may be preferred. Using a diverse range of data collection methods can help to maximize the participation of different groups in the community. Alternatives to written forms of evaluation data collection include:

- **observational data**, where the evaluator observes, in a systematic way, activities within the community for evidence of indicators of process or outcomes. For example, the evaluator may observe how community members contribute to leadership in community meetings.

- **group interviews**, such as focus groups or 'yarning circles' (a term used by some Aboriginal people), where an evaluator meets community members to evaluate the progress (or otherwise) of community work activity.

- **interviews with individuals**. While this can be time-consuming, it can be helpful when seeking to gain insights into a diversity of views and experiences of community members and other stakeholders.

The analysis of evaluation data is primarily focused on promoting understanding of what works, and what needs to change in order to achieve process, outcomes and output objectives. Using established social science research techniques can help to achieve a transparent and credible analysis. The analysis of quantitative data may include descriptive techniques, particularly the analysis of frequencies of indicators, and trends over time, such as evidence of increased involvement of community members in leading community groups. The qualitative data should be analysed thematically to draw out stakeholders' experiences and perceptions of the success, or otherwise, of community work practice for achieving identified processes, outcomes and outputs.

Consistent with the community work objective of building community members' capacity to act collectively on shared concerns, the community worker should facilitate community participation in interpreting and acting on evaluation findings (Wadsworth, 2011). This means that the evaluation must be presented in an accessible format, such as a short report with key messages clearly spelt out and readily available to the community. The community worker can further facilitate community involvement by meeting community members to discuss the evaluation outcomes and to consider how the findings may improve our ongoing work with the community.

Conclusion

In this chapter, we have discussed community work as a method of social work practice. While some social workers may choose to specialize in community work practice, it is important also that all social workers are aware of this method of practice. Community work practice has a great deal to offer social workers as way of working alongside people to foster the collective capacities of communities to build on their strengths and to address concerns facing them.

Review Questions

1. Why is it important for social workers to engage in community work practice?

2. What are the five types of community work practice defined in this chapter?

3. What are the differences between community work with identity-based and locality-based communities?

4. Why is it important to pay attention to community needs and strengths in building a community profile?

5. What strategies can social workers use to promote community members' participation in defining practice goals and evaluating community practice outcomes?

Critical Reflection Questions

1. What do you see as the similarities and differences between social work practice with individuals and with communities?

2. Compare and contrast consensus and conflict-based approaches to community work practice.

3. Considerable difference of opinion exists about whether community work should be considered a method of social work practice or an entirely distinct field of practice. What is your view on this longstanding debate?

Practice Exercise

Imagine you are working in a disadvantaged neighbourhood on the outskirts of a large city. The neighbourhood is characterized by high levels of unemployment, particularly among young people up to 25 years old. The proportion of people from culturally and linguistically diverse communities is higher than the national average, with many of those migrating to the area being refugees from war-torn parts of Africa and the Middle East. The crime rate is substantially above the national average, with older people in the neighbourhood reporting that they are afraid to go out in the evening.

Recently, a young man, a recently arrived refugee from Asia, was arrested for a violent robbery of an older person in the community. The older woman was hospitalized as a result of her injuries. Newspaper and television media have highlighted the case, with recent news items including pictures of the badly beaten older person in her hospital bed. These images have ignited tensions in the community, with groups of residents organizing around the issue. While some residents are organizing to seek a reduction in the number of refugees arriving in the community, others, such as leaders of the culturally and linguistically diverse communities, want to see better acceptance of young people from their communities in the neighbourhood. These leaders claim that young people from culturally and linguistically diverse backgrounds experience discrimination in local schools and are excluded from training and employment opportunities. The multicultural support worker in your agency has asked for your support in addressing the tensions in the community and in ensuring that the people from culturally and linguistically diverse communities are welcomed into the neighbourhood.

1. Identify the strengths and challenges facing the community as presented in this case study.

2. Discuss how you might facilitate the participation of community members in addressing the challenges facing this community.

Further Reading

● Alinsky, S. (1969) *Reveille for Radicals*. New York: Vintage Books.

● Alinksy, S. (1971) *Rules for Radicals*. New York: Random House.

These two books outline Alinsky's vision, theory and tactics for community-based activism. They were integral to the development of the community organizing tradition and, as such, are a must read for all those interested in understanding the history and diversity of approaches to community work and as a guide to the practice of community organizing.

● Freire, P. (1997) *Pedagogy of the Oppressed*. New York: Continuum.

In this classic work, Freire outlines the theory and practice of popular education. This approach has provided a foundation for popular education in a range of community work practice contexts globally. Is essential reading for all students and practitioners who plan to be involved in any form of community education whether within community work practice or other social work practice contexts.

● Hawtin, M. and Percy-Smith, J. (2007) *Community Profiling: A Practical Guide*. Maidenhead: Open University Press.

Provides a step-by-step guide to developing and presenting a community profile. Presents community profiling as part of community development activity and so emphasizes the importance of citizen participation in all elements of developing and presenting the profile. Is rich in practical tips for every step in developing a community profile.

● Henderson, P. and Thomas, D. (2002) *Skills in Neighbourhood Work*, 3rd edn. London: Routledge.

The first edition was published more than three decades ago, yet the book offers an enduring contribution to community development work in neighbourhoods. Offers a step-by-step guide to community work practice that is likely to be particularly valuable to the student and novice neighbourhood worker.

● Ohmer, M. and DeMasi, K. (2009) *Consensus Organizing: A Community Development Workbook*. Thousand Oaks, CA: Sage.

Offers a comprehensive guide to designing, implementing and evaluating community change initiatives, primarily within neighbourhoods. Includes numerous practice examples and exercises that could be used by community workers to train community members in community-building skills.

● Twelvetrees, A. (2008) *Community Work*, 4th edn. Basingstoke: Palgrave Macmillan.

Now in its fourth edition, this classic text on community work provides an accessible overview of the history and types of community work practice. Offers a broad range of practice examples that are useful for the beginning practitioner to understand how they can deploy community work strategies, whether working as a social worker or in a specialist community work role. Includes information of foundational and advanced community work practice and, as such, is relevant to a broad range of community work audiences.

8

Policy Practice

In this chapter, I consider social workers' roles in shaping and implementing social policy with and for service users and communities. I adopt Chapin's (2007, p. 1) definition of social policies as the 'laws, rules, and regulations that govern the benefits and services provided by governmental and private organizations to assist people in meeting their needs'. Government and health and welfare services organizations develop and use social policies to assist them in making decisions about how to ration limited resources in the context of unlimited needs and competing views about how those needs are to be met (Chapin, 2007). While social policies affect all members of the population, in social work practice we are often involved with policies shaping the scope and nature of resources available to vulnerable populations, such as children in need of out-of-home care, people with chronic mental and physical health challenges and disabilities (Rocha, 2007). Social workers have an important role to play ensuring that social policies are responsive to the needs of the service users and communities with whom they work and in promoting opportunities for these citizens to participate in the policy process.

In this chapter, I define policy practice as a method of social work practice and I discuss why all social workers need to actively engage with policy practice. I outline six phases of the policy process in which social workers may be involved with, and on behalf of, service users and other citizens. I discuss how social workers can bring the humanist values underpinning our practice to bear on policy work and, in particular, to facilitate citizen involvement in social policy processes.

Policy Practice: What it is and Why it Matters

Policy practice refers to practice involving the design, implementation, evaluation or reform of policies through which governments or health and welfare service organizations govern the provision of benefits and services to people (Chapin, 2007; Rocha, 2007). Social workers need to be actively involved in policy practice because social policies determine the scope of our practice and the benefits and services available to service users (Fawcett et al., 2010; see also Chapin, 2007). Jansson (2008, p. 104) asserts that: 'Policy advocacy is, in short, a *professional* intervention because, like direct service work, it is geared to improving the well-being of citizens and clients.'

The term 'policy' refers to 'a formally adopted statement that reflects goals and strategies or agreements on a settled course of action' (Netting et al., 2008, p. 331). Some examples of policy include a statement by government about how public housing resources are to be rationed to meet the housing needs in the community or a statement by a nongovernment community service agency on its approach to working with vulnerable families. Policies help to clarify the objectives of government and organizations, eligibility for services or resources (such as financial aid), and principles for decision-making in the rationing of resources. While a range of government and organizational policies impact on service users' access to services and other resources (Weiss et al., 2006), such as education and employment, in this chapter we focus primarily on policy practice in relation to social policies. Fawcett et al. (2010) identify that social policy is associated with the governance of three types of resources:

- **Cash benefits:** such as pensions and other income supplements (known as direct payments) or cash rebates through the taxation system (known as indirect payments). Health and welfare service agencies can also be involved in the provision of cash benefits, such as short-term financial aid. Of course, policies related to cash benefits vary considerably among nations.

- **Services:** such as the provision of family and individual support services. Governments and health and welfare services seek to achieve many of their social policy objectives through the delivery of services. Consequently, social policies often involve statements about the nature and scope of the service to be provided and principles of eligibility to receive services. For example, a young parents' support service is likely to have age-related eligibility criteria for receipt of services. These criteria help to ensure that the services are targeted to those for whom they are intended.

- **Regulations:** the 'implementation of rules governing what organizations and individuals can and cannot do' (Fawcett et al., 2010, p. 9). A wide variety of regulations shape the scope of the work undertaken by the agencies where social workers practice. Social workers may, for example, be bound by statutory law or other regulations to report on certain concerns, such as child abuse or public health (see Chapter 4). Other regulations shaping our practice include occupational health and safety and anti-discrimination legislation. As practitioners, we also need to be aware of the regulations shaping the practice of the sectors with which our work intersects. For example, we may need knowledge of housing, tenancy or employment regulations to ensure that the service users and community members with whom we work are being treated justly under these regulations.

The increasing influence of managerialism on government institutions in many countries has contributed to a separation between state agencies that create social policies and other sectors, such as for-profit and non-profit, that play a larger role in implementing them (Healy, 2009; McDonald, 2006). This distance means that those formally responsible for designing policy may have limited knowledge of the lived experience of people on the receiving end of policy interventions, or of the complexities of service delivery or community development activities with the vulnerable communities and individuals to whom social policies are often directed (Mullaly, 1997). In this context, the participation of social workers and the people they work with can enhance the responsiveness of social policy to the needs and interests of service users.

The social policies of the organizations where we are employed shape our work by influencing how the resources of our employing organization, including the external funding received by them, will be allocated to benefits and service provision. The social policies of health and welfare services are shaped by government social policies, as government funders will require that prescribed policy objectives and legal obligations are met by the organization. The social policies of health and welfare service organizations are also influenced by local factors, particularly the agency's mission, the institutional philosophy, and the extent to which the agency has mechanisms for service providers and service users to participate in the formation of social policies. Social workers' opportunities to directly influence the policies of the health and welfare service organization vary according to the size of the organization, with direct participation more difficult in large, hierarchical organizations, and the extent to which mechanisms exist within organizations for service provider and service user participation in policy design, implementation and evaluation. Even in the absence of such mechanisms, social workers can still influence policies within their organizational environment through building a base of knowledge about the relative effectiveness of the organization's social policies for achieving service delivery objectives (Jansson, 2008).

Over to you ...

Consider a group of service users or community who you have an interest in working with or with whom you have some experience, for example children in out-of-home care or people with intellectual disabilities.

1. What do you see as the social policies impacting on this group of service users or their community?

2. In what ways do existing social policies have a positive influence on these people's lives?

3. In what ways do these policies have a negative influence on these people's lives? For example, are service users or the community systematically excluded from access to the services or other resources they require as a result of these policies?

Social Workers and Policy Practice

All social workers are involved with social policy processes. Some social workers specialize in policy practice as their core method of practice, and are sometimes referred to as 'policy experts' (Wyers, cited in Rocha, 2007, p. 2). Social workers who are policy experts may work in a wide variety of policy practice roles, such as policy-makers working in government bureaucracies designing, implementing and evaluating social policies. Just like the other methods we have considered throughout this book, involvement in policy practice methods is not unique to social workers. Indeed, social workers often work alongside policy workers from a range of other disciplinary backgrounds, such as politics, management and law.

While only some social workers may work as policy experts, most social workers are involved in policy practice by virtue of their employment in publicly funded health and welfare service agencies. These agencies are accountable to government funding bodies, as well as to their own organizational social policies, for the achievement of defined social policy objectives. For example, a community-based mental health service may be required, as a condition of its funding, to demonstrate how its service approach assists government to achieve policy objectives, such as reducing inpatient admissions among people living with mental illness. In this chapter, we are concerned with the foundations of policy work for all social workers, not only those who are, or seek to become, policy experts.

Social workers need to be informed and active users of social policy because these policies shape the parameters of what we do as social workers and the entitlements of those with whom we work (Chapin, 2007). Social workers' theoretical base, particularly our emphasis on improving the interaction between people and their environment, requires that we incorporate social policy methods into our work (Jansson, 2008; Netting et al., 2008). Similarly, from a social justice value position, it is imperative that we understand social policies in order to ensure that service users gain access to their entitlements under government and organizational policies (Netting et al., 2008). For example, when working with a young family that is vulnerable to homelessness, we will need knowledge of a range of social policies including income support policies and housing policies that shape the young family's entitlements under government legislation and policy. To assist the young family, we may also need to know the policies of the service agencies relevant to them, for example we need to understand which agencies provide emergency accommodation and their policies regarding the allocation of accommodation.

One way social workers shape social policy is through interpretation of, and decision-making about, social and organizational policies. Lipsky (1980) coined the phrase 'street-level bureaucrat' to highlight that social workers', and other frontline workers', use of discretion in the interpretation of policy objectives has profound effects on the recognition of service user needs, rights and entitlements. As street-level bureaucrats, social workers 'make a significant difference to who gets services and why, and what services they get and how' (Fawcett et al., 2010, p. 124). For example, in a study of family group meetings (FGM) in child protection services in Queensland, Australia, we found considerable variation in the extent to which individual family group convenors interpreted families' rights to inclusion in decision-making under Queensland child protection legislation (Healy et al., 2011). Using the principles of family group conferences established in New Zealand, some FGM convenors sought to achieve the policy objective of family inclusion by meeting family members on several occasions before the meeting to explain the decision-making process, to prepare families to participate in the decision-making process, and to consider how absent family members, such as young children, would be represented at the meeting. Other convenors interpreted the legislation and policy regarding family inclusion more minimally to focus on ensuring that the parents were aware of and, where possible, present at the meeting, with little, if any emphasis, on engaging with the family prior to the meeting. Although social workers, like other frontline health and welfare service workers, exercise discretion that shapes the delivery of social policy objectives, we also acknowledge that the influence of managerialism on social service agencies has constrained decision-making opportunities at the front line (Walton, 2005).

Another way social workers shape policy is through active participation in 'efforts to change policies in legislative, agency, and community settings, whether by establishing new policies, improving existing ones, or defeating the policy initiatives of other people' (Jansson, 2008, p. 14). Social workers engage in policy reform to assist relatively powerless people to achieve better recognition of and response to their needs by governments and service organizations (Jansson, 2008). Social workers' involvement in policy change work is complicated by their multiple roles in the service systems that impact on service users' lives. In particular, as discussed in Chapter 4, social workers are necessarily involved in the provision of statutory services, which is experienced as oppressive by some groups of service users. Yet social workers have participated alongside service users, community members and other stakeholders to achieve recognition of and response to a range of social concerns by governments and service agencies, such as the needs of parents whose children are in out-of-home care (Dumbrill, 2010), women who have survived domestic violence (Danis and Lockhart, 2003) and people who experience chronic mental health challenges (Carpenter, 2002).

Engaging in Social Policy Debates: A Policy Dilemma Exercise

I have suggested that all social workers are involved with social policies. Often these social policies raise ethical issues as we may experience tensions between the humanist values that underpin social work and the values influencing policy development and implementation. One of the most obvious tensions is that of the dissonance between neoliberal economic values that have influenced government policy, such as an emphasis on open markets and competition, and the values of social justice and fairness that lead many social workers to challenge the ascendancy of neoliberal values (Healy, 2005; McDonald, 2006). Sometimes the tensions between social work values and social policies can be more subtle and contested. For example, the achievement of the goal of child protection may involve the containment of the self-determination of some service users, such as parents, over others, such as vulnerable children. In the imperfect world of social work practice and policy-making, we may have to compromise aspects of one value, such as access to services, to another value, such as self-determination. As we participate in the policy process, it is important that we are able to think strategically about the short and longer term implications of a policy position for the achievement of our policy objectives. I have chosen the next example from a situation I was involved in when working at a support service for homeless people. The example concerns a debate that emerged within the service about a proposal from a local business to provide food to clients of our service in exchange for our service's willingness to recognize them as a donor. The proposal raised many ethical challenges about the dignity of service users and the value of collaboration with business and other sectors. As you read through the example, consider what values you think are important in this case and what policy position you would propose the organization adopt in response to the issue.

Over to you ...

Imagine you work at a youth service that provides support to vulnerable young people. Many of the young people are homeless or in substandard accommodation, most are on low incomes and few have family support. The local bakery has offered to provide your service with bakery goods that are no longer sellable, such as bread and buns that were baked two or three days previously. The baker states that the goods are edible but that his customers prefer goods baked on the same day. The bakery describes his proposal to provide the older goods to your service as 'giving back' to disadvantaged young people. The owner of the bakery has also asked if he could advertise that his business supports your agency, if your agency agrees to accept the bakery goods. Your manager has presented this proposal to your staff meeting. Your manager states that she has spoken with the young people who use the service and they are keen to go ahead with the proposal. You are also aware that the manager is under pressure as part of her funding contract to demonstrate that the youth service is forming partnerships with local business agencies.

Discuss the ethical dilemmas arising from the manager's proposal to accept the bakery's offer to provide non-saleable bakery goods to young people using the service.

As I said, the above practice example was drawn from a real example where considerable debate ensued about whether or not the service should accept the offer of support. Those in favour of the proposal argued that many young people using the service often went hungry and that, although the food being offered was not of high quality, it was comparable or better than the young person would access. They also emphasized the value of partnerships with the local business community. Those against the proposal argued that it compromised the human dignity of the young people accessing the service and that we should only accept offers of support that were consistent with the mission of the service to achieve social justice and enhance recognition of the human dignity of the service user. Those arguing against the proposal also claimed that the partnership with the business was not sustainable because it was based on a view of the young people as objects of charity rather than as valued citizens. The proposal was defeated.

Community Participation in Policy Processes

Citizen participation in policy process involves more than their representation by policy experts. Rocha (2007, p. 33) defines participation as 'the deliberate involvement of the people for whom we advocate in the decision-making of the goals and strategies chosen for the policy intervention'. The participation of citizens in policy practice reaches beyond consultation on their views on a predefined problem to involving them in defining the problem in their terms, developing alternatives to existing policy responses, and evaluating policies that affect them.

In many fields of government service provision, it is increasingly recognized that citizens have a right to have a say in the development and evaluation of policies. Indeed, in some fields of policy, governments may be obliged to consult with citizens and specific stakeholder groups about how the proposed policies will affect them (Althaus et al., 2007). Aside from the legal obligations government may bear for consulting with citizens, involving citizens in policy-making is likely to have many practical benefits. Policy practice is more likely to be effective with community involvement and support because such involvement will lead to more relevant policy proposals and participants will gain ownership of the policy process. There are numerous examples of policy failure arising from policy-makers paying inadequate attention to the involvement of service users in policy formation and thus failing to learn from service users about the potential practical obstacles to the achievement of policy objectives (Chapin, 2007).

Service user participation is also consistent with social workers' values of promoting 'human dignity and worth; service to humanity; and social justice' (Banks, 2006, p. 47). We recognize human dignity and worth by ensuring that service users and community members have a say over the policies that so profoundly shape their lives. We promote social justice when we work to ensure that policies facilitate the access of marginalized groups to the resources they need to participate in society, such as improved access to education and training. The theoretical perspectives guiding social work practice in most cases emphasize collaboration between social workers and service users or community members. A strengths-based approach requires us to recognize the strengths and capacities of service users and community members represented by, and involved in, the policy process (Chapin, 2007). A critical approach means being sensitive to issues of power differences at every phase of the policy-making process. Together, critical and strengths-based perspectives involve recognizing service users' needs arising from disadvantage or exclusion as evidence not of individual failure but of the need for change in the systems impacting on service users' lives (Chapin, 2007). These perspectives also require that we recognize and build the capacities of service users in creating change in the systems that shape their opportunities.

Social workers involved in policy practice need to be mindful of the challenges involving service users and community members in the policy process. One of the challenges is that community members and service users may feel alienated from policy processes. They may view policy-making as the domain of policy experts and removed from the everyday struggles they face as service users. In addition, service users may lack access to the specialist knowledge and skills that may be needed to participate in policy processes. For example, terminology that is widely used in policy processes may need to be explained to people who do not have formal experience of policy processes. A further challenge may be that governments and health and welfare service agencies may, in fact, be ambivalent about whether certain groups of service users have a right to have a say in policy processes. For example, governments may be ambivalent about recognizing parents in child protection service systems as participants in policy-making because parents may be seen, in part, as perpetrators of abuse and neglect rather than as partners in policy-making (Dumbrill, 2010).

To overcome these challenges, we need to ensure that our approach to policy practice is democratic, inclusive and builds the capacities of community members to participate in policy processes (Rocha, 2007). As we consider the skills involved in each phase of the policy process, I will consider how we, as social workers, can involve service users in these processes.

Phases of the Policy Process

In many social policy texts, there is reference to distinct phases of policy processes or the 'policy cycle' (see Althaus et al., 2007; Fawcett et al., 2010; Jansson, 2008). While there is variation in the terminology used, these typologies of the policy process usually refer to a temporal element to policy work by distinguishing between the beginning, middle and end phases of the policy process. It is widely acknowledged that the reference to policy phases or policy cycles is a heuristic device used to make sense of the range of knowledge and skills needed at different points in what is often a nonlinear process (Fawcett et al., 2010). In other words, policy processes are often complex and messy but in order to explain these processes, we need to refer to distinct phases; the reader must understand that, in practice, these phases may not proceed in a distinct or linear order. I now discuss the skills that practitioners need to participate and facilitate the participation of others in the six phases of the policy process.

Figure 8.1 outlines the phases of the policy process considered in the remainder of the chapter. The focus is on the phases of the policy process that you, as a frontline or professional social work practitioner, and service users or communities are likely to have the opportunity to participate in. Policy experts, that is, workers who specialize in policy practice, are likely to be involved in a larger range of policy activities, such as the coordination of stakeholder submissions and synthesis of these submissions and other expert advice in order to advise political leaders (Althaus et al., 2007; Rocha, 2007).

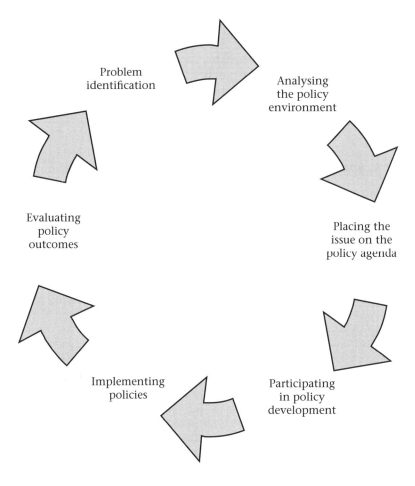

Figure 8.1 Phases of social workers' involvement in policy practice

While all social workers participate in policy processes by virtue of their role in implementing policy, it is not always possible for social workers to participate overtly in policy development and policy change (Chapin, 2007). For example, some workers may be compelled by the conditions of their employment not to directly participate in policy activities that might invite external public scrutiny of their organization or the funding body. Even if you cannot directly participate in the policy process, understanding the phases of the policy process where the input of social workers and service users may be most influential can help you to work collaboratively with those in your organization or in the health and welfare services sector who have formal responsibilities for policy work. For instance, you may work with the policy expert in your agency or within a policy advocacy network to involve service users in preparing a public comment submission for a forthcoming community consultation process. As an illustration, when working as a social worker with a support service for young homeless parents, I introduced the young parents to a policy advocacy worker who then drew on the parents' life experiences to advocate for improvement in the provision of affordable housing for vulnerable young families.

Over to you ...

The rest of this chapter outlines the objectives of each phase of the policy process and the skills that social workers need to participate in these phases. I will use a practical example of a social worker seeking to improve access to mental health services for service users from culturally and linguistically diverse backgrounds.

As we go through the policy phases, I want you to imagine you are a social worker working in a nongovernment agency that supports people from culturally and linguistically diverse backgrounds who settle into your local community. The majority of individuals and families accessing your service are from diverse cultural groups in Asia and Africa, with a small proportion from the Middle East. About half the service users are refugees, with many of them traumatized either by events in their own country or their experiences in refugee camps while they waited for resettlement.

Caseworkers at your service offer supportive case management and groupwork programmes for service users experiencing trauma and grief arising from their experiences in their home country or in the resettlement process. However, the frontline social workers describe feeling ill-equipped to respond to the psychological trauma experienced by the majority of refugees who come to the service. They also report great difficulty in gaining access to specialist mental health services for two main reasons. The first is the lack of access to affordable mental health specialists, with waiting times of several months for publicly funded mental health services and, second, the lack of interpreter services to assist service users in seeking appropriate treatment and support. Hence, even when the individual or family has access to a service, they may require an interpreter to accompany them to the service in order to express the individual or family need.

Before we turn to considering each phase of the policy process, note your answers to the following questions:

1. Why would it be important for social workers to engage in policy practice in this situation?

2. What are the challenges you might face in engaging in policy practice with, and on behalf of, this population if you were a social worker with this group?

Phase 1: Problem Identification

The first step of the policy practice is to identify the problems facing service users or citizens as a concern for policy-makers. In this phase, we are seeking to examine the extent to which the 'personal' issue facing service users can be considered a public concern. According to Chapin (2007, p. 120), in order to make the case that the problem warrants a policy rather than a case-based response, 'it is usually necessary to convince at least a sizeable segment of the public that a problem or need exists that warrants intervention'. Many problems we encounter in practice that have gained recognition as social policy issues were once considered primarily private problems, for example domestic violence, child abuse in the family and abuse in institutional care. By naming the problem and collecting information on it, we start to make the problem visible as a policy concern.

In this phase, we need to provide policy-makers with information about the scope of the problem, specifically the number of people who are affected, if they are to be persuaded of the need for policy change. An issue that affects only a small proportion of the population seen by an agency might be better dealt with on a case-by-case basis or through the use of professional discretion rather than by policy change. We also need to identify the characteristics of the people affected by a problem. Governments and organizational decision-makers are likely to be persuaded of the need for policy change if it can be demonstrated that certain population groups are systematically excluded from or disadvantaged by existing policies. In such instances, problem identification can centre on the discriminatory or nonresponsive nature of existing policy to specific groups. For example, referring to our case example, we might argue that people from culturally and linguistically diverse backgrounds are systematically excluded from mental health service provision where these services do not also incorporate interpreter services.

Once we have identified the scope of the problem, we need to identify how citizens, or, more specifically, recipients of the service provided by the government authority or service agency, are affected by the problem. Here, we, and those with whom we collaborate, may identify and elaborate on the direct and indirect ways that existing policies negatively affect service users' lives generally and the achievement of service outcomes. For example, referring to our case study, we might argue that a lack of access to these services for this specific group of citizens is associated with higher rates of serious mental health-related incidents of self-harm and suicide.

If service users and other stakeholders are to develop ownership of the policy solution, it is important they are involved in the problem identification phase (Chapin, 2007). There are several ways social workers can facilitate service user participation in the problem identification phase. One approach is to invite service users with a lived experience of the policy problem to participate in a project reference group that can advise on data collection sources and interpretation of information gathered in the process. The reference group can draw on their lived experiences to help the worker interpret findings and to formulate the policy problem (see Wadsworth, 2011). Another way is use participatory action research processes to involve service users in each phase of data collection, analysis and action (Kindon et al., 2007; Wadsworth, 2011). A third option is for the social worker to initiate opportunities for community feedback through, for example, community forums and community surveys at different points of the policy process. The advantages of this option are that it is less demanding of individual community members' time and levels of commitment and also allows for a larger group of community members to participate in problem identification. The disadvantage is that the social worker remains central to facilitating community members' involvement in the policy process and thus may reduce community members' sense of ownership of the policy outcomes.

There are several sources to which we can turn to gain information about the population affected by a specific policy concern and the nature of the impact of the problem on citizens' lives. It is important that in defining the scope and nature of the policy problem, we draw on sources that are widely recognized as credible and, preferably, sources recognized by the audience we seek to influence. Credible sources of population data can include:

● Population census figures

● Government reports, such as annual reports, which may include information about the number of people served or seeking a government-funded service

● Reports from health and welfare service agencies.

Administrative reports, such as annual reports, from government and health and welfare service agencies may reveal information about the number of people served by the agencies, outcomes of service provision and estimates of unmet need.

In identifying and defining the policy problem, we also need to articulate how people are affected by a problem and the factors in the social environment that exacerbate specific kinds of problems service users' experience (Jansson, 2008). For example, we may argue that people who have experienced traumatic events, such as living in a refugee camp, are at increased risk for complex mental health conditions and that these conditions substantially interfere with their ability to adapt to a new country of residence. Understanding how people are affected by a policy issue can assist in bringing the issue to life for policy-makers. There are several types of information (or data) that we can draw on to understand the impact of a policy issue:

- **Analysis of agency records:** we could undertake an analysis of agency data to analyse how some service users' lack of access to culturally and linguistically appropriate mental health services is associated with difficulties in adapting to, and participating in, the community where they now reside.

- **Case studies:** we may involve people with experience of the problem in identifying how this policy problem has had practical effects upon their lives.

- **Participatory action research:** we could involve service users in analysing their own and other service users' experiences of the policy problem.

Turning to our practice example, in identifying the policy problem, you could collect and analyse information about:

- The number of asylum seekers and refugees in our country and within the region where our service is based

- The characteristics of these people, including the range of languages they speak

- Government and service records, such as the types of mental health challenges they face

- Their experiences of seeking service provision and the challenges they have experienced as a result of delayed or inappropriate services.

Phase 2: Analysing the Policy Environment

Our objective in this phase is to analyse previous and current policies in relation to the identified issues. This information is vital for avoiding repetition of past policy failures and for building credible policy alternatives based on an understanding of what works and on partnerships with individuals and groups seeking similar policy change (Rocha, 2007).

Our social work values are central to our analysis of the policy environment, just as these values are core to our approach to any other method of social work practice. Drawing on the strengths perspective, Chapin (2007, p. 133) suggests that we begin our analysis by focusing on the structural barriers that prevent service users and communities from meeting their needs, and that our approach should 'reflect the basic social work values of self-determination and social justice'. Because social work is a values-based profession, it is important that we are able to articulate the values that guide us in our analysis of the policy environment.

Our analysis of the policy environment is intended to inform action. Our analysis must then be grounded in knowledge of past and current policies with the objective of informing further policy development. Questions that can assist our analysis of the policy environment include:

● How are the existing policy approaches contributing to, or failing to adequately address, the problem?

● What past policy responses existed in relation to this issue and why were they superseded?

● Who is also currently working on this issue?

● What are the costs of failure to address the issue and the potential cost savings of alternative policy approaches?

● What are the likely points of resistance to, and support for, change?

I turn now to consider how we might use these questions to guide us in practice.

As social work practitioners, we will often have some insight into the policy environment shaping a particular concern because we have had direct experience of negotiating that environment with service users. In our practice as social workers, we often become aware of how existing social policies at the government or organizational level exacerbate the problems and challenges facing service users or at least fail to address these problems. Often the problem may not be in the intention of the policy but in the failure of policy-makers to adequately consider these issues in the implementation process. Hence, some policies may, in practice, have negative and unintended consequences or simply fail to achieve outcomes for service user groups (Rocha, 2007). For example, in relation to our case study, we may be aware that although certain groups of asylum seekers and refugees qualify for access to mental health services, government funding for interpreter services may be so limited as to prevent the group using the available services.

In analysing the policy environment, we need to consider the policies directed at the problem and also policies that may indirectly shape the achievement of policy objectives. In relation to our practice example, the policies that will directly influence the policy problem are those concerning the availability and appropriateness of mental health policies to people from culturally and linguistically diverse backgrounds, particularly those who are refugees and asylum seekers. These policies may include statements about eligibility for mental health services and the scope of mental health service provision. Policies that may indirectly shape the policy problem of asylum seeker access to mental health services include those regarding interpreter services, public transport and, of course, the processing of asylum seeker and refugee applications that may exacerbate the stresses facing people experiencing the policy problem.

In developing credible policy alternatives, we also need to demonstrate an understanding of previous policy solutions so that any new policy proposals build on previous policy successes and avoid perceived failures of the past (Rocha, 2007). At a minimum, our review of policy should be cognizant of major policy shifts in relation to the policy problem over several decades and should demonstrate a more detailed understanding of policy responses in the past decade. For example, in relation to the provision of mental health services, one would review the shift away from institutionalized services to community-based services, and how governments responded (or failed to respond) to the mental health needs of earlier waves of asylum seekers and refugees and the outcomes of these policies, such as the longer positive and adverse consequences of these policies.

Analysis of the cost of existing policy approaches and relative cost savings that can be achieved through alternative approaches can be a powerful way of convincing policy-makers and organizational leaders of the need for policy change. As social workers, we should highlight the social as well as the economic costs of existing policy approaches that we seek to challenge. Moreover, we may need to draw attention to the short- and long-term costs of existing policy approaches. For example, we may argue that short-term cost-cutting measures can be shown to increase longer term costs for vulnerable populations or the general population who, as taxpayers, fund a range of health and welfare services. Turning to our practice example, the social costs of failing to provide adequate mental health service responses to asylum seekers and refugees with complex mental health needs arising from traumatic experiences may include unnecessary and prolonged distress to these people and their families. The economic costs may include the need for more expensive inpatient psychiatric treatment for this population who are at increased risk of complex post-traumatic stress disorders should the government fail to address this policy problem in a timely and appropriate way.

Phase 3: Placing the Issue on the Policy Agenda

Once we have identified the policy problem, we may then need to convince formal policy-makers to recognize the problem as a policy problem that requires either a government or organizational response. I use the term 'placing the issue on the policy agenda' to refer to the phase in which we focus on gaining government or organizational recognition that an issue requires a policy response. Sometimes this phase may be skipped if there is already recognition of the concern and well-developed mechanisms exist for policy-makers to consult with communities on the issue. In seeking to place an issue on the policy agency, we need to identify the government departments and health and welfare service organizations responsible for the policy, or field of policy, of your concern. There may be several departments or agencies involved. We are more likely to be successful in achieving policy change if we can identify one agency on which we will concentrate our change efforts and that department (or organization) should be the one with greatest responsibility for the issue of concern.

Making contact with policy-makers within these formal sites of policy formation is often the first step towards placing an issue on the policy agenda. Ideally, we seek to work collaboratively with policy-makers to achieve recognition of our policy concerns and to work together to achieve policy changes that benefit service users. As Jansson (2008, p. 94) observes:

> policy practitioners need to use persuasive and coalition-building competencies ... they need to convince others that an issue is relevant to their beliefs, that important political threats or opportunities exist, or that credible people take an interest in the issue.

In my experience, creating opportunities for policy-makers to meet service users and other citizens directly affected by a policy concern can be a powerful strategy for convincing policy-makers of the existence and importance of a policy concern.

We may encounter several barriers from policy-makers to their recognition of the issue we have identified as a policy concern. One barrier may be that the government or health and welfare service organization may not recognize the problem as a policy problem but as an individual or private matter not requiring policy attention. To convince policy-makers otherwise, we need to show how the problem affects a substantial segment of the population for whom the policy-makers are responsible and that existing policy responses are inadequate for addressing the specific concern (Chapin, 2007). For example, we might show that a larger proportion of asylum seekers face certain kinds of mental health problems, due to greater exposure to experiences of torture and trauma, than the rest of the population and that current policy responses do not achieve humane and effective responses to their needs.

Policy-makers may also argue that the identified problem is outside the scope of the responsibilities of the government department or their organization. Hence, in identifying the policy problem, we need to demonstrate how this problem is relevant, even central, to the concerns of the government or organization to which you refer. For example, we may need to demonstrate why mental health policy-makers should develop policies in relation to a population, such as asylum seekers, who they may see as the responsibility of other government agencies, such as agencies responsible for immigration.

Even where it is agreed that a policy problem exists, policy-makers may regard it as a low priority compared to other policy issues. Again, in formulating the policy problem, we need to show why the problem demands attention of the government or the health and welfare service organization. The data we collected in phases 1 and 2 can be vital to encouraging policy-makers to recognize the problem and act on this information. Jansson (2008, p. 93) observes that: 'When current data point to a problem's severity and trend data track the problem over time, decision makers are likely to believe that it demands immediate attention.' In short, the data we present should highlight to policy-makers the costs of failing to act on the policy issue. Timing can also be crucial to encouraging recognition and action on a concern. For example, if our organization is seeking increased government funding to address a particular concern, such as increased funding for interpreter services, we might build a campaign about this issue several months before government annual budgets are announced, rather than in the period immediately after these announcements. We also need to be ready to seize opportunities created by events in the public domain (Jansson, 2008). For example, media coverage of a sudden spike in mental health hospital admissions may provide an opportunity to bring our campaign for better mental health policies for asylum seekers and refugees to the government's attention.

In circumstances where we encounter continued resistance to recognition of the policy concerns we have identified, it may be necessary to place external pressure on policy-makers. This may involve presenting our policy issue directly to politicians in the case of government agencies or to the boards of directors in nongovernment services. In some instances, we may involve the media, through, for example, letter writing campaigns, publication of opinion pieces by experts who are sympathetic to our policy position, or by encouraging journalists to write articles highlighting the policy concern. There are several guides to involving citizens in public campaigns generally and working with the media in particular, and these should be consulted before involving the media in policy campaigns (see Bensley and Brookins-Fisher, 2009). Although little is yet written on the topic, social media is fast becoming an important site for communicating with your community, social campaigning and for raising community concerns in the public domain.

Phase 4: Participating in Policy Development

Once policy-makers and policy leaders are convinced there is a social issue that needs to be addressed by policy, they may then initiate a public consultation process. In some contexts, policy-makers may invite participation in the policy process, for example through a formal consultation process. In other situations, policy-makers may choose to develop policy without formal consultation. In either case, it is important for social workers to work alongside the service users and communities with whom they work to facilitate their participation in the policy process (Chapin, 2007). In this section, we will focus our attention on how to participate, and to facilitate the participation of others, in a formal public consultation process (also referred to as community consultations).

Public consultations can be conducted in person, such as where government representatives meet citizens to discuss the policy concerns, and also through written submissions, such as calls for public comment or community opinion submissions, or citizen surveys. Governments and other agencies may use a variety of modes to distribute information about public consultation activities and these are likely to include advertisements in newspapers, information on government or agency websites about consultation opportunities, and, more rarely, through mailouts to citizens most likely to be affected by a policy proposal. As social workers seeking to engage in policy-making activities, it is important that we identify how government and other agencies in our field of service activity disseminate information about community consultation activities. It is also important to identify the range of departments and other agencies whose policies may affect the citizens with whom are concerned. For example, if you are working with homeless families, it is likely that a range of government departments, such as housing, child protection, employment and income security, all impact on these clients, so it is important that you are aware of opportunities to participate in policy development in these fields. Some state or national governments have registers with information about forthcoming community consultations, such as online community consultation registries. It may also be possible to register with government agencies or community advocacy associations for email alerts about forthcoming consultation activities.

Over to you ...

Thinking of our practice example, where we are concerned about ensuring that government policy achieves fair outcomes in the delivery of mental health services to people from culturally and linguistically diverse backgrounds, particularly those who are refugees and asylum seekers, consider how you could ensure that you, and the community you are working with, were aware of public consultations being conducted that might affect this group of citizens. Make a list of the health and social policy fields relevant to the mental health needs of people from culturally and linguistically diverse communities generally, and refugee and asylum seeker communities in particular. Conduct an online search to see what, if any, consultations were recently or are currently being undertaken by governments or other service agencies that might be relevant to your group.

Preparation is vital for effective participation in public consultation activities whether these are public meetings or written submissions. Our preparation involves understanding the scope of the consultation. This includes understanding the 'terms of reference' (TOR) for the consultation, which refers to the matters to be considered and the proposed outcomes of the consultation. We enhance the likelihood of our concerns being acknowledged and solutions fostered, if we can demonstrate how they are relevant to the TOR of the consultation. Using our example of addressing the mental health needs of asylum seekers from culturally and linguistically diverse communities, we may also encourage this group to participate in community consultations in other social policy fields such as public and community housing policy by showing how the resource of public and community housing has implications for the mental health of asylum seekers. In addition to accessing the TOR, we should also familiarize ourselves with any policy documents or position papers presented by the organization responsible for the consultation. These documents are likely to reveal the organization's history of involvement with the policy concern and its areas of priority. Again, understanding how those conducting the consultation see the policy problem can help us to communicate our concerns more effectively with them.

Our preparation should also involve attention to the resources we seek and our rationale for claiming these resources. As Chapin (2007, p. 131) observes: 'Even if policy makers agree that a need exists, they may not necessarily agree that the need deserves to be met ... a compelling claim for resources must be made.' These are several grounds on which we can advance our policy proposal as preferable to existing or competing approaches. These grounds include:

- **A value-based argument:** We may refer to the liberal humanist values guiding social work as a framework for our argument (Jansson, 2008). For example, we may argue that existing social policies are unfair because they place some groups at a comparative disadvantage in accessing the same services or resources available to others within the broader population. Values-based arguments are most likely to hold weight when they appeal to a shared value base with the government or organizational agency to whom we are addressing our claim for policy change.

- **Cost–benefit arguments:** We may also refer to the comparative costs and benefits of existing policies and our proposed alternatives. Governments and health and welfare service organizations face considerable pressure to demonstrate efficient use of public resources and so we are likely to enhance interest in our proposal if we can demonstrate the social and economic costs of existing policies and the reduced costs and enhanced benefits of alternative solutions (Chapin, 2007). For example, in advocating for improved early intervention mental health services with asylum seekers, we may show how these services promote improved mental health and reduce longer term human suffering and the use of costly inpatient services.

- **Rights and obligation-based arguments:** We may argue for our policy proposals by demonstrating how these proposals enable governments or health and welfare service organizations to better meet their obligations, such as obligations under existing law or to international conventions to which they are a signatory. For example, we might highlight how an early intervention approach to mental health service provision with asylum seekers is consistent with the state's obligations to refugees in accordance with United Nations 1951 Convention Relating to the Status of Refugees (UNHCR, 1951).

As mentioned, public meetings are one forum in which you, as a social worker, and the citizens with whom you practise may participate in the policy process. Public meetings refer to a meeting where all citizens are invited to engage in a dialogue about an issue of public concern. While public meetings can be large, with hundreds of attendees for meetings about issues that affect the population generally, the numbers of citizens attending locality-based community consultations addressing specific health or welfare issues tends to be smaller. For example, a national government consultation on changes to transport infrastructure is likely to attract a much larger number of attendees than a community consultation meeting conducted in a local government area about the mental health needs of vulnerable community members. Rocha (2007) suggests that in preparation for public meetings, one should aim to:

- maximize attendance of citizens who share your concerns about the policy issue
- find out who will be present, such as politicians and policy-makers and address your argument to them
- identify the key points you and your group of constituents want to see covered and make sure that you express these points in ways that are relevant to the scope of the consultation
- find out how long you and those with whom you are collaborating have to state your case
- make sure that you have your speeches or talking points planned beforehand.

In a public consultation process, you may have the opportunity to submit a written comment. The advantage of submitting a written public comment is that you are likely to have the opportunity to present the evidence for your claims and policy alternatives in more detail than is usually possible in a public meeting. One of the disadvantages is that your submission may be one among many (possibly thousands) and so it is important that you maximize your chances of making an impact in the context of many other views competing for policy-makers' attention (Chapin, 2007). I have written about public comment submissions elsewhere (see Healy and Mulholland, 2007) and here I will just briefly review the key points in making an impact in written public comment submissions. For our written public comment submission to make an impact on policy-makers and to maximize the chances of your ideas, and those of the community with whom you are working, being included in development process, we should be:

- **engaging:** When advocating with and for citizens, we should seek to capture the hearts and minds of our audience, who are the policy-makers. We should ensure that our submission conveys the lived experiences of citizens who directly encounter the policy issue. Whereas policy experts may seek to adopt an emotionally neutral tone, as frontline workers we have a right, and perhaps also a responsibility, to highlight the human dimensions of the problem being faced by a particular community with whom we are working.

- **cognizant of our audience:** Our audience will be policy-makers and just like any other form of effective writing, we should show that we understand their frame of reference, particularly the policy challenge they are seeking to resolve (Jansson, 2008, Ch. 8). A level of balance here, where we acknowledge the possible benefits or successes of existing policy approaches while also advocating for change, may assist the audience to be more receptive to your message.

- **credible:** This means that we should incorporate factual information from recognized data sources, such as national statistical bureaus. Furthermore, our argument should be logical and supported by relevant examples. These examples may include anecdotal evidence from the lived experience of citizens with direct experience of the policy problem. Of course, these citizens must at the very least give permission for their experiences to be conveyed in this context, and, where possible, citizens should be involved in conveying their experience.

- **succinct:** Given that policy-makers may be reviewing many submissions, it can help to ensure that you remain focused on the core policy concerns and convey your argument as succinctly as possible.

● **feasible:** We enhance our chances of our proposal being incorporated into policy-making if we can show how our policy recommendations enable policy-makers to achieve their policy goals in ways that are at least as efficient and effective as existing policy approaches. It is vital that the proposals are feasible in terms of the time and cost parameters outlined in the government or health and welfare service organization's consultation documents. For example, if the government states that it is seeking to implement new and innovative approaches to mental health provision in the next one to three years, our recommendations should be consistent with this time frame.

Phase 5: Implementing Policies

Once the consultation process is complete, a government or an organization may then decide on policy goals and objectives. They may then seek the assistance of the service agencies and communities in achieving these goals and objectives. Social workers have an important role to play in policy implementation through, for example, designing practice-based projects that integrate policy objectives with service user and community members' preferences for service provision or community-building activities. In this phase, we, as service providers, may have the opportunity to participate in policy implementation by applying for programme funding under new policy initiatives.

There are a variety of ways in which social workers may participate in implementing policy goals. Social workers may be directed by their agency or their funder to work towards the achievement of policy goals by changing the way they, the social workers, do their work. For example, an agency may be required to ensure that their service is accessible and responsive to people from culturally and linguistically diverse backgrounds. Directives to achieve policy goals often entail changes in the way services are delivered or how community development processes are engaged in. At the front line of service delivery, social workers will have varying degrees of discretion in how they respond to directives from their employers or funders to reorient their services towards the achievement of new policy goals. Nonetheless, by gathering evidence about the impact of policy shifts on our direct service activities, we increase our chances of having a base from which to influence managers and policy-makers.

Another way governments implement policy goals is by directing funding towards the achievement of those goals. In this process, governments may offer nongovernment (for-profit and not-for-profit) agencies and, in some instances, service delivery agencies within the government the opportunity to apply for funding that is tied to the achievement of policy goals and objectives. If governments want to strictly define how policy objectives will be implemented, they may offer 'contracts' to service agencies to provide services within well-defined terms (Coley and Scheinberg, 2008). By contrast, if governments want to provide direct service agencies with the opportunity to create more flexible and locally relevant approaches to achieving a policy goal, they may instead offer 'grants' (Coley and Scheinberg, 2008). The difference between a contract and a grant is that in the contract, the service provider agency will be compelled not only to seek to achieve prescribed policy goals but to do so in a way that is strictly defined by the funder, while the recipient of a grant, who will also be required to work towards the achievement of prescribed policy goals, will have the opportunity for flexibility in how these services are achieved (Coley and Scheinberg, 2008; Healy and Mulholland, 2007).

There is a vast literature on the strategies and skills involved in writing funding applications, which you should consult if you have the opportunity to apply for funding contracts and grants (Coley and Scheinberg, 2008; Healy and Mulholland, 2007; Jansson, 2008). In brief, though, you increase your chances of attracting funding or other resources for your proposal if you:

- **present an appropriate and effective response/solution to the policy problem:** one that is also consistent with the proposed policy direction.

- **have a feasible project and project plan:** Rocha (2007, p. 19) suggests that we should 'choose interventions that have the least costs and the most potential benefits'. We should also demonstrate that our project has clear objectives and a realistic plan for realizing those objectives (Jansson, 2008).

- **have an innovative approach:** governments and health and welfare service organizations will be aware of the strengths and limitations of existing programmes and may be willing to try new ways of addressing a problem, particularly if the innovation addresses the weaknesses of existing responses to a policy concern.

- **have an inclusive proposal:** given that many social policy problems are linked to social marginalization, governments and health and welfare service organizations are likely to prefer proposals that will actively promote the inclusion of community members. Indeed, in some contexts, governments or other funding bodies will require that proposals for services are inclusive of particular populations that might otherwise be excluded from service or community development activities.

● **show that your organization is well placed to achieve agreed policy objectives:** for example, in our policy example, we might emphasize that our organization has a well-established history of service delivery and/or strong connections to the community or population to whom the policy is addressed.

Frontline social work practitioners play in an important role in shaping how policy objectives are achieved in practice. As social workers in direct practice, we often need to engage in a constructive dialogue with government about how policy objectives are to be achieved within local communities so as to ensure that our services are responsive to local conditions and government policy objectives. Evaluation of the outcomes of existing and previous initiatives for achieving policy goals is helpful to ensuring that emerging policies are consistent with the available evidence about what works in achieving social policy outcomes.

Phase 6: Evaluating Policy Outcomes

As part of the policy cycle, governments and health and welfare service organizations may seek to evaluate social policy outcomes. Indeed, they may be required by law to evaluate policy outcomes or they may face immense public pressure to demonstrate the effectiveness or efficiency of policy outcomes. Evaluations of policy help to inform policy-makers about the extent to which existing policies are achieving the desired goals and objectives. A range of data may be used to inform policy evaluations including rigorous empirical studies, informal observations and service administrative data from the services and populations affected by the policies (Jansson, 2008).

Social workers have an important role to play in ensuring that the experiences and perspectives of service users and community members, as well as the experiences of frontline service providers, are included in policy evaluation. This role is important because governments and health and welfare service organizations may emphasize administrative goals, such as the demonstration of financial efficiency. Both sets of goals, those of policy-makers and clients (and community members), need to be considered. Furthermore, unless client and other community members' experiences and perspectives are incorporated into policy evaluation, we run the risk of contributing to policies that are unresponsive, or irrelevant, to service users and community members. Understanding what policies work from a service user and community member perspective places us in a stronger position to advocate to policy-makers for the retention and development of effective policies.

Chapin (2007) observes that is important to think about ways of involving clients' and community members' perspectives early in the policy enactment process if these stakeholders' views are to be meaningfully included in the evaluation of policy. There are several ways of incorporating clients' and community members' views in evaluating policy.

First, it is helpful to gain agreement between policy-makers and clients and other community members about the outcomes they would like to achieve from the social policies impacting on them (Chapin, 2007). For example, the government may have the goal of reducing costs associated with inpatient psychiatric care, while clients may want to see community-based early intervention. Together, policy-makers and clients may agree on the goals of reduced rates of inpatient treatment and increased voluntary use of community-based mental health services.

Second, the social worker should work with, and on behalf of, community members to develop meaningful measures for the achievement of policy goals. As Chapin (2007, p. 169) observes: 'it is important to think about outcome measures that include client goals as well as policy makers' goals'. For example, for people living with mental illness, an important outcome of community-based early intervention services might focus on improvements in quality of life generally, not only specific mental health concerns, while government policy-makers may want evidence of the cost-effectiveness of new policy interventions. Hence, it may be important to include quality of life measures, such as measures of increased social connection, as well as financial cost–benefit indicators. Measures taken at the outset of policy implementation, referred to as 'baseline measures', can be important for measuring the extent interventions are associated with the achievement of agreed policy goals (Chapin, 2007, p. 170). Indeed, from an ethical perspective, it is important that we continually monitor whether the intervention in which we are involved is assisting those with whom we work to achieve agreed goals as, in some instances, monitoring may reveal that interventions are ineffective or, worse still, contribute to a deterioration in the service user or community member's circumstances. Through monitoring these effects, we can improve our practice and also reduce the chances that our interventions may cause harm.

Third, service users and community members should have the opportunity to participate in the evaluation of policies and programmes. At a minimum, service users and community members affected by a policy should have opportunities to comment directly on those policies. Better still, social workers can incorporate strategies for more actively involving service users and community members in evaluating policy from the outset of policy implementation. Seeking the active involvement of service users and community members over the period of policy implementation is likely to yield more relevant and useful feedback on policy than selecting a single point in time at which to conduct an evaluation. This is because service users and community members will have the opportunity to reflect on what has worked, and what has not, at different phases of the policy process.

Several evaluation researchers in the social policy field have outlined the value of participatory action research strategies for involving service users and community members in the evaluation of policy and other forms of direct health and welfare service intervention (Kindon et al., 2007; Wadsworth, 2011). Drawing on participatory action research principles, Wadsworth (2011) advocates that evaluators foster the development of a 'critical reference group' to ensure that their evaluation incorporates the views of service users and marginalized community members. The critical reference group comprises the relatively powerless members who are the subject of a policy intervention but whose voices might not otherwise be heard in a formal evaluation process. So, for example, if we were to conduct an evaluation of a policy intervention aimed at improving community-based mental health services to asylum seekers and refugees, we would involve people from this community to participate in a critical reference group. The critical reference group is like a steering committee that often guides evaluations, except that the critical reference group uses their lived experience of the policy concern, rather professional expertise, as the basis for advising the evaluator. Like a steering committee, the number of people participating in a critical reference group needs to be limited to a number that can meaningfully contribute to regular group discussions of an issue. The group also needs to commit to meeting several times over the course of an evaluation to inform the evaluator. There are advantages to involving those directly affected by a policy problem in an active way in the evaluation, including that it enhances the relevance of evaluation outcomes to the lived experience of those to whom the policy is directed, and it can alert policy-makers to hidden problems in policy implementation and in so doing improve the effectiveness of policies (Wadsworth, 2011).

Conclusion

In this chapter I have defined policy practice and discussed its importance to professional social work practice. Although only some social workers become policy experts, that is, practitioners who specialize in policy work, all social workers are involved in policy processes. I have outlined six phases of the policy process in which direct practice social workers, service users and other community members may be involved with social policy processes. At a minimum, social workers are involved in the implementation of policy. However, we can also contribute to the improvement of policies by involving service users and community members in identifying policy issues, shaping strategies for policy implementation, and evaluating policy outcomes. Social policies profoundly shape our practice as social workers, not only by determining what resources are available to those with whom we work but also by shaping what is regarded by governments and health and welfare service organizations as the legitimate scope of direct social work practice.

Review Questions

1. What does the term 'street-level bureaucrat' mean?

2. What are the six phases of the policy process outlined in this chapter?

3. What strategies might you use to increase your chances of attracting funding or other resources for your policy proposal?

Critical Reflection Questions

1. The influential ecosystems perspective requires that social workers seek to enhance the interactions between the individuals and the institutions shaping service users' lives. To what extent do you consider social workers' involvement in policy work essential to improving the interaction between service users and the institutions with which we practise?

2. What do you see as the benefits and challenges of involving service users in all phases of the policy process?

Further Reading

● Chapin, R. (2007) *Social Policy for Effective Practice: A Strengths Approach*. Boston: McGraw-Hill.

Engaging introduction to social policy work as a method of social work practice. Outlines the history and rationale for social workers' involvement in policy work as a complement to other methods of intervention. Demonstrates how social workers can apply strengths-based principles in policy practice. Numerous examples are presented to show how social workers in frontline practice can participate in policy work.

- Jansson, B. (2008) *Becoming an Effective Policy Advocate: From Policy Practice to Social Justice*, 4th edn. Belmont: Thomson Higher Education.

  Outlines the history of social workers' involvement in policy work, starting with the work of social work pioneer, Jane Addams. Detailed introduction to strategies for effective policy work at all phases of the policy process. Case studies from student and practitioner policy work help to illuminate how social workers integrate policy work into their professional practice. Detailed guide to policy work; useful for social workers who seek to become policy specialists as well as those who aim to incorporate policy methods into their professional social work practice.

- Rocha, C.J. (2007) *Essentials of Social Work Policy Practice*. Hoboken, NJ: John Wiley & Sons.

  Practical guide to influencing social policy in the public sector and within the organizations where social workers practise. Makes clear links between social work values and theory, and explains how social work values can influence policy. Provides helpful insights into maximizing service user and citizen involvement in policy processes.

9

Conclusion: Creating a Context for Change

In this book I have provided an introduction to the history, current debates and skills pertaining to a diverse range of social work practice methods. In this final chapter, I outline the key messages about social work methods and skills underpinning this book and I discuss strategies for creating change in the organizational contexts of social work practice.

Throughout this book, the diversity of social work practice methods has been emphasized. Social workers are diverse in their theoretical outlook, context of practice and methods of practice deployed. The range of practice methods is a source of tension within the profession, as commentators debate the relevance of various theoretical and methodological approaches to practice (see Gray and Webb, 2009; Healy, 2005). Yet the diversity of theoretical and methodological bases is also a rich resource for practitioners, service users and community members. A comprehensive methodological base enables social workers to respond flexibly and creatively to the challenges facing service users and community members. Of course, social workers are not always in a position to deploy the broad range of practice methods outlined in this book as, for example, our organizational context of practice and formal occupational role may require that we focus on certain methods and limit our involvement in others. Nonetheless, as social workers with a solid foundation in the uses and limitations of diverse practice methods, we can refer service users to services that deploy methods that best meet their specific practice needs. For example, a statutory social worker working with a young person in trouble with the law may focus their work on dealing with the legal issues facing the young person, while referring the young person and their family to a family therapist to address the conflict that may be contributing to the young person's antisocial behaviour. Similarly, a hospital social worker can assist an older person address issues of social isolation by referring them to community support services that deploy group and community methods to facilitate the development of new skills and social networks. A key message of this book is that diverse social work methods can complement each other

231

and enable us to achieve better outcomes for service users and communities than is possible with single method approaches.

While the profession's methodological diversity is a strength, it is also a source of vulnerability because we lack exclusive ownership of the methods we use. Practitioners from a variety of fields use elements of interpersonal work, family work, groupwork, community work and policy skills. The lack of exclusive ownership of these methods has contributed to debates about the level of specialist expertise that social workers can be said to have in any of them. For example, the breadth of our methodological base has contributed to debates about whether all social workers are qualified to provide counselling (Seden, 1999) or child protection services (Healy and Meagher, 2007), and whether interpersonal forms of social work are compatible with community work practice (Reisch, 2005). These debates are well established and may deepen as managerial reforms lead to increasing pressure on professions to demonstrate specific domains of practice competency (Healy, 2009). Our capacity to maintain the methodological diversity of social work practice will depend, in part, on social workers' ability to articulate and justify this diversity to stakeholders, such as employers, funding bodies, service users and the communities with whom we work.

In this book, some common themes have underpinned the discussion of the range of social work practice methods. One theme is the importance of social workers working collaboratively with service users and community members. Across all the methods of practice, social workers should seek to facilitate service users' and community members' involvement in defining the nature of the challenges facing them, identifying the strengths and capacities they bring to resolving those challenges, and working alongside them to create change. We need to reject the position of the professional expert who 'knows better' than the service user or the community, although we should acknowledge our expertise in practice methods to facilitate change with individuals, families, groups and communities. The theme of working alongside service users is a practical expression of the professional value of respect. This value is important because we recognize that we are working with fellow human beings, rather than objects of professional intervention. There is also substantial evidence to show that service users, both in and beyond social work services, are more likely to participate in and benefit from intervention plans they have participated in developing (Reid and Epstein, 1972; Trotter, 2006). This is because such plans are likely to be more relevant to service users' lives and because the service user or community member 'owns' the plan.

A second theme underpinning this book is the importance of evaluating our practice. Building knowledge about what works and what can be improved in our practice helps us to continuously improve the quality of our work (Trotter, 2004). As we have considered each method of practice, we have also discussed how to evaluate our practice in relation to these methods. Evaluating our practice is our professional responsibility, essential to ensuring that we provide the best practice possible in the context of our practice. It is also important for the survival of professional social work as under conditions of managerialism, social workers are increasingly required to demonstrate practice effectiveness and efficiency.

Our professional responsibility to critically reflect on our practice is a third theme that unites the diverse practice methods discussed in this book. A critical reflection approach recognizes that we transform formal knowledge and build new knowledge in our practice (Fook and Gardiner, 2007). Critical reflection helps us to articulate our learning about ourselves and our practice and, as such, can complement other forms of knowledge building in practice, such as formal evaluation and research evidence. One of the reasons critical reflection is important is that social work is a contextually variable activity. Even where research evidence is available about our practice methods, our use of these methods will vary with different service user groups and in varying institutional contexts of practice. These local variations mean that we cannot be passive users of knowledge but must actively construct knowledge in practice.

Recognition of cultural diversity in social work practice is a fourth theme that underpins the communication skills and methods of practice considered in this book. Cultural diversity involves being informed about, and respectful of, the cultural differences that influence every dimension of social work practice when we are working with people from cultures other than our own. For example, we need to be sensitive to different communication practices if we are to create an effective working relationship with culturally diverse individuals and communities (see Chapter 2). We also need to resist making assumptions and sweeping generalizations about people from cultures and linguistic groups other than our own. We can improve our capacity for culturally responsive practice by being alert to the communication practices of the people with whom we are working and by consulting with members of culturally and linguistically diverse communities.

To recognize the diversity of methods is not to argue against specialization within the profession. The complexity of practice in many fields, such as mental health, health services, child protection and prison services, demands a depth of knowledge that can be difficult to achieve without some level of specialization in fields of practice (Healy and Meagher, 2007). In addition, the complexity of different fields of social work may require that some practitioners develop a depth of expertise in a set of specific methods within the field in which they practise. To acknowledge the value of expertise in specific fields and methods of practice does not negate the importance of social workers maintaining a broad methods base.

While I have presented social work as a contextually and methodologically diverse profession (see also Healy, 2005), I want to acknowledge the common threats now facing social workers seeking to deploy diverse methods. One of the many challenges facing the profession today is that of defending our rich and diverse methodological base from the assaults of neoliberalism and managerialism (Healy, 2009; McDonald, 2006; McLaughlin, 2007). Managerialism is predicated on a view that governments, which fund the majority of social services and community work activity, should be 'steering rather than rowing', in other words, governments should direct services not provide them (Osborne and Gaebler, 1993, p. 25). This means that decisions about how services are to be 'delivered' and who 'delivers' them may be made by administrators with little or no consultation with those providing or the individuals and communities receiving those services. Managerialist reforms are associated with the fragmentation of social work practice into units of activities and a preoccupation with calculating the final value of individual social work activities (see Annison et al., 2008). For example, in their review of the impact of managerialism on Finnish community mental health services, Saario and Stepney (2009, p. 27) remark that:

> Professional work becomes designated as 'individual therapy', 'emergency duty counselling', or 'home visit' or with a financial value attached ... AHO [a mental health practice audit tool] has therefore helped to make practitioners' work visible in a highly selective manner. To be precise, it is not possible for practitioners to make all their tasks and functions visible because codes do not exist for every activity.

One danger of the influence of managerialism on social service and community work agencies is that some essential activities may be devalued because they are less visible to those who construct auditing tools than to the service providers and service users who may have little, if any, say over what should be valued in practice. The fragmentation of social work activity proposed by managerialism is a clear and present threat to social workers' capacities to respond flexibly and creatively with the service users and communities with whom we work.

Creating Organizational Change

I want now to discuss how social workers can create organizational change, particularly to challenge the most negative effects of managerialism on diverse methods of direct social work practice. It is important that as social workers, we are critically aware of, and where necessary promote change in, our organizational environment because this environment defines our practice and the resources available to service users (Netting et al., 2008). I recognize that frontline social workers, particularly those who are newly qualified, may hold little formal authority to achieve organizational change. This limited authority does not mean that we are completely powerless; however, it does mean that we need to be careful to practise self care as we work towards change and also learn to celebrate small and incremental steps when working towards positive change within health and welfare service organizations.

I want to turn first to how social workers might challenge the negative and pervasive influence of neoliberalism and managerialism on health and welfare service organizations (see Healy and Meagher, 2004; McDonald, 2006; Saario and Stepney, 2009). While it seems likely that managerialism will continue to shape the organization of health and welfare services for the foreseeable future, social workers can still challenge some elements of this influence by understanding points of contradiction and vulnerability of this discourse. In order to achieve this, it is important for social workers to have a firm understanding of the features of this discourse; specifically, what the discourse values and what it marginalizes. Managerialism demands a focus on economic efficiencies in part through making visible and calculating service activities (Meagher and Healy, 2003). The managerialist discourse also reconstitutes social work activity away from the provision of holistic, comprehensive services to a focus on the management of risk (McDonald, 2006). This focus threatens to marginalize those elements of social work that are not readily calculable and which do not appear central to a narrow definition of social work activity as managing risk.

Social workers can challenge the influence of managerialism by making visible those aspects of our practice that are devalued by this discourse. Throughout this book, I have emphasized the importance of rigorous practice evaluation for improving our practice but it also has another use, which is to make visible those aspects of our practice that may be difficult to measure but are central to successful outcomes with service users and communities. Managerialism is associated with a distrust by managers of professionals' claims to unique expertise or value positions and so social workers, like other professionals, must now articulate and defend the assumptions underpinning our practice. In part, we can do this by invoking practice research evidence demonstrating, for example, that collaboration between social workers and service users contributes to positive outcomes for service users and the goals of the agencies working with them, such as keeping children safe and reducing recidivism (see Annison et al., 2008; Trotter, 2006). We also achieve recognition of the value of this work by ensuring that our evaluations of practice enable us to build an evidence base around those often less visible elements of our practice, such as the value of comprehensive or multi-method approaches for achieving practice outcomes in an economically efficient way.

Alongside the threats posed by managerialism, there is the ongoing challenge of ensuring that our services are structured in ways that best meet their mission to the clients and communities whom they are intended to serve. Health and welfare service organizations are dynamic and over time the organization may evolve in ways that create contradictions or limitations in the capacity of the organization to deliver on its mission (Netting et al., 2008). Moreover, the inherently moral, practical nature of social work (Parton and O'Byrne, 2000) requires that social workers engage in critical reflection on the extent to which their individual practice as well as the organizational practice enables the achievement of core practice values. Elliot (2008, p. 283) argues that:

> An active culture of analysis, critique and demands by professionals for ethical standards within a supportive practice context is a means for maintaining a balance between the 'moral voices' of practice and a restraint on the drift to an amoral instrumentalism.

As social workers, we have an ethical responsibility to critically reflect on the extent to which our organization meets the mission for which it was established. In a spirit of collaboration, we should initiate and engage in opportunities to critically reflect on the ongoing relevance of the organization's stated mission and its capacity to meet that mission. While such discussions can be incorporated into regular meetings with colleagues, new initiatives may also provide opportunities to critically reflect on the effectiveness of our organization in meeting its mission or drifting from its mission. For example, social workers in nongovernment organizations may need to raise concerns within their organization about whether acceptance of particular funding initiatives from government or business will associate the organization with a social policy that contradicts our organizational mission or that may unacceptably reshape how we deliver services or engage with communities.

Engaging colleagues in critical reflection on the organizational mission can itself be a challenging task and is likely to be highly emotive. There are several reasons for this. Social work practice operates in zones of uncertainty in which the evidence for best practice is contested. This lack of certainty is an inevitable feature of social work but can make rational debate difficult because such a debate may require us to recognize that the evidence for our position about practice is partial and imperfect. In addition, the work itself is emotional, it demands that we engage in relationships with service users and communities in ways that are often deeply affecting and distressing. Our individual experiences of the work and of witness to the lived experience of clients can reinforce a sense of correctness in our outlook that may, in turn, make openness to different viewpoints about change difficult to achieve. We also have our different value frames (including differences in our interpretation of professional value statements) and differences in our willingness to tolerate levels of accommodation or trade-offs for the achievement of the organizational mission. For example, one advocacy group may be willing to accept funding from the government department against which it is advocating in order to build a professional advocacy service, while another advocacy organization may regard the receipt of such funding as an unacceptable compromise of their mission.

How then do we engage in the difficult conversations with colleagues and managers necessary to achieve organizational change? Several points are important:

● Establish (and follow) ground rules for respectful engagement. First and foremost this means focusing on the organizational change issues and avoiding personalizing differences of opinion about the organization's mission or capacity to deliver on that mission. If there is a chair for meetings about organizational change, ask the chair to establish and reinforce ground rules for respectful engagement.

● Build your knowledge of what works and what prevents the organization from achieving its mission. This knowledge can be built from the research literature on social work practice and also from your own evaluations.

● Focus on persuading colleagues of your viewpoint by use of logical argument and evidence from research literature and evaluations taken within the organization. Avoid seeing your own position as inherently superior and instead try to build a logical and evidence-based case for your position. Expression of emotion about your position may be inevitable, and may also show that you genuinely care about the issues, but you should also avoid alienating colleagues who may hold a different viewpoint from you.

● Seek to keep an open mind to any counterarguments presented by your colleagues, even where you might find these arguments challenging to your outlook and evidence base. In some instances, these discussions may be personally confronting to you and then it may help to critically reflect with a supervisor or peer (not involved in the change process) about the challenges you are experiencing. This is not to suggest that you let go of your position but rather to ensure that your personally held views do not prevent you from recognizing possible merits in the arguments of others.

● Be prepared to make reasonable compromises and trade-offs, particularly where decisions will have minimal impact on service users or community members or where the evidence for outcomes is ambivalent. The health and welfare service field, like most fields of service provision, involves some trade-offs because of unlimited human needs, imperfect service systems and limited resources. It is important for you to critically reflect on your evolving practice framework, perhaps with the help a peer or supervisor external to your organization, in order to establish what compromises you can work with as well as areas that are non-negotiable. In some situations, you may feel that you have no option but to place external pressure on the organization, such as through whistle-blowing on practices that are unethical or illegal, or to leave the organization itself. These are significant decisions and need to be undertaken with due consideration of the costs to the service user and community of such decisions.

A further way we can ensure that health and welfare service organizations meet their mission to the service users and communities they are intended to serve is to create pathways for service users to participate in defining the mission of the organization. I refer here to the development of democratic organizational processes that facilitate the involvement of service users and service providers in decision-making and, in so doing, develop services that recognize those experiences.

The foundation of citizen involvement in organizational design is our expression of respect for service users as partners in our organizations. As an expression of respect, it is important for us to recognize and challenge those aspects of organizational policy and design that pathologize the service user. Instead, if we are to engage with service users as partners, we need to 'push for definitions of problems and solutions that are grounded in people's lived realities' (Mullaly, 2007, p. 323). In essence, the definitions of problems need to recognize, and respond to, the social, economic and political circumstances of people's lives.

One further way of democratizing the health and welfare service organization is by developing a clear policy on, or charter about, the rights of service user participation and then by working with service users to ensure this policy is implemented at each level of the organization. Admittedly, these processes are more readily implemented where there is some degree of voluntary engagement between social workers and service user communities and where community identities are well developed; rather than in the contexts where options for partnership are complicated by the statutory authority of the social worker or lack of service user identification with a community. Another complementary way of assuring service user involvement in changing health and welfare service organizations is through supporting the development of citizen advocacy associations and unions, where service users are empowered to collectively voice and act upon their shared concerns (Dumbrill, 2010).

Protecting and Sustaining Ourselves

Drawing on external sources of support can also assist us to create change in our organizations. By participating in change-oriented collectives or associations, we gain external reference points for our change activity, and we also reduce our risk of burnout and personal reprisals against us from those who oppose the changes we seek. In the health and welfare services field, there are at least three forms of external organizational support that are important to social workers seeking to create organizational change.

Advocacy groups, both citizen and professionally led, can provide support for organizational change activity. Citizen advocacy networks that are established to promote social justice for the service users and communities with whom we work can provide one form of support for organizational change activity. In a range of health and welfare fields, advocacy networks and associations have developed to provide a collective base for articulating and defending the needs and interests of service users, such as young people leaving care or people living with disability or mental illness (Healy, 2005). Often these networks involve, and may be led by, people with experience as service users or by professionals who are closely connected to these service user communities. Another form of advocacy network are research networks, which seek to generate research evidence for achieving best policy and practice in a specific domain of practice. These research networks exist in a broad range of health and welfare domains such as child protection and youth justice. The networks provide an opportunity for interdisciplinary and interinstitutional research and in so doing enable academic researchers to collaborate with policy-makers, evaluation researchers and practitioners to develop an evidence base for change. Advocacy groups and networks can support social workers by informing us about what service users want and need from our services and providing evidence about policies and practices that have been demonstrated to work in other health and welfare service contexts.

Industrial unions provide another level of support for organizational change activity. Unions have an important role in protecting our democratic rights as social workers to participate in some forms of organizational change activity and, where necessary, to seek support for change outside our organization. In addition, the unions that represent social workers, and other health and welfare service workers, often share the humanist values on which these professions are based. Because of this shared value base, social workers' unions may play an important role, not only in protecting the industrial rights of workers but also in defending the values of the profession and the rights of service users against the inroads being made by managerialism (Healy and Meagher, 2004).

Finally, *professional associations* can also provide support for organizational change activity. The core responsibilities of professional associations in social work, as in other fields, are to promote the profession they represent and protect the public from incompetent or unethical practices in their domain of professional practice. Of course, there is considerable debate about whether professional associations do in fact achieve the aim of public protection and whether the eligibility requirements of professional associations promote elitism (see Briggs et al., 2007; Healy and Meagher, 2004; McDonald, 2006). Notwithstanding these debates, professional associations provide an external reference point and support for our organizational change activities by outlining the values that guide professional practice. More generally, professional associations have a pivotal role to play in advocating for the reprofessionalization of social service agencies. This is critical, for without a clear identity grounded in the humanist values of social work, frontline practice lacks 'a readily defensible and principled identify beyond whatever the policy-makers of the day deem to be proper for it' (Elliott, 2008, p. 282).

There is considerable variation internationally in the extent to which professional associations are also industrial unions. For example, in Scandinavia, the professional social work associations are also unions; this differs from Australia, the UK and the USA, where professional social work associations have separate responsibilities from unions, although they may collaborate with them. In countries where professional associations and industrial unions are separated, coalitions between these entities are also important for defending the workplace conditions required for social workers to practise critically and creatively (Healy and Meagher, 2004).

Conclusion

Social work practice is complex because the social world is inherently complex. Social workers practise in the grey areas of the human condition where we often confront difficult personal and social challenges in service users' and community members' lives. These challenges defy simple or single method solutions. Embracing a diverse methodological base is not easy or comfortable, but is necessary if we are to practise flexibly and creatively with individuals, families, groups and communities. In this final chapter, we have considered how social workers might work collaboratively within and outside our organizations to create organizational change. Such change is oriented towards creating organizational environments that support us to achieve best outcomes with, and for, the service users and communities with whom we practise.

I hope that in this introduction to the diverse foundations of professional practice I have provided a base for you, the reader, to go ahead with confidence into the social work field. Social workers, like members of all other professions, have made mistakes and members of the profession have sometimes inadvertently and sometimes deliberately contributed to the pain and suffering of people who should have been able to rely on us. Yet social workers have also contributed to achieving a share of social justice with the individuals and communities with whom they have practised. Social workers are committed to making a positive difference in the lives of people, particularly those who are vulnerable and socially excluded. This is our driving goal and it involves awesome responsibilities. I wish you well on your journey as a member of this vital and challenging profession.

Further Reading

- Brophy, R. (2005) *Effectively Managing Human Service Organizations*. Thousand Oaks, CA: Sage.

- Patti, R. (2009) *The Handbook of Human Services Management*. Los Angeles, CA: Sage.

  Many of the recent books on health and welfare service organizations are focused on health and welfare services management rather than organizational change. Nonetheless, understanding how health and welfare service organizations operate and are best managed is an excellent basis for working for change in organizations. The above texts provide a comprehensive overview of management and leadership in health and welfare service organizations. I also recommend the journals *Administration in Social Work* and *Social Policy and Administration*, which regularly publish articles on organizational change.

References

Addams, J. (1910) *Twenty Years at Hull-House: With Autobiographical Notes*. New York: Macmillan.

Allen, G. and Langford, D. (2008) *Effective Interviewing in Social Work and Social Care: A Practical Guide*. Basingstoke: Palgrave Macmillan.

Alinksy, S. (1971) *Rules for Radicals*. New York: Random House.

Althaus, C., Bridgman, P. and Davis, G. (2007) *The Australian Policy Handbook*. Crows Nest, Sydney: Allen & Unwin.

Anning, A., Cottrell, D., Frost, N. et al. (2006) *Developing Multi-professional Teamwork for Integrated Children' s Services*. Maidenhead: Open University Press.

Annison, J., Eadie, T. and Knight, C. (2008) People first: probation officer perspectives on probation work. *Probation Journal: The Journal of Community and Criminal Justice*, 55(3), 259–71.

Australian Institute of Health and Welfare (2001) *Family Support Services in Australia 2000*. AIHW cat. no. CFS 4. Canberra: AIHW.

Aveyard, H. and Sharp, P. (2009) *A Beginner's Guide to Evidence Based Practice in Health and Social Care Professions*. Maidenhead: Open University Press.

Bailey, R. and Brake, M. (1975) *Radical Social Work*. London: Edward Arnold.

Banks, S. (2006) *Ethics and Values in Social Work*, 3rd edn. Basingstoke: Palgrave Macmillan.

Barak, M., Levin, A., Nissly, J. and Lane, C. (2006) Why do they leave? Modeling child welfare workers' turnover intentions. *Children and Youth Services Review*, 28(5), 548–77.

Bensley, R.J. and Brookins-Fisher, J. (2009) *Community Health Education Methods: A Practical Guide*. Sudbury, MA: Jones and Bartlett.

Berg, I.S. and Kelly, S. (2000) *Building Solutions in Child Protection Services*. New York: Norton.

Blieszner, R. (2009) Who are the aging families? In Qualls, S. and Zarit, S. (eds) *Aging Families and Caregiving* (pp. 1–18). Hoboken, NJ: John Wiley & Sons.

Boyle, S., Hull, G., Mather, J., Smith, L. and Farley, O.W. (2006) *Direct Practice in Social Work*. Boston: Pearson Education.

Briggs, C., Meagher, G. and Healy, K. (2007) Becoming an industry: the struggle of social and community workers for award coverage, 1976–2001. *Journal of Industrial Relations*, 49(4), 497–521.

Bunyan, P. (2008) Broad-based organizing in the UK: reasserting the centrality of political activity in community development. *Community Development Journal*, 45(1), 111–27.

Butler, E., Lee, T. and Gross, J. (2007) Emotion regulation and culture: are the social consequences of emotion suppression culture-specific? *Emotion*, 7(1), 30–48.

Carpenter, J. (2002) Mental health recovery paradigm: implications for social work. *Health and Social Work*, 27(2), 86–72.

Carr, S. (2004) *Has Service User Participation Made a Difference to Social Care Services?* London: Social Care Institute for Excellence.

Chapin, R. (2007) *Social Policy for Effective Practice: A Strengths Approach*. Boston: McGraw-Hill.

Chen, M.-W. and Han, Y.S. (2001) Cross-cultural group counseling with Asians: a stage-specific interactive approach. *The Journal for Specialists in Group Work*, **26**(2), 111–28.

Christensen, D.N., Todahl, J. and Barrett, W. (1999) *Solution-based Casework: An Introduction to Clinical and Case Management Skills in Casework Practice*. New York: Aldine de Gruyter.

Coley, S.M. and Scheinberg, C.A. (2008) *Proposal Writing: Effective Grantsmanship*, 3rd edn. Thousand Oaks, CA: Sage.

Commission to Inquire into Child Abuse (2009) The investigation committee report on institutions. Dublin: Commission to Inquire into Child Abuse (available at http://www.childabusecommission.ie/).

Compass (2002) *Saving Claymore*. Sydney: Australian Broadcasting Commission.

Corporal, S. (2007) Getting to know the community. In Darlington, Y., Garland, L. and Hall, K. (eds) *Listening with Respect: Strengthening Communication with Aboriginal and Torres Strait Islander Australians* (pp. 11–15). St Lucia, Brisbane: School of Social Work and Human Services, University of Queensland.

Coulshed, V. and Orme, J. (2006) *Social Work Practice: An Introduction*, 3rd edn. Basingstoke: Palgrave Macmillan.

Crago, H. (2008) Preserving family therapy's legacy. *Australian and New Zealand Journal of Family Therapy*, **29**(2), 70–6.

Crichton-Hill, Y. (2009) Working with families. In Maidment, J. and Egan, R. (eds) *Practice Skills in Social Work and Welfare: More Than Just Common Sense*, 2nd edn (pp. 181–202). Crows Nest, Sydney: Allen & Unwin.

Crossley, M. and Crossley, N. (2001) 'Patient' voices, social movements and the habitus: how psychiatric survivors 'speak out'. *Social Science and Medicine*, **52**(1), 1477–87.

Danis, F. and Lockhart, L. (2003) Domestic violence and social work: what do we know, what do we need to know? *Journal of Social Work Education*, **39**(2), 215–24.

De Jong, P. and Berg, I.K. (2001) Co-constructing cooperation with mandated clients. *Social Work*, **46**(4), 361–74.

Department of Justice and Attorney General (2000) *Aboriginal English in the Courts: A Handbook*. Brisbane: Queensland Government.

Doel, M. (2006) *Using Groupwork*. London: Routledge.

Dominelli, L. (2002) Anti-oppressive practice in context. In Adams, R., Dominelli, L. and Payne, M. (eds) *Social Work: Themes, Issues and Critical Debates*, 2nd edn (pp. 3–19). Basingstoke: Palgrave Macmillan.

Dominelli, L. (2006) *Women and Community Action*, rev. 2nd edn. Bristol: Policy Press.

Doolan, M. (2004) The family group conference: a mainstream approach in child welfare decision-making. Paper presented at the Conference on Family Group Decision Making.

Douglas, H. and Walsh T. (2010) Mothers, domestic violence and child protection. *Violence Against Women*, **16**(5), 489–508.

Dumbrill, G.C. (2010) Power and child protection: the need for a child welfare service users' union or association. *Australian Social Work*, **63**(2), 194–206.

Egan, G. (2010) *The Skilled Helper: A Problem-management and Opportunity-development Approach to Helping*, 9th edn. Belmont, CA: Brooks/Cole Cengage Learning.

Elliott, N. (2008) The global vortex: social welfare in a networked world. *Social Work Practice*, **2**(3), 269–87.

Eriksson, L. (2010) Community development and social pedagogy: traditions for understanding mobilization for collective self-development. *Community Development Journal*, advanced access, doi: 10.1093/cdj/bsq008.

Fawcett, B., Goodwin, S., Meagher, G. and Phillips, P. (2010) *Social Policy for Social Change*. Melbourne: Palgrave Macmillan.

Ferguson, H. (2011) *Child Protection Practice*. Basingstoke: Palgrave Macmillan.

Fischer, J. (1973) Is casework effective? A review. *Social Work*, **18**(1), 5–20.

Fischer, J. and Corcoran, K. (2007) *Measures for Clinical Practice and Research: A Sourcebook*. New York: Open University Press.

Fisher, R. (2005) History, context and emerging issues for community practice. In Weil, M. (ed.) *The Handbook of Community Practice* (pp. 34–58). Thousand Oaks, CA: Sage.

Fook, J. (1993) *Radical Casework: A Theory of Practice*. St Leonards, Sydney: Allen & Unwin.

Fook, J. (2002) *Social Work: Critical Theory and Practice*. London: Sage.

Fook, J. and Gardner, F. (2007) *Practising Critical Reflection: A Resource Handbook*. Maidenhead: Open University Press.

Fook, J., Ryan, M. and Hawkins, L. (2000) *Professional Expertise: Practice, Theory and Education for Working in Uncertainty*. London: Whiting & Birch.

Frederick, J. and Goddard, C. (2008) Sweet and sour charity: experiences of receiving emergency relief in Australia. *Australian Social Work*, **61**(3), 269–84.

Freire, P. (1997) *Pedagogy of the Oppressed*. New York: Continuum.

Gant, L. (2004) Evaluation of group work. In Garvin, C.D., Gutierrez, L.M. and Galinsky, M.J. (eds) *Handbook of Social Work with Groups* (pp. 461–75). New York: Guilford Press.

Garvin, C.D., Gutierrez, L.M. and Galinsky, M.J. (2004) *Handbook of Social Work with Groups*. London: Guilford Press.

Germain, C. (1970) Casework and science: a historical encounter. In Roberts, R. and Nee, R. (eds) *Theories of Social Casework* (pp. 5–32). Chicago: University of Chicago Press.

Germain, C. and Gitterman, A. (1996) *The Life Model of Social Work Practice: Advances in Theory and Practice,* 2nd edn. New York: Columbia.

Gibelman, M. (1999) The search for identity: defining social work – past, present, future. *Social Work*, **44**(4), 298–310.

Gillingham, P. and Humphreys, C. (2010) Child protection practitioners and decision-making tools: observations and reflections from the front line. *British Journal of Social Work*, **40**(8), 2598–616.

Gray, M. and Webb, S. (eds) (2009) *Social Work: Theories and Methods*. Los Angeles, CA: Sage.

Green, G. and Haines, A. (2002) *Asset Building and Community Development*. Thousand Oaks, CA: Sage.

Hall, C. and Slembrouck, S. (2001) Parent participation in social work meetings: the case of child protection conferences, *European Journal of Social Work*, **4**(2), 143–60.

Harms, L. (2007) *Working with People: Communication Skills for Reflective Practice*. Melbourne: Oxford University Press.

Hartman, A. (1995) Diagrammatic assessment of family relationships. *Families in Society*, **76**(2), 111–22.

Hawtin, M. and Percy-Smith, J. (2007) *Community Profiling: A Practical Guide*. Maidenhead: Open University Press.

Healy, K. (2000) *Social Work Practices: Contemporary Perspectives on Change*. London: Sage.

Healy, K. (2005) *Social Work Theories in Context: Creating Frameworks for Practice*. Basingstoke: Palgrave Macmillan.

Healy, K. (2006) Community education. In O'Hara, A. and Weber, Z. (eds) *Skills for Human Services Practice: Working with Individuals, Communities and Organisations* (pp. 247–58). Melbourne: Oxford University Press.

Healy, K. (2009) A case of mistaken identity: social welfare professions and new public management. *Journal of Sociology,* **45**(4), 401–18.

Healy, K. and Darlington, Y. (1999) Family support and social inclusion: practice and policy issues in Australia. *Just Policy,* 16, 3–10.

Healy, K. and Darlington, Y. (2009) Enhancing participation in child protection: principles for practice. *Child and Family Social Work,* **14**(4), 420–30.

Healy, K. and Meagher, G. (2004) The re-professionalisation of social work: collaborative approaches for achieving professional recognition. *British Journal of Social Work,* **34**(2), 243–60.

Healy, K. and Meagher, G. (2007) Social workers' preparation for child protection: revising the question of specialisation. *Australian Social Work,* **60**(3), 321–35.

Healy, K. and Mulholland, J. (2007) *Writing Skills for Social Workers.* London: Sage.

Healy, K. and Oltedal, S. (2010) An institutional comparison of child protection systems in Australia and Norway focused on workforce retention. *Journal of Social Policy,* **39**(2), 255–74.

Healy, K., Darlington, Y. and Yellowlees, J. (2011) Family participation in child protection practice: an observational study of family group meetings. *Child and Family Social Work.* DOI: 10.1111/j.1365-2206.2011.00767.x.

Healy, K., Meagher, G. and Cullin, J. (2009) Retaining novices to become expert practitioners: creating career pathways in direct practice. *British Journal of Social Work,* **39**(2), 299–317.

Henderson, P. and Thomas, D. (2002) *Skills in Neighbourhood Work,* 3rd edn. London: Routledge.

Hoatson, L. (2003) The scope of Australian community practice. In Weeks, W., Hoatson, L. and Dixon, J. (eds) *Community Practice in Australia* (pp. 23–32). Melbourne: Pearson Education.

Holland, S. and O' Neill, S. (2006) 'We had to be there to make sure it was what we wanted': enabling children's participation in family decision-making through the family group conference. *Childhood,* **13**(1), 91–111.

Hutchins, S. and McLucas, J. (2004) *Forgotten Australians: A Report on Australians Who Experienced Institutional or Out-of-home Care.* Canberra: Senate, Community Affairs References Committee.

Hutchinson, G.S. (2009) The mandate for community work in the Nordic welfare states. In Strand Hutchinson, G. (ed.) *Community Work in Nordic Countries: New Trends* (pp. 15–37). Oslo: Universitetsforlaget.

IFSW (2000) *Definition of Social Work.* Retrieved 1 June 2011 from http://www.ifsw.org/f38000138.html.

IFSW/IASSW (2004) *Ethics in Social Work: Statement of Principles.* International Federation of Social Workers (IFSW) and International Association of Schools of Social Work (IASSW). Retrieved 1 June 2011 from http://www.ifsw.org/p38000324.html.

Jansson, B.S. (2008) *Becoming an Effective Policy Advocate: From Policy Practice to Social Justice,* 5th edn. Belmont, CA: Thomson Higher Education.

Johnson, N.E., Saccuzzo, D.P. and Koen, W.J. (2005) Child custody mediation in cases of domestic violence: empirical evidence of a failure to protect. *Violence Against Women,* **11**(8), 1022–53.

Johnson, Y. and Munch, S. (2009) Fundamental contradictions in cultural competence. *Social Work,* **54**(3), 220–31.

Kane, L. (2010) Community development: learning from popular education in Latin America. *Community Development Journal,* **45**(3), 276–86.

Killen, K. (1996) How far have we come in dealing with the emotional challenge of abuse and neglect? *Child Abuse and Neglect,* **20**(9), 791–5.

Kindon, S., Pain, R. and Kesby, M. (2007) *Participatory Action Research Approaches: Connecting People, Participation and Place*. Abingdon: Routledge.

Kretzmann, J. and McKnight, J. (1993) *Building Communities from the Inside Out: A Path Toward Finding and Mobilizing a Community's Assets*. Evanston, IL: The Asset Based Community Development Institute, Northwestern University.

Leathard, A. (2003) Introduction. In Leathard, A. (ed.) *Interprofessional Collaboration: From Policy to Practice in Health and Social Care* (pp. 3–11). Hove: Brunner-Routledge.

Le Riche, P. (1998) The dimensions of observation: objective reality or subjective interpretation. In Le Riche, P. and Tanner, K. (eds) *Observation and its Application in Social Work: Rather Like Breathing* (pp. 17–38). London: Jessica Kingsley.

Lincourt, P., Kuettel, T.J. and Bombardier, C.H. (2002) Motivational interviewing in a group setting with mandated clients: a pilot study. *Addictive Behaviors, 27*(3), 381–91.

Lipsky, M. (1980) *Street-level Bureaucracy: Dilemmas of the Individual in Public Services*. New York: Russell Sage Foundation.

Lonne, B., Parton, N., Thomson, J. and Harries, M. (2009) *Reforming Child Protection*. Abingdon: Routledge.

McDermott, F. (2002) *Inside Group Work: A Guide to Reflective Practice*. Crows Nest, Sydney: Allen & Unwin.

McDonald, C. (2006) *Challenging Social Work: The Institutional Context of Practice*. Basingstoke: Palgrave Macmillan.

McGoldrick, M., Gerson, R. and Petry, S. (2008) *Genograms: Assessment and Intervention*. New York: WW Norton.

McLaughlin, K. (2007) Regulation and risk in social work: the general social care council and the social care register in context. *British Journal of Social Work, 37*(7), 1263–77.

McMaster, K. (2009) Facilitating change through groupwork. In Maidment, J. and Egan, R. (eds) *Practice Skills in Social Work and Welfare: More Than Just Common Sense*, 2nd edn (pp. 205–17). Crows Nest, Sydney: Allen & Unwin.

Magen, R. (2004) Measurement issues. In Garvin, C.D., Gutierrez, L.M. and Galinsky, M.J. (eds) *Handbook of Social Work with Groups* (pp. 447–60). New York: Guilford Press.

Maiter, S. (2009) Using an anti-racist framework for assessment and intervention in clinical practice with families from diverse ethno-racial backgrounds. *Clinical Social Work Journal, 37*(4), 267–76.

Maiter, S., Palmer, S. and Manji, S. (2006) Strengthening social worker-client relationships in child protection services: addressing power imbalances and 'ruptured' relationships. *Qualitative Social Work, 5*(2), 161–86.

Marshall, M., Preston, M., Scott, E. and Winnicott, P. (eds) (1979) *Teamwork for and Against: An Appraisal of Multi-disciplinary Practice*. London: British Journal of Social Workers.

Martin, V. and Rogers, A. (2004) *Leading Interprofessional Teams in Health and Social Care*. Abingdon: Routledge.

Mathie, A. and Cunningham, G. (2003) From clients to citizens: asset-based community development as a strategy for community-driven development. *Development in Practice, 13*(5), 474–86.

Mayo, M. (1975) Community development: a radical alternative? In Bailey, R. and Brake, M. (eds) *Radical Social Work* (pp. 129–43). New York: Pantheon Books.

Meagher, G. and Healy, K. (2003) Caring, controlling, contracting and counting: governments and non-profits in community services. *Australian Journal of Public Administration, 62*(3), 40–51.

Midgley, J. and Livermore, M. (2005) Development theory and community practice. In Weil, M. (ed.) *The Handbook of Community Practice* (pp. 153–68). Thousand Oaks, CA: Sage.

Miller, R. (2009) Engagement with families involved in the statutory system. In Maidment, J. and Egan, R. (eds) *Practice Skills in Social Work and Welfare: More Than Just Common Sense,* 2nd edn (pp. 114–30). Crows Nest, Sydney: Allen & Unwin.

Mitchell, J. and Correa-Velez, I. (2010) Community development with survivors of torture and trauma: an evaluation framework. *Community Development Journal,* 45(1), 90–110.

Mojtabai, R. and Olfson, M. (2008) National trends in psychotherapy by office-based psychiatrists. *Archives of General Psychiatry,* 65(8), 962–70.

Morris, K. and Connolly, M. (2010) Family decision making in child welfare: challenges in developing a knowledge base for practice. *Child Abuse Review,* DOI: 10.1002/car.1143.

Mowbray, M. (2005) Community capacity building or state opportunism. *Community Development Journal,* 40(3), 255–64.

Mullaly, B. (2007) *The New Structural Social Work,* 3rd edn. Don Mills, Ontario: Oxford University Press.

Mullaly, R. (1997) *Structural Social Work: Ideology, Theory and Practice,* 2nd edn. Toronto: Oxford University Press.

Mullender, A. and Ward, D. (1991) Empowerment through social action groupwork: the 'self-directed' approach. In Vinik, A. and Levine, M. (eds) *Social Action in Group Work* (pp. 125–40). London: Haworth.

Munro, E. (2008) *Effective Child Protection.* Los Angeles, CA: Sage.

NASW (2005) *NASW Standards for Clinical Social work in Social Work Practice.* Washington DC: NASW.

Netting, F.E., Kettner, P.M. and McMurtry, S.L. (2008) *Social Work Macro Practice,* 4th edn. Boston: Pearson Education.

Ohmer, M. and DeMasi, K. (2009) *Consensus Organizing: A Community Development Workbook.* Thousand Oaks, CA: Sage.

Opie, A. (1995) *Beyond Good Intentions: Support Work with Older People.* Wellington: Institute of Policy Studies.

Orme, J. (2001) *Gender and Community Care: Social Work and Social Care Perspectives.* Basingstoke: Palgrave – now Palgrave Macmillan.

Osborne, D. and Gaebler, T. (1993) *Reinventing Government: How the Entrepreneurial Spirit is Transforming the Public Sector.* New York: Plume Books.

Parton, N. and O' Byrne, P. (2000) *Constructive Social Work: Towards New Practice.* Basingstoke: Macmillan – now Palgrave Macmillan.

Perlman, H.H. (1957) *Social Casework: A Problem-solving Process.* Chicago: University of Chicago Press.

Perlman, H.H. (1968) Can casework work? *The Social Service Review,* 42(4), 435–47.

Pincus, A. and Minahan, A. (1973) *Social Work Practice: Model and Method.* Itasca, IL: FE Peacock.

Plath, D. (2006) Evidence-based practice: current issues and future directions. *Australian Social Work,* 59(1), 56–72.

Preston-Shoot, M. (2007) *Effective Groupwork,* 2nd edn. Basingstoke: Palgrave Macmillan.

QAA (2008) *Subject Benchmark Statement: Social Work.* Mansfield: Quality Assurance Agency for Higher Education.

Qualls, S.H. and Zarit, S.H. (eds) (2009) *Aging Families and Caregiving.* Hoboken, NJ: John Wiley & Sons.

Quinney, A. (2006) *Collaborative Social Work Practice.* Exeter: Learning Matters.

Rasheed, J., Rasheed, M. and Marley, J. (2011) *Family Therapy: Models and Techniques*. Thousand Oaks, CA: Sage.

Reid, W.J. (1978) *The Task-centered System*. New York: Columbia University Press.

Reid, W.J. and Epstein, L. (1972) *Task-centered Casework*. New York: Columbia University Press.

Reid, W.J. and Shyne, A. (1969) *Brief and Extended Casework*. New York: Columbia University Press.

Reisch, M. (2005) Radical community organising. In Weil, M. (ed.) *The Handbook of Community Practice* (pp. 287–304). Thousand Oaks, CA: Sage.

Reynolds, A. and Valentine, D. (2004) *Guide to Cross-cultural Communication*. Upper Saddle River, NJ: Pearson Prentice Hall.

Richmond, M.E. (1917) *Social Diagnosis*. New York: Russell Sage Foundation.

Roberts-DeGennaro, M. (2008) Case management: using the integrative and collaborative process of evidence-based practice paradigm. In Mizrahi, T. and Davis, L. (eds) *Encyclopedia of Social Work*, 20th edn. New York: Oxford University Press.

Rocha, C.J. (2007) *Essentials of Social Work Policy Practice*. Hoboken, NJ: John Wiley & Sons.

Rojek, C., Peacock, C. and Collins, S. (1988) *Social Work and Received Ideas*. London: Sage.

Ronnby, A. (2009) Empowering people by building community. In Strand Hutchinson, G. (ed.) *Community Work in Nordic Countries: New Trends* (pp. 119–47). Oslo: Universitetsforlaget.

Rothman, J. (2001) Approaches to community intervention. In Rothman, J., Erlich, J. and Tropman, J. (eds) *Strategies of Community Intervention* (pp. 27–64). Itasca, IL: FE Peacock.

Rubin, A. and Babbie, E. (2007) *Essential Research Methods for Social Work*. Belmont, CA: Brooks/Cole/Wadsworth.

Saario, S. and Stepney, P. (2009) Managerial audit and community mental health: a study of rationalising practices in Finnish psychiatric outpatient clinics. *European Journal of Social Work*, **12**(1), 41–56.

Saleebey, D. (ed.) (2006) *The Strengths Perspective in Social Work Practice*, 4th edn. Boston: Pearson/Allyn & Bacon.

Schön, D. (1983) *The Reflective Practitioner: How Professionals Think in Action*. New York: Basic Books.

Seden, J. (1999) *Counselling Skills in Social Work Practice*. Buckingham: Open University Press.

Seymour, C. and Seymour, R. (2007) *Courtroom Skills for Social Workers*. Exeter: Learning Matters.

Sheafor, B. and Horejsi, C. (2006) *Techniques and Guidelines for Social Work Practice*, 7th edn. Boston: Pearson Educational.

Sheldon, B. (1995) *Cognitive Behavioural Therapy: Research, Practice and Philosophy*. London: Routledge.

Sheldon, B. and Macdonald, G. (2009) *A Textbook of Social Work*. Abingdon: Routledge.

Shlonsky, A. and Wagner, D. (2005) The next step: integrating actuarial risk assessment and clinical judgment into an evidence-based practice framework in CPS case management. *Children and Youth Services Review*, **27**(4), 409–27.

Shlonsky, A., Schumaker, K., Cook, C. et al. (2009) Family group decision making for children at risk of abuse and neglect (Protocol). *The Cochrane Library 3*.

Skuse, V. (2007) It's not what you do but how you do it. In Darlington, Y., Garland, L. and Hall, K. (eds) *Listening with Respect: Strengthening Communication with Aboriginal and Torres Strait Islander Australians* (pp. 21–7). St Lucia, Brisbane: School of Social Work and Human Services, University of Queensland.

Specht, H. and Courtney, M.E. (1994) *Unfaithful Angels: How Social Work has Abandoned its Mission.* New York: The Free Press.

Stepney, P. and Popple, K. (2008) *Social Work and the Community: A Critical Context for Practice.* Basingstoke: Palgrave Macmillan.

Sue, D.W. and Sue, D. (1977) Barriers to effective cross-cultural counseling. *Journal of Counseling Psychology,* **24**(5), 420–9.

Sundell, K. and Vinnerljung, B. (2004) Outcomes of family group conferencing in Sweden: a 3-year follow-up. *Child Abuse and Neglect,* **28**(3), 267–87.

Tanner, K. (1998) Introduction. In Le Riche, P. and Tanner, K. (eds) *Observation and its Application to Social Work: Rather Like Breathing* (pp. 9–16). London: Jessica Kingsley.

Tesoriero, F. (2010) *Community Development: Community-based Alternatives in an Age of Globalisation,* 4th edn. Frenchs Forest, NSW: Pearson Australia.

Tham, P. (2007) Why are they leaving? Factors affecting intention to leave among social workers in child welfare. *British Journal of Social Work,* **37**(7), 1225–46.

Toseland, R. and Rivas, R. (2009) *An Introduction to Group Work Practice,* 6th edn. Boston: Pearson Education.

Trevithick, P. (2005) *Social Work Skills: A Practice Handbook,* 2nd edn. Buckingham: Open University Press.

Trotter, C. (2002) Worker skill and client outcome in child protection. *Child Abuse Review,* **11**(1), 38–50.

Trotter, C. (2004) *Helping Abused Children and Their Families,* 2nd edn. St Leonards, Sydney: Allen & Unwin.

Trotter, C. (2006) *Working with Involuntary Clients: A Guide to Practice,* 2nd edn. Crows Nest, Sydney: Allen & Unwin.

Trotter, C. (2008) What does client satisfaction tell us about effectiveness? *Child Abuse Review,* **17**(4), 262–74.

Trowell, J. and Miles, G. (1991) *The Place of an Introduction to Child to Young Child Observation in Social Work Training.* London: CCETSW.

Tuckman, B. (1965) Development sequence in small groups. *Psychological Bulletin,* **63**(6), 384–99.

Tuckman, B. and Jensen, M. (1977) Stages of small group development revisited. *Group Organization Management,* **2**(4), 419–27.

Turnell, A. and Edwards, S. (1999) *Signs of Safety: A Solution and Safety Oriented Approach to Child Protection Casework.* New York: Norton.

Turnell, A. and Parker, S. (2009) *New and Revised Introduction to the Signs of Safety Approach to Child Protection Casework.* Perth: Resolutions Consultancy.

Turunen, P. (2009) Nordic community work in transition. In Strand Hutchinson, G. (ed.) *Community Work in Nordic Countries: New Trends* (pp. 38–63). Oslo: Universitetsforlaget.

Twelvetrees, A. (2008) *Community Work,* 4th edn. Basingstoke: Palgrave Macmillan.

UNHCR (1951) *Convention Relating to the Status of Refugees.* Geneva: Office of the United Nations High Commissioner for Refugees.

Vinson, T. (2007) *Dropping off the Edge: The Distribution of Disadvantage in Australia.* Richmond, Victoria: Jesuit Social Services.

Wadsworth, Y. (2011) *Everyday Evaluation on the Run: The User-friendly Guide to Effective Evaluation,* 3rd edn. Crows Nest, Sydney: Allen & Unwin.

Walton, R. (2005) Social work as a social institution. *British Journal of Social Work,* **35**(5), 587–607.

Weil, M. and Gamble, D. (2005) Evolution, models and the changing context of community practice. In Weil, M. (ed.) *The Handbook of Community Practice* (pp. 117–49). Thousand Oaks, CA: Sage.

Weiss, I., Gal, J. and Katan, J. (2006) Social policy for social work: a teaching agenda. *British Journal of Social Work,* **36**(5), 789–806.

Westoby, P. and Dowling, P. (2009) *Dialogical Community Development: With Depth, Solidarity and Hospitality*. West End, Brisbane: Tafina Press.

White, M. (1995) *Re-authoring Lives: Interviews and Essays*. Adelaide: Dulwich Centre.

Wildeman, C. (2009) Parental imprisonment, the prison boom and the concentration of childhood disadvantage. *Demography,* **46**(2), 265–80.

Woods, M.E. and Hollis, F. (1990) *Casework: A Psychosocial Therapy*. New York: McGraw-Hill.

Yan, M.C. (2008) Exploring cultural tensions in cross-cultural social work practice. *Social Work,* **53**(1), 312–28.

Index